AN EAGLE'S ODYSSEY

AN EAGLE'S ODYSSEY
My Decade as a Pilot in Hitler's Luftwaffe

Johannes Kaufmann

Translated by John Weal

Foreword by Richard Overy

Greenhill Books

Greenhill Books

An Eagle's Odyssey
This edition published in 2019 by Greenhill Books
c/o Pen & Sword Books Ltd,
47 Church Street, Barnsley,
S. Yorkshire, S70 2AS

Publishing History
Johannes Kaufmann's *Mein Flugberichte* 1935-1945 was first published by
Journal Verlagshaus Schwend in 1989. This is the first English language translation
and includes a new foreword by Richard Overy.

www.greenhillbooks.com
contact@greenhillbooks.com

Greenhill Books ISBN: 978-1-78438-253-7

Front cover image colourised by Jon Wilkinson

CIP data records for this title are available from the British Library

Typeset in Miller by MATS typesetters, Leigh-on-Sea

Printed and bound in England by TJ International Ltd., Cornwall

Contents

Foreword

Captain Johannes Kaufmann was a lucky man. Where thousands of German pilots perished in combat or accidents over the wartime years, Kaufmann survived some 212 combat operations, a number of years as a Luftwaffe instructor, and numerous ferrying and test flights, often in atrocious weather. His luck held throughout this ten-year 'Eagle's Odyssey', from his first training flights in 1935 as a novice twenty-year-old, to his last operation escorting suicide aircraft in April 1945, flown by pilots who, unlike Kaufmann, embraced death rather than defeat.

Survival was a lottery in every air force, but it is clear from Kaufmann's account that it was not just luck. He was evidently an outstanding pilot, utterly at home in the cockpit and able on numerous occasions, detailed throughout his autobiographical account, to extricate himself from crisis after crisis. These qualities picked him out as a natural instructor and most of the first half of his career as a pilot in the Luftwaffe was spent training others to the same high technical and practical standards he set himself. As a result, he did not see his first combat operation until June 1941 when as a re-trained heavy-fighter pilot flying the Messerschmitt Bf 110 he took part in the opening months of the German 'Barbarossa' campaign against the Soviet Union.

It is here that his account really comes to life. He recalls that his years as an instructor were fulfilling enough but lacked the excitement and challenges of combat. His narrative of life as a junior Luftwaffe pilot spans the whole story of Hitler's war from the ground-support operations in 1941 to help the German Panzer forces rout the Red Army, to the final desperate effort to stem the remorseless bomber offensive, when as a squadron commander he took off day after day knowing that this might well be his last mission. In the interval he flew at Stalingrad, engaged in maritime operations with Kampfgeschwader 40, based in western France, returned to Germany to be trained in turn as a single-seat fighter pilot, followed by action at Arnhem, during the Battle of the Bulge, and in the doomed effort to stem the tide of Soviet advance on Berlin. Kaufmann's often vivid recounting of flights and operations will appeal to everyone with a desire to understand just what it was like to fly mission after dangerous mission.

Several things stand out from what is a simple and straightforward account by an ordinary pilot of the revival and decline of German air power in the 1930s and 1940s. Kaufmann provides a good deal of background detail on what life in the air force was like, from the accommodation (lavish by most standards in the new air force quarters built in the 1930s, Spartan once in the field), the food (he almost never complains of being hungry), to the schedules and curricula of the various training stations where he both learned and taught the art of flying. He is unstinting in his praise of the ground crews, that essential branch of the air force that kept aircraft in good shape, repaired damage in a day or less, and coped with the shrinking supply of spare parts. He is much less enthusiastic about his superiors who often failed at briefings to provide pilots with full or precise instructions, gave haphazard meteorological information, and then complained at debriefing if the crews had not achieved what they were intended to.

The second striking feature of Kaufmann's story is the extent to which the Luftwaffe improvised or cut corners to cope with the numerous demands created by Hitler's strategy. The peripatetic career that Kaufmann himself enjoyed, switching from one kind of aircraft to another, moving from front to front seemingly at random, is testament to just how difficult it was for the Luftwaffe to cope with multiple demands for ground-support, counter-force operations, maritime air warfare and defence against bombing. Kaufmann's own judgement, seen from the worm's eye view, was that better use might have been made of what air resources were available. When he was switched to a ground-support role in Russia he had had almost no experience, received quite inadequate training, and like many others developed his tactical skills and operational awareness in the harsh apprenticeship of combat. Improvements in tactical behaviour seem often enough to have been the fruit of post-operation discussions between the pilots themselves rather than directed from above. Luckily for him, Kaufmann was a quick learner so that the move from one aircraft type to another did not affect him much. He even flew in a unit designed to test and then adopt the ill-fated Me 210 replacement for the ageing Bf 110, an aircraft in which a good many pilots died because of poor handling qualities. Kaufmann flew the aircraft without incident though he does judge it here to have been a design 'disaster'. He ended up flying the Messerschmitt Bf 109, but proved just as adept as a single-engine fighter pilot as he had been on the heavy twin-engine Bf 110, though by late 1944 he reckoned the latest Spitfire mark to be a much superior aircraft.

The most curious aspect of this autobiography is the almost complete absence of the wider world in which he lived and operated. A reader might be forgiven for not realizing that Kaufmann served one of the most brutal dictatorships of the twentieth century. He even records a flight over the village of Dachau in 1936 with no mention of the camp that lay below him. Kaufmann himself notes that he and his companions knew it was prudent 'to keep our views on current events to ourselves', but even then it is hard to believe that he was not aware of or affected by the existence of the state's repression or, in service on the Eastern Front, that he saw nothing of the atrocities performed all around him. His account fits perfectly with the image of the 'clean' Wehrmacht, which was strongly defended in the first decades after the end of the war in 1945. But his memoir, first published in 1989, came at just the time that German historians were scrutinizing the archive to discover how compromised the German armed forces were in undertaking routine atrocities and assisting the genocide of the Jews. Only a few years later a major exhibition was mounted on the 'Crimes of the Wehrmacht' which prompted a harsh public debate about the extent to which German servicemen either aided or knew about the criminal activities on the Eastern front. Kaufmann's account would have added grist to the mill of those who argued that most of the Wehrmacht was innocent of the crimes committed in the East and elsewhere. It is true that Kaufmann may well not have witnessed anything himself, but rumour was rife among those serving in the East. He clearly made the decision when he wrote his memoir to remain 'prudent' when it came to commenting on anything but his flying. The one time he steps out of this mould is his account of a visit to a Hitler speech in 1942. It was, he records, a three-hour monologue but he sat with 'rapt attention'. He seems to have been too naïve to realize that this was not a very prudent admission for his postwar audience.

He is also reticent about the campaigns in which he was involved. On a number of occasions in the book he records how little he and his fellow pilots knew about what was going on, and it is certainly the case that historians all too easily forget that the ordinary airman or soldier knows only his small patch and really has no idea what the overall strategy and intentions of those at the top might be. When he found himself posted to the East just prior to the start of 'Barbarossa', he and his friends speculated that the Soviet Union might have granted Hitler's forces the right to cross Soviet territory to the Middle East in order to hit the British in Egypt from the rear. Kaufmann might well have chosen to colour his account with the knowledge of hindsight, but instead the story he tells gives a more honest rendering of the little effort made by the authorities, both military and political, to keep frontline forces informed. Nevertheless, he seems not to have questioned the legitimacy of what he was doing in Russia. His account suggests a kind of neutrality when it comes to estimating rights and wrongs. The real concern for Kaufmann and his colleagues as the war drew to an end was what would happen to them once it was over, not that German defeat was a just recompense for years of aggression.

His matter-of-fact approach to the war reflects a modest personality and a professional rectitude. He seldom steps out from behind the mask of the obedient serviceman, doing what he is told to do without much question. Occasional glimpses of an emotional life are there when he loses a close companion, but fear or anxiety he keeps hidden. His philosophy seems to have been to get on with the job at hand and no griping. Even in his account of his last operations with the *Selbstopfer* – the suicide pilots – he remains singularly detached, observing that they had only enough fuel to reach their designated target and no parachutes. Not for him this final act of futile heroism. Kaufmann, the veteran pilot, survived, while all around him went down in flames.

Richard Overy,
University of Exeter

Introduction by the Translator

This volume fills a long-standing gap in the library of Luftwaffe literature for it chronicles not the exploits of some well-known highly successful fighter ace, but rather the experiences of an 'ordinary' flyer during an extraordinary ten-year career as a pilot in the air arm of the Third Reich.

Born in 1915, the author left school with few qualifications in his early teens to start work as an apprentice in an aircraft factory. In 1934 his ambition to fly led him to volunteer for service in the then still embryonic Luftwaffe, where he steadily rose through the ranks finally to end the war as a Hauptmann in command of a Staffel of Bf 109 fighters.

Yet when Johannes Kaufmann's book first appeared in its original German soft-cover version thirty years ago (*Meine Flugberichte*; Journal Verlag Schwend, 1989) it met with a mixed reception. As one reviewer observed: '...Herr Kaufmann has a remarkable and fascinating story to tell ... all the more pity, therefore, that he feels obliged to regale us with the exact times of take-off and landing for almost every flight he describes ... this constant repetition does little to add to the narrative, rather it detracts from it ...'

It was valid comment. Johannes Kaufmann does indeed have a fascinating tale to tell. But when putting it down on paper it is clearly apparent that he had his meticulously kept flying logbooks – detailing the precise times, duration and distance of every one of his nearly 6,000 flights – on the desk in front of him. And it was presumably his all-too-frequent references to these details which so irritated the unnamed reviewer.

This revised and enlarged English edition of the book attempts to rectify that situation by reducing the number of such details to an acceptable minimum. It also puts the many events described by the author into their correct chronological order and, for the benefit of English readers, provides additional background information on the units Johannes Kaufmann served in, together with their locations, as well as the campaigns he fought in.

What emerges is a unique insight into one man's ten years service as a pilot in the German Luftwaffe – in peace and in war – from its earliest formative months until its final days in the skies above Berlin.

Although he spent lengthy periods as a flying-instructor – with all the humour and all the risks that such a job entailed – Johannes Kaufmann was also involved, either directly or indirectly, in some of the most important and historic events, battles and campaigns of those turbulent years: the reoccupation of the Rhineland, the annexation of Austria, the attack on Poland, the aftermath of the Blitzkrieg in the West, the invasion of Russia, Stalingrad, the campaign in the Caucasus, the D-Day landings, and the Battles of Arnhem, the Ardennes and Berlin, before his final surrender to British forces at Leck in Schleswig-Holstein on 4 May 1945.

A modern-day odyssey in the truest sense of the word.

John Weal

PART I – THE PEACETIME YEARS

Chapter 1
Fliegerschule Magdeburg

The ruins of Berlin slid past beneath my wings. Although the weather on this morning of 1 May 1945 was good, I was unable to make out any details of the ground fighting amidst the smoking devastation below. As I banked the Bf 109 away from the capital and set course for base, I little realised that this brief but abortive reconnaissance sortie was to be the final mission of my Luftwaffe flying career – a career that stretched back ten years almost to the day.

It had all begun the moment the wheels of the little Focke-Wulf Fw 44 '*Stieglitz*' (Goldfinch) biplane trainer lifted off from the grassy surface of a runway some 120km to the south-west of my present position. The date was 27 April 1935. The time exactly 10.26 hours. And the place Magdeburg.

The newly-opened *Fliegerschule* Magdeburg (Magdeburg Flying Training School) had been established on land adjoining the city's then main municipal airport of Magdeburg-Ost. As its name implies, the airport was situated on the eastern outskirts of the city along the road leading out towards Potsdam and beyond to Berlin.

Located on the northern side of this road, the school's accommodation blocks were ultra-modern in style. It was said that their design owed a lot to the clean lines of contemporary Italian Fascist architecture. They were certainly a far cry from the traditional Prussian military barracks of old with their grimly forbidding air of brick-built fortresses. The rooms were well appointed, light and spacious. They not only offered comfortable living quarters but, equally importantly, were also ideally suited to long periods of

1

undisturbed study. In addition, there were ample facilities for sport and more formal military duties close to hand. A swimming pool and the rifle range were both nearby.

The airfield itself was situated on the southern side of the Potsdam road. As was standard at that time, it was grass-surfaced and circular in area. Spaced at intervals around its perimeter were an administration block – which housed the station HQ and the flying control office – a workshop and aircraft hangars, plus all the necessary equipment and supply stores, fuel dump and the like.

The field had two parallel runways, one for take-offs and the other for landings, marked out by rows of flags. The area between the two, known as the 'neutral zone', enabled returning aircraft to turn off the runway at the end of their landing run and taxi back to the take-off point in perfect safety. This ensured a constant and uninterrupted flow of traffic. All aircraft movements on the field were controlled from the so-called '*Startwagen*', which was simply a two-wheeled pushcart used as a mobile desk by the duty time-keeping clerk to log all take-offs and landings. Usually positioned close to the runway, its exact location was indicated by a large white flag bearing a black diagonal cross which made it clearly visible to all.

For night flying the runway marker flags were replaced by portable lamps. Any obstacles on, or in the immediate vicinity of the field were also illuminated. But as yet the school had no kind of any base approach lighting.

The *Fliegerschule* Magdeburg was commanded at this time by a Major Sturm. He was assisted by a relatively small administrative staff. The flying instructors were a mix of service and civilian personnel, headed jointly by Hauptmann Heinzinger and Herr von Bornstedt. We pupils belonged to the trainee company, which was led by Leutnant *Freiherr* von Sichardt. The company consisted of two groups, the first of which had already commenced their flying training in October 1934. I was part of the second group, whose training began towards the end of April 1935.

My maiden flight on that 27 April, with group instructor Feldwebel Bachmann in Focke-Wulf Fw 44 '*Stieglitz*' D-EQEM, lasted all of twenty minutes. It was the first of five such introductory flights spread over a period of four days. Their purpose was twofold:

to familiarize us newcomers with the airfield's immediate surroundings, and also to give us the opportunity to experience for
ourselves how the aircraft responded to the controls. At first we were
allowed to hold the stick only very loosely, following the instructor's
every movement and simply getting used to the feel of being in the
air. It was a fascinating experience and ideal preparation for the
weeks of intensive training that lay ahead of us.

In fact, it took a good two months of thorough schooling, both
practical and theoretical, before I made my first solo flight. Then, on
4 July, came the big day. One last check flight with test instructor
Oberfeldwebel Schmidt. He was apparently satisfied with my
progress, for he climbed out of the aircraft with a perfunctory 'That'll
do' and turned for a few brief words with my flying instructor,
Gefreiter Schaffranek, who promptly ordered an airman to attach
two long red pennants to the wing struts of my machine.

These colourful strips of cloth served as a warning to any other
aircraft flying in the vicinity of the field to give me a wide berth.
There was no sense of shame or stigma involved in having to display
the tell-tale red pennants. They were simply a sensible precaution.
But they did rob the tyro pilot of his comforting cloak of anonymity
as he concentrated on completing that all-important first solo
without mishap.

As for myself, I must confess to feeling nervous but confident as I
sat in the cockpit, engine ticking over, waiting for permission to take
off. The usual crowd of fellow trainees had gathered at the start line.
They were watching the proceedings with interest, laughing and
joking as they always did on these occasions.

At last I saw the duty NCO wave the large white flag with the
diagonal green cross on it. Cleared for take-off! From then on
everything went like clockwork. I eased the throttle forward and
'*Stieglitz*' D-EPYF began to roll. I held her straight as she gathered
speed across the grass. After lifting off I performed a single circuit of
the field as ordered and, exactly four minutes later, put her down
again in a textbook three-pointer, main wheels and tailskid all
touching the ground simultaneously.

My first solo, which had been my eighty-second flight in all, had
thankfully gone off without a hitch. To go solo for the first time was

a major milestone in any pilot's flying career and I can vividly recall my main emotion as being one of jubilant satisfaction, tempered by not a little relief – sentiments shared, no doubt, by my instructor!

Four more flights followed in quick succession. All went equally smoothly; the last of them bringing to an end my flying duties on what had been a truly memorable day. But there was no party that evening. We were all still very much beginners and it was made clear to us that there was no justification for celebrations at this early stage of our training. The sense of personal achievement was deemed reward enough.

Order and discipline were paramount throughout our training and each and every one of us tried to conduct himself accordingly. Our superiors were demanding but not unreasonably so. They were strict, fair and solicitous. The standards we were expected to meet were exceptionally high, but attainable with perseverance and practice.

As well as flying training, we had to master a comprehensive theoretical programme on all matters aeronautical. In addition, a major part of what little off-duty time we *did* have was devoted to sport, which was designed to keep us fit and healthy. The purely military side of our basic training – 'square-bashing', if you will – was confined to Saturdays. Sundays were given over to rest, personal chores and quiet contemplation. There was no weekend leave at the start of the course, although 24-hour Sunday passes were sometimes granted under special circumstances.

We trainees all had the same aim: to gain our pilot's licence. We wanted to avoid being washed off the course at all costs. Comradeship and self-discipline were the order of the day. And despite the many demands made upon us, our little group displayed an air of quiet determination.

Training continued apace and very soon it was time for us to take our first flying tests. To get through them would require all our new-found flying skills – plus a good helping of luck. The ultimate goal was to win the coveted Class B-2 pilot's licence (soon to be renamed the Military Pilot's Licence). This was achieved in three stages, the first of which was covered by the Class A-2 training programme. To successfully complete the A-2 programme, the trainee pilot had to carry out the following:

17 precision landings on his home field, plus a number of flights under various set conditions;

12 open country landings on outlying, unmarked and unprepared fields or meadows, and take-offs from same;

1 high-altitude flight of one hour's duration at 3,000m above mean sea level;

2 cross-country flights each to include an intermediate landing; and

1 cross-country flight with two intermediate landings.

In the early years of the Luftwaffe great emphasis was laid on pilot training. It was extraordinarily thorough and very nearly four months were to pass before I attained my A-2 licence. Between 27 April and 23 August 1935 I made no fewer than 241 training flights totalling 37 hours and 58 minutes flying time in all. The aircraft used during this initial stage were the Focke-Wulf Fw 44 '*Stieglitz*' and the Heinkel He 72 '*Kadett*' basic trainer biplanes.

There was no let-up in our busy schedule. Just one day after gaining my A-2 licence I began training for the B-1. This second phase of our schooling was appreciably shorter and more concentrated than the first. In the space of just over five weeks I clocked up another 65 hours (and one minute!) in the course of 150 flights. The training exercises themselves were not dissimilar to those needed for the A-2, but the requirements were now more stringent. We were flying heavier, more powerful advanced trainers – notably the Arado Ar 66 and the Albatros L 75 – and were having to master the arts of aerobatic, formation and night flying.

Included at intervals among the 150 flights that led to my gaining my B-1 licence on 1 October were the following specific tests, every one of which had to be performed to the instructors' complete satisfaction:

1 high-altitude flight of one hour's duration at 4,000m above mean sea level;

4 open country landings in the Ar 66 on unprepared fields;

14 aerobatic flights totalling 10 hours and 55 minutes (including one 33-minute training flight in the company of an instructor);

1 aerobatic final examination flight;

12 formation flights each lasting 1 hour and 55 minutes;

8 night flights totalling 5 hours and 58 minutes;

2 orientation flights of 1 hour and 7 minutes duration (to be flown at an altitude of less than 50m); and

24 cross-country flights involving 11 intermediate landings on unfamiliar airfields (and covering a total distance of 4,658km).

The third and final part of the Magdeburg course not only added considerably to our piloting skills, it also broadened our overall experiences of flying to a marked degree. Whereas the A-2 and B-1 training schedules had taught us, step by methodical step, the mechanics of controlling an aircraft in flight, this last phase imposed more demands on us as individuals. As the training progressed, every single one of us was being assessed; our strengths built upon and encouraged, our weaknesses noted and, if possible, rectified.

This was to have a direct effect on our subsequent Luftwaffe careers – and ultimate fates. For it was during this stage that the school staff and instructors were having to decide which arm of the service we were best suited for; which of us, for example, displayed the flair and dash that would make a good fighter pilot, and which of us had temperaments and abilities more suited to flying bombers or reconnaissance aircraft. Naturally, we were aware of what was going on, and the pressure upon us was enormous.

The B-2 course introduced us to a wide range of new and diverse aircraft types. Among them were the single-seat Focke-Wulf Fw 56 'Stösser' (Falcon), a sleek high-wing advanced trainer and home defence fighter, the much more cumbersome Heinkel He 45 and He 46, which were bomber and tactical reconnaissance aircraft respectively, and the Junkers W 33 and W 34 light transports. The two Heinkel types were used primarily to practise formation flying, while the Junkers duo were employed mostly for lengthy cross-country flights.

In all, I was to log a further 142 flights – a total of 52 hours and 50 minutes flying time – before attaining my B-2 licence on 12 December 1935. More than eleven of those hours had been spent on blind-flying training. We were not expected to do any navigating during these exercises. Their sole purpose was to make us fully conversant with flying the aircraft on instruments alone. We sat behind blacked-out windows in the left-hand pilot's seat of the Junkers' cockpit, while the instructor occupied the right-hand seat monitoring our progress and keeping an eye on the navigation.

Devoid of all external vision, we were required to carry out a number of specific manoeuvres using just the instruments on the control panel in front of us. These manoeuvres included:

Maintaining a given height by means of the precision altimeter;
Keeping to a set course by following the needle of the magnetic (repeater) compass;
Performing a controlled turn at a constant rate of two degrees per second; the full circle to be completed in three minutes; and
Gaining and losing height by use of the variometer (rate-of-climb/descent indicator) at a constant rate of plus/minus 2m per second within set altitude datum marks.

Considering the relatively short time devoted to blind-flying training, these exacting requirements were difficult to meet. It meant a lot of hard work and dedication on our part. The instructors were constantly demanding the very utmost from us and we couldn't afford even a moment's lapse of concentration. The training may have been hard, but it would prove its worth and we were to be hugely grateful for it in the months and years ahead.

Such was the intensity of the training schedule at Magdeburg that we had to put in some very long hours. Take 13 September, for example, a particularly hectic day in the middle of the B-1 course: first take-off at 09.29 hours, end of the day flying programme 16.30 hours; start of the night-flying schedule 19.42 hours, final landing at 02.50 hours the following morning.

And it should perhaps be pointed out that our working day did not begin from the time we climbed into the cockpit. We were also required to help beforehand with the preparations for the day's flying by pushing the aircraft out of the hangar onto the apron and setting up the flags marking the take-off and landing strips. And when flying was finally finished for the day we had to assist the ground personnel with the maintenance and readying of the machines for the next day's programme.

Between, and in addition to the hours we spent in the air, we were given a very thorough schooling in the many specialist subjects relating to all things aeronautical. In fact, the basics of aviation had already been imparted to us during day-long sessions in the classroom before we were even allowed anywhere near an aircraft. The individual subjects covered during these opening stages of the course had included

Aerodynamics;
The science of flight;
Aero-engines;
Instrumentation;
Introduction to the aircraft;
Air traffic rules and regulations;
The marking of the airfield and of obstacles;
Meteorology;
Navigation and map-reading;
Actions to be taken in cases of emergency; and
Introduction to the flying training programme.

And once flying training commenced, the majority of these subjects were enlarged upon and tailored to match our progress in the air. At the end of the course we had to sit a written examination in each subject; some even requiring an additional oral exam as well. Just as with our practical training, the work in the classroom also made great demands upon us. The school staff expected nothing but total commitment on our part. They pushed us hard, but it was a policy that was to pay enormous dividends.

Another highly valuable part of the course was the time we spent helping the ground crews service the school's aircraft. This benefitted us in two ways. Not only did we acquire a good basic understanding of the workings of an aircraft, we also established a personal rapport with the mechanics and an appreciation for the vital yet often unsung tasks that they performed.

On occasion we would also be ordered to report for duty in the aircraft repair workshops. Here we had the opportunity to experience at first hand the more specialized work required to keep the engines, airframes and instrumentation of the machines in perfect working order. This added significantly to our growing pool of knowledge and was of particular benefit to the less technically gifted among our number.

I have deliberately described our initial training in some detail in order to illustrate just how much importance the Luftwaffe attached to giving its new recruits a thorough grounding in those early years. Inevitably, however, the quality of training such as we were fortunate enough to receive was to become a casualty of the approaching World War. After the start of hostilities, and as the conflict progressed, so the standards steadily declined and the courses grew ever shorter until, by the closing stages of the war, the training programmes for new young pilots were being measured not in months and weeks, but in hours – and even in minutes!

But that disastrous state of affairs still lay ten years into the future and, despite the thoroughness of our own training, things didn't always go strictly according to plan, even in the brave new Luftwaffe of the mid-1930s.

The aforementioned 13 September was a case in point. After an early start I had completed my daylight flying schedule by late afternoon. I then had a break of very nearly three hours, during which time I was able to get some rest and grab a bite to eat, before taking off on the first of my night-flying exercises at exactly 19.42 hours. With further short breaks, night-flying training then continued until well into the early hours of the following morning.

My last flight had been a thirty-minute test which, happily, I managed to get through to the apparent satisfaction of my instructor. Pleased as I was, I was not sorry when I finally touched down again at 02.50 hours. It was the end of a strenuous twenty-hour day and as I clambered out of Arado Ar 66, coded D-IHAQ, I was feeling absolutely drained.

At the close of each day's flying it was customary for the trainees to get out of the aircraft at the end of the landing run and make their way back to the hangar on foot, leaving the instructors to taxi in on their own. As I wearily set off across the field in the company of a small group of my fellow pupils, I consoled myself with the thought that they must be feeling just as exhausted as I was. But one of our number clearly did not relish the prospect of the long trudge back across the grass and had decided to do something about it – as we were soon to discover.

Unnoticed by any of us Gefreiter Müller, an irrepressible Berliner who never missed a trick, had quietly climbed back aboard one of the idling Arados hoping to get a free lift back to the hangar. Unfortunately, the machine he had chosen to stow away in was the one being flown by an instructor named Lonzius, who was also something of a character. And, for reasons best known to himself, Lonzius had decided on this particular night not to join the steady procession of machines heading back to the hangar, but instead to return to the start line. There he briefly gunned his engine before promptly taking off again for a spot of impromptu nocturnal aerobatics.

He had just reached the top of a loop, hanging inverted and almost motionless, when the still air of the night was rent by a banshee wailing. Thoroughly unnerved – 'for a moment I honestly thought that I'd disturbed some ghostly spirit' – Lonzius lost no time in getting back down on the ground again.

There the mystery was quickly solved when a querulous voice complained in an unmistakably thick Berlin accent, 'Herr Flying Instructor, I almost fell out!' As indeed he had, without a parachute and not having bothered to strap himself in, Müller had had to cling on for dear life as the Arado teetered on its back at the top of the loop. The shaken Lonzius was absolutely incandescent and proceeded to give the stowaway a dressing down of truly epic proportions. But there the matter rested. If the instructor had reported it to the higher authorities our comrade Müller would almost certainly have been facing disciplinary action, but then too so would Lonzius himself for his unauthorized aerobatic activities.

Just over a fortnight later I had a spot of excitement of my own. It was on 30 September, the penultimate day of the B-1 course, and I had been ordered to carry out a lengthy solo cross-country flight in Albatros L 75, coded D-IRIQ. The route itself was fairly straightforward: Magdeburg to Böblingen and back – a distance of close on 900km in all.

The weather at Magdeburg was fine, hardly a cloud in the sky and near perfect visibility. The forecast for Böblingen was also good. The only thing I didn't know was what the conditions were like between the two and that, as it turned out, was the important bit.

I didn't call in to the weather office before my flight. This was something that the instructors had always done on our behalf before deciding on the day's flying programme. In fairness, I should perhaps also mention that at this relatively early stage of our training our knowledge of matters meteorological still left a lot to be desired. Not one of us would have been able to form an accurate picture of the overall weather conditions from the confusion of maps and charts available for inspection in the station weather office.

For navigational purposes I had been issued with a single route map. These maps, to a scale of 1:300,000, were produced for every cross-country training flight. They came in the form of a continuous roll, some 20cm in width, and were fitted into small rectangular aluminium boxes. The course to be followed was clearly marked and, as the flight progressed, the trainee pilot could gradually unroll the map by turning a small knob on the side of the box and thus keep abreast of the landscape unfolding beneath him. The map box had to be hung around the pilot's neck so that it was readily available to him at all times, and also to ensure that he didn't drop it on the floor of the cockpit or lose it overboard.

It should be borne in mind that we were flying in open-cockpit aircraft with just a small plexiglass windscreen to protect us from the buffeting of the airstream. A pair of large awkwardly-fitting goggles, which were a constant nuisance, went some way towards protecting our eyes but, at the same time, greatly reduced our peripheral field of vision.

Our flying gear comprised a one-piece flying suit – lightweight for summer, fleece-lined for winter – flying helmet, boots and gloves. We also wore a parachute harness to which we attached our seat parachute. The whole outfit was not exactly what you would call comfortable, but it was necessary.

I took off for Böblingen at 09.18 hours. All went smoothly, as did the first part of the flight. By slowly unrolling the map I was able to keep a check on my position at all times and follow the route indicated.

Meanwhile, however, the weather was slowly worsening. It began to get slightly hazy and it was not long before I noticed a bank of high clouds gathering in the otherwise clear blue sky. I paid them little attention at first but gradually, almost imperceptibly, they began to form into a solid unbroken blanket. Barely an hour after leaving Magdeburg I found myself flying over an extensive area of low rolling hills. This was the region known as the Thuringian Basin. Ahead of me, to left and right, the twin towns of Erfurt and Gotha were clearly visible despite the haze. I was bang on course.

The picturesque valley I was following ended abruptly as the ground rose steeply in front of me. This was the start of the more mountainous Thuringian Forest, the dark line of tall trees along its ridge standing out sharply against the now pale grey sky. And above this narrow strip of clear sky the solid cloud was hanging like a curtain about to fall.

Up to this point I hadn't really paid much attention to the deteriorating weather conditions. The thought of abandoning the flight and turning back hadn't entered my head. Although admittedly narrow, the gap of clear sky between the forest ridge and the cloud base above did not pose any great difficulty and gave me little cause for concern. I was on course. I was on time. And so I set out to cross the 2,000km^2 expanse of the Thuringian Forest.

But it was not long before the wind started to pick up and very soon the Albatros was being buffeted by squally gusts. Then, quite unexpectedly, it began to rain. It got darker and the machine shook violently as the gusts of wind grew stronger. Suddenly the first ragged wisps of low-lying cloud were whipping past my wingtips. In my efforts to keep sight of the ground I had forfeited so much altitude that by this time I was flying at little more than treetop height.

Everything had happened so quickly that all I could do now was to try to keep the crate in the air and not smash into some hidden mountainside or other. I grappled with the controls as D-IRIQ fought her way through this witches' brew. Turn back? Yes, I'd thought of that the moment it had begun to rain. But by then it was far too late. The weather had already closed in behind me and the way back to Magdeburg was completely blocked.

I had no alternative but to struggle on, peering through the rain-lashed windscreen, my fate entirely in the hands of the weather gods. Fortunately they soon grew tired of toying with me. Conditions began to ease, and after about another ten minutes I caught a glimpse of an airfield below me, its name spelled out in large white letters: Meiningen. This lay directly on my course! I remembered the name from studying the route map before I set out. Although badly shaken by my recent experience, a false sense of pride prevented me from putting down for an intermediate landing.

Instead I pressed on, making steady if somewhat erratic progress by heading from one patch of clearing sky to the next. Not surprisingly, this played havoc with my course keeping and within a very short space of time I realized that I was totally lost. I'd had to lay the metal map case to one side quite a while ago. It was getting in the way as I fought to keep the aircraft under control. The L 75 had more than its fair share of foibles, especially in blustery weather, and could be a tricky beast to fly.

Aircraft compasses back in those days were quite basic and mine had been bouncing about with every jolt and judder of the Albatros as it battled its way through the continuing severe turbulence. This meant that I was able to maintain only a very rough heading. I was still much too low to see enough of the landscape between the banks of scudding grey cloud to gain a visual fix. It was not until I spotted the unmistakable saw-tooth course of the River Main ahead of me that I was able to re-establish my exact position.

The weather improved rapidly from this point on and I finally landed safe and sound, albeit very late, in Böblingen at 12.55 hours. Thirty minutes later I was in the air again and on my way back to Magdeburg. I had been informed that conditions en route had quietened down and so it proved. After an uneventful flight of just over two hours – little more than half the time the outward leg had taken – I touched down at my home field.

It had been a memorable day and one I would not forget in a hurry. It had impressed upon me the vital importance that the weather played in a pilot's life. From that day on I took a keen interest in meteorology and everything associated with it. This was to prove not merely useful, but at times absolutely crucial in the years to come.

I subsequently learned that what I had just experienced was by no means uncommon. Many others had also encountered severe conditions in this area. And not everyone had got away with it as lightly as I had done. There had been a number of fatal crashes. Thuringia prided itself on being the 'Green Heart' of Germany. The Bf 109s and Fw 190s of Jagdgeschwader 54, one of the most successful Luftwaffe fighter groups of the war, would later wear the 'Green Heart' as their unit badge. But the very heart of that 'Green Heart' – the Thuringian Forest itself – acquired a far more sinister reputation during the early days of the Luftwaffe when it was frequently referred to as the 'Flyers' Graveyard'. Sadly, it was a reputation that it lived up to all too often.

My respect for the weather in all its moods, both good and bad, was reinforced by another incident just over three weeks later. On 22 October, together with two fellow trainees, I was ordered to proceed by rail to Schleissheim, an airfield outside Munich. There we were to pick up a trio of Albatros L 101 trainers and ferry them back to Magdeburg. The L 101 was a parasol-wing design that was inevitably nicknamed the 'Umbrella'. The machine assigned to me was coded D-EZAZ. Because time was pressing, the handover procedure was confined to just a few essential formalities which were gone through in very much of a hurry.

As there were three of us, we decided that we would fly in line-astern formation with the senior man taking the lead. I should perhaps mention that this formation was not specified in our orders. It was simply something that we three young pilots, in our total ignorance, thought would be the most suitable for the flight back to Magdeburg. But events were soon to prove just how wrong we were.

Our pre-flight briefing was not merely rushed, it was also based on two false premises. We were told that we would have the benefit of a tail wind whereas, in fact, the wind was coming from the quarter. This meant that we would not be flying at the estimated speed of 150km/h, but would be lucky to make 110km/h. Furthermore, as the distance from Schleissheim to Magdeburg was 442km, it was confidently predicted that the flight would take us no more than 2 hours and 40 minutes. The combination of our own inexperience, plus a sloppy briefing was, in short, a recipe for disaster – and a disaster is what it very nearly turned out to be.

We lifted off from Schleissheim at 13.30 hours and quickly got ourselves into formation. The weather was fine and the first hour passed without incident. Our three 'Umbrellas' crawled slowly across the Bavarian landscape and we looked forward to a pleasant and leisurely flight home. Maintaining formation was proving a lot trickier than we had at first imagined, however. We were so busy juggling stick and throttle that we weren't able to pay enough attention to our maps. We had to snatch brief glances at them in the odd intervals when we were not totally preoccupied with keeping station on each other. In this way, slowly but surely, we began to lose our orientation.

After ninety minutes in the air Bayreuth airfield appeared in front of us – so even though we were not yet halfway, we were at least still on course. It was at this point that our leader, who had been casting enquiring looks over his shoulder at us with increasing frequency for the past quarter-of-an-hour, indicated by hand signal that he intended to make an intermediate landing. We duly broke formation and a few minutes later, at 15.08 hours, touched down at Bayreuth.

After a brief discussion, and despite some misgivings, we decided not to abort the flight, but to continue with our journey. Bearing in mind the distance we still had to cover and the relatively early time of sunset, we were anxious to be on our way and so were back in the air again little more than twenty minutes later.

The weather was still good as we bumbled happily towards the southern foothills of the Thuringian Forest. But the sun was already beginning to sink low in the sky under our port wingtips and soon the first tendrils of ground mist could be seen seeping along the valley floors below us. This was not uncommon at this time of year, of course, but it did give me the first slight prickle of unease.

I noticed too that the air speed indicator was no longer registering the speeds it had been earlier in the flight. The wind must have increased and was now slowing us down even more. I began to have serious doubts about continuing the flight. It seemed to me that an emergency landing was the only sensible way out of what was rapidly becoming a dangerous situation.

There were no airfields in the immediate vicinity and to have carried on flying after night had fallen would be asking for all kinds of trouble. My two comrades must have been thinking along similar lines if the hand signals we were exchanging and the shaking of heads were anything to go by.

Our formation leader, who had served in the infantry before volunteering for the Luftwaffe, settled matters by vigorously pumping his arm up and down. This was the accepted military signal for 'Follow me' and we each raised a hand in reply to indicate that we had understood. We slid into a wide line-abreast-right formation and started searching for somewhere to land. It was not long before we spotted a suitable looking meadow ahead of us in the gathering dusk.

We all three landed safely and in quick succession. The time was exactly 16.45 hours, a good thirty minutes *after* our original ETA in Magdeburg, even though we had still only covered about three-quarters of the distance back to base. After climbing from our cockpits we gathered in a tight, self-conscious little group and attempted to pretend that nothing out of the ordinary had happened. In truth, each was trying to hide his embarrassment from the others and was acting as if it were the most natural thing in the world to be standing in the half-light beside a trio of cooling, gently ticking aircraft in the middle of an empty field.

Soon, however, we were surrounded by a crowd of curious locals from the nearby community of Kunitz which, we were told, was some 5km north of Jena. The mayor and councillors bade us welcome and invited us to be their guests for the night. A group of volunteers offered to stand guard over our aircraft and so, with darkness rapidly falling, we left our 'emergency landing meadow' and made our way to the mayor's house where we were received with genuine warmth and hospitality.

The first thing our leader Schulz did was to telephone through to Magdeburg, as per standing orders, to report on what had happened to us. He didn't say much after replacing the receiver, just that our reception in Magdeburg was unlikely to be as warm and friendly as here in Kunitz – but we'd already come to that conclusion ourselves.

The following morning we found the meadow blanketed in a thick layer of mist. It was slow to clear, which gave us ample time to thank our kind hosts and to prepare for our departure. The three of us paced out a likely looking take-off strip through the long damp grass to ensure that there were no hidden obstacles and agreed that it was suitable. Along the edge of the field, however, we were shocked to discover a row of tall iron stakes, which were probably used to support wires for drying hay. They were dangerously close to where we had landed late the previous afternoon and had we hit them the results could have been catastrophic.

It was not until 11.25 hours that we lifted off for the third and final part of our eventful ferry flight. The sun was now shining brightly and it took us just over an hour-and-a-quarter to reach Magdeburg. But on this last leg, having decided that we had had enough of long-distance formation flying for the time being, each made his own way back to base.

Our reception at Magdeburg turned out not to be as frosty as we had at first feared. Rather than being faced with disciplinary action, we were told to regard the matter as a valuable lesson learned. I think the school authorities were secretly as relieved as we were that all had ended well, and that three pilots and three new aircraft had arrived safe and sound; especially in the light of the grievous losses that our course had suffered back in August.

My time at Magdeburg was nearing its end. I had thoroughly enjoyed the whole experience of learning to fly and had found everything I had been taught, both in the air and on the ground, hugely interesting. At 15.10 hours on 12 December 1935 I touched down in an Arado Ar 64 for my final landing at Magdeburg. The first stage of my flying training was over and I took my leave of my instructors and superiors. I owe them a great debt of thanks and have retained lasting memories of them all to this day.

Chapter 2
Fliegerschule (S) Schleissheim

After successfully completing my basic flying training at Magdeburg, my next destination was to be the historic airfield at Schleissheim, home to the Luftwaffe's premier fighter training wing.

In the aftermath of the First World War a defeated Germany had been prohibited by the terms of the Versailles Treaty from indulging in any form of military aviation activity. But the post-war Weimar Republic found a number of ways to circumvent this blanket ban. One of them involved the signing of an agreement with the Soviet Union for the setting up of a secret fighter training school for German personnel at Lipezk, some 400km to the south of Moscow.

Training had commenced there in the summer of 1925 and over the course of the next seven years Lipezk produced about a hundred German fighter pilots, many of them later to become well-known names in the wartime Luftwaffe. But circumstances changed with the rise to power of Adolf Hitler. The elaborate subterfuge of Lipezk was brought to an end, the last German trainees departed in August 1933, and a new fighter training school was established in Germany. The site chosen was Schleissheim, near Munich.

The resurgent German air arm was still very much a clandestine force, however. Its existence had to be kept secret from the Allies. For the first year of its being the school therefore operated under the guise of the '*Deutsche Verkehrsfliegerschule GmbH, Zweigstelle Schleiss-heim*', or 'German Commercial Pilots' School Ltd., Schleissheim Branch'.

Hitler finally unveiled his new Luftwaffe to the world in the spring of 1935. But even then a degree of secrecy was retained. Every unit, irrespective of its type, was given the same generic title of *Fliegergruppe* (Air Wing), followed by the name of its home base. This system of designation offered no clue as to the unit's specific

18

role (fighter, bomber, etc.), nor as to its position within the Luft-waffe's table of organization as a whole.

The Luftwaffe's foremost fighter training establishment, com-manded now by Major Gerd Massow, thus emerged as the *Fliegergruppe (S)* Schleissheim – the '*S*' in brackets denoting 'Schule' or school – and it was to Schleissheim that our entire Magdeburg course was posted *en bloc* to become trainee fighter pilots.

We set off by rail on 17 December 1935. Like a bunch of excited children going on holiday, we were full of high spirits as we journeyed south. Not only were we now the proud possessors of B-2 flying licences, we were also looking forward to the myriad pleasures the big city of Munich had in store for us.

We pulled into Munich's main station early on the morning of 18 December and made good use of the wait for our connection to Schleissheim by strolling into the city centre for a hearty breakfast of white sausage, a local delicacy recommended by the Bavarians in our party, who were only too keen to introduce us to the culinary delights of their capital city.

Replete and somewhat weary, we reached Schleissheim airfield around mid-day. Upon reporting our arrival, we were welcomed in a very efficient but friendly fashion by the station Senior Warrant Officer – more commonly referred to as the '*Spiess*', or 'Chiefy' – who assigned us to our quarters. As was only to be expected, everything seemed to be run on very efficient lines and, despite the unfamiliarity of our surroundings, we were all very quickly assigned our quarters and informed what our duties would be.

When we fell in on parade the next morning we were told that, because of the approach of Christmas and the consequent break in the school's training schedules, we were all being granted leave for the entire festive period up to and including Three Kings Day, or 6 January; another very welcome surprise!

With leave over, we all met up again at Schleissheim, rested and refreshed, ready to start what would prove to be a very tough period in our flying careers. This new school was altogether different from what we had been used to at Magdeburg. There, training had been conducted more or less along civilian lines – almost like a civil flying club, in fact – whereas here at Schleissheim every day was very strictly regimented. The only off-duty time we had was from midday on Saturdays until 21.00 hours on Sundays, the hour that the retreat was sounded. Weekend passes were sometimes granted upon request, however, and this gave us the opportunity to get to know the city of Munich and its beautiful surroundings a little better. I still have a lot of happy memories of visiting Munich's many museums and art galleries, and of exploring the picturesque lakes and mountains of Bavaria.

Reveille was at 06.00 hours each day and training commenced at 07.00 hours. Getting up this early wasn't too much of a hardship as we all had to be in bed by 21.00 hours every evening. This timetable was very strictly enforced. But it certainly did us no harm; quite the opposite, in fact, if the relaxed attitude of our little group was anything to go by.

But Schleissheim *was* similar to Magdeburg in one respect. Our training was still divided into two very distinct parts: the theoretical and the practical – or, as we said, 'the classroom and the cockpit'. Our extra-curricular military duties accounted for only a few hours of the overall weekly schedule. They were mostly taken up by rifle practice at the butts, or by sport. The highlight of our sporting activities was without doubt the few days we spent skiing in the Kreuzberg region south of Partenkirchen. The school had its own ski chalet down there and this provided the perfect opportunity for us to become better acquainted with the flying instructors who had accompanied us on the trip. Each day on the slopes ended in a convivial evening spent chatting in front of a blazing log fire. Another treat was to be able to visit the Winter Olympics, which had opened in neighbouring Garmisch on 6 February.

The theoretical side of our schooling always took place in the mornings. Building upon the basics we had been taught at Magdeburg, it was designed to give us a deeper and more complete understanding of aerodynamics, aero engine technology, navigation and meteorology. Mastery of these subjects was vitally important. At times they could spell the difference between life or death. Both theoretical and practical aspects of the training programme were carefully co-ordinated to make a cohesive whole and provide us with a solid foundation for a successful career as fighter pilots.

It was clear to us that we had to learn to fly an aircraft to the very limit of its capabilities. This was essential if we were to survive in a dogfight which was, after all, the whole point of our present training. And this was where the theory part came in. A good grasp of the maximum performance of the machine we were flying was of the utmost importance, and we were given ample opportunity to put our newly-gained classroom knowledge to the test during our hours in the air.

Aerial tactics also featured prominently in the curriculum. At this still relatively early stage in the history of aviation, our teaching was said to be based primarily on the current known practices, strengths and equipment of foreign air forces. But it quickly became apparent, even to us, that much of what was being drummed into us harked back to the days of the Great War.

The flying part of our Schleissheim training had begun on Thursday, 9 January 1936 with a few circuits in the Focke-Wulf Fw 56 '*Stösser*' single-seat advanced trainer. In the days that followed we were introduced to the Arado Ar 65 and the Heinkel He 50. These latter were both operational types. Entering service in 1933, the Ar 65 had been the first fighter aircraft to equip the then still clandestine Luftwaffe. The He 50 was a very different kettle of fish. A sturdy two-seat biplane, it had served briefly with the Luftwaffe's first dive-bomber unit before being relegated to training duties.

On 20 January, after thoroughly familiarizing ourselves on these two machines under all conceivable flight conditions – a procedure commonly known in the Luftwaffe as '*einfliegen*', or 'flying oneself in' – we were split into small groups, each of about six in number, to commence an exceptionally intensive and rigorous regime of individual training.

Each group was led by an officer-instructor. Our particular group was headed by a 24-year-old graduate from Lipezk named Günther Lützow. Leutnant Lützow was an example to us all, a gifted flyer and an outstanding instructor. We had no idea at the time, of course, that our lowly Leutnant Lützow was destined to become one of the true greats of the wartime Luftwaffe.

This next stage of the training programme required us to carry out some very demanding and complex practice flights, each of which could last for up to an hour or more. Before every take-off we were given a meticulous pre-flight briefing setting out in great detail exactly what it was that we were being ordered to do. It would have been well-nigh impossible to memorize the minute-by-minute sequence of manoeuvres that went to make up such a flight, but fortunately for us it was all printed out in time-table form on a sheet of paper. This sheet could then be attached to a small clipboard strapped around the pilot's thigh, which allowed him to refer to it throughout the course of the exercise.

A typical sheet would have looked something like this:

Time (Minutes)	Manoeuvre
0 – 6	Take off individually, 50m intervals, climb line-astern to altitude 3,000m, proceed overland to exercise area. Order of flight (followed by a list of names)
6 – 11	Change formation; in-line Immelmann turns
11 – 15	Climbs and dives
15 – 20	Loops and Immelmann turns
20 – 23	Formate in left-hand turn above Puchheim railway station
23 – 29	'Zirkus' (a series of intricate aerobatic figures to be flown in line-astern)
29 – 40	Re-formate in pairs and fly route designated
40 – 46	Return flight from end point of exercise to Schleissheim airfield; descend to altitude of 300m en route
46 – 50	Break individual pairs formation and land individually in following order (list of names).

Each of the groups had its own strictly defined airspace in which to practise. Our area, which was roughly triangular in shape, lay to the west of Munich and was bounded by the railway lines fanning out from Pasing to Fürstenfeldbruck and from Pasing to Maisach. Our rendezvous point was always Puchheim railway station situated approximately midway between the two.

In such a confined space the risk of a mid-air collision was ever-present. Every single manoeuvre therefore required total concentration, and each figure had to be flown with absolute precision. In addition to this, we also had to keep strictly to the times specified for each separate part of the exercise. This was one of the primary functions of the Schleissheim course: to teach us how to master and co-ordinate these two vital disciplines – complete control of the aircraft combined with accurate timekeeping.

These exercises would sometimes be flown above a solid blanket of cloud. Climbing and descending through thick layers of cloud was always done in tight line-astern formation. In order to minimize the risks, preparations for flights on those days when the sky was overcast were even more meticulous than usual. And we were very closely monitored while carrying them out. The instructor would suddenly appear off a pupil's wingtip, indicating by hand signals what he was doing wrong and what action needed to be taken to correct it. After landing, a thorough debriefing would then review and analyse all the mistakes made and the correct remedial actions explained and discussed.

This procedure was hugely beneficial to us all. We felt that our training was coming on in leaps and bounds. And the reason for this wasn't hard to find. All our instructors were excellent flyers, of course. But it was their enthusiasm, encouragement and natural ability to pass on their knowledge and skills that made them truly exceptional. I flew seventeen of these complex practice flights during my time at Schleissheim; logging exactly 17 hours and 31 minutes in the process. But the Schleissheim training programme also included a number of other, much shorter exercises – in my case twenty-four in all; totalling just over four hours in the air.

Many of these shorter flights were deliberately flown in bad weather; the object being to provide us with as much experience as possible of operating in adverse conditions. Very often the cloud base would be less than 100m off the ground and visibility one or two kilometres at best. Under conditions such as these we would be ordered up in the single-seat Fw 56s to carry out local orientation exercises. We would, of necessity, be forced to fly at little more than treetop height, and the aim was to teach us how to follow a set course with absolute accuracy in the most difficult of circumstances.

Such flights were always carried out when the weather was at its worst so that there was no possibility of anyone cheating. In other words, the given course really *did* have to be flown at treetop level. There was no chance of anybody gaining a little surreptitious altitude every now and again to have a quick look around and get his bearings. 'Eat birds or die!' was the somewhat enigmatic watchword.

None of us actually died on 27 January 1936 – but it was a close-run thing. That Monday morning the weather was atrocious. The clouds were hanging very low, visibility was extremely poor and there were intermittent heavy showers. On this occasion the pre-flight briefing was kept quite short. Each of us was simply given the course he was to follow, reminded of the obligatory precautions and measures to be taken in cases of emergency, and told to get going!

At the height we would be flying, we would need all our concentration to keep the aircraft straight and level. There would be time for only the occasional quick glance down at the maps strapped to our thighs. So it was imperative that we establish firmly in our minds beforehand any distinctive terrain features along the route we would be following, together with the fixed turning points where the flight plan required us to alter course.

And it was the sheer number and frequency of these turning points along my given route that was very nearly my undoing. After thirty minutes spent battling against the driving rain and deteriorating visibility I was hopelessly lost. Back in those days there was no Autobahn network with its many identifiable interchanges to help you on your way. The only available aid to navigation was to find a railway line, follow it, 'dive-bomb' the first station to appear and read its name. But this, of course, was strictly forbidden to us trainees. Anybody caught committing such a heinous crime was immediately placed on a charge.

Fortunately, I was spared 'a meeting with Father Philip' – our expression at the time for being sent to the detention cells – by the gradual emergence out of the murk of the twin spires of the monastery of Markt Indersdorf. I no longer needed a railway station to tell me my position. I knew at once that I was only some 35km to the north-west of Munich and quickly got back on course.

I was just approaching the village of Dachau when Leutnant

Lützow's machine suddenly slid up beside me. He signalled for me to return to base. The exercise had obviously been called off which, I have to admit, came as something of a relief. Our instructor must have been out rounding up all his lost lambs and sending them home, for he then peeled away in a steep left turn and was gone again as quickly as he had come.

Not everyone made it back to Schleissheim in one piece. Some of my comrades had opted to make emergency landings rather than continue their battle with the elements. Although all survived, the result was that the remains of several rather bent '*Stössers*' lay scattered about the Bavarian countryside. This did not go down at all well with our course leader Hauptmann Karl Vieck, who made his feelings known with some vehemence at the post-exercise debriefing.

Hauptmann Vieck may have been mourning the loss of one or two of his precious aircraft, but there was a great deal of hilarity and mirth over dinner in the mess that evening as we regaled each other with accounts of our experiences in the chaos and confusion of this day's memorable but ultimately abortive exercise.

In fact, our entire time at Schleissheim was memorable, and the style of training we received must have been well-nigh unique. Despite the brevity of the course both in terms of calendar days and actual hours flown, the results achieved were quite remarkable. Any initial doubts or fears we may have had in the beginning about meeting the high standards expected of us were quickly dispelled. And the personal example set by every single instructor, their commitment to get the very best out of us, and their total readiness to take full responsibility for the orders they gave us, were, in my opinion, the bedrock upon which the success of the school was built.

The entire course was extremely demanding, given the average age of the trainees – most of us were between twenty and twenty-five years old – and our limited flying experience prior to the start of our fighter pilot training. It would be no exaggeration to say that when we walked past the guardroom and out through the gates of Schleissheim for the last time we were all much more mature, much more self-confident, and far tougher than we had been when we first arrived.

But our fledgling careers as fighter pilots had come at a cost. During the time of our training a number of very serious accidents had taken place, including several mid-air collisions involving loss of life. The majority of these had occurred during the complex air exercises that we had all been required to fly. But others had happened during 'normal' training flights, for it should not be forgotten that, at this time, single-seat fighters had no electronic navigational aids, nor any communications systems, either air-to-air or ground-to-air. Today, many decades later, it hardly seems credible that we tyros were sent up in the worst kind of weather conditions – heavy rain, low-lying cloud, appalling visibility – and expected to perform manoeuvres of the most complicated kind.

In short, and I can't say it often enough, the Schleissheim training programme was incredibly hard. But it was designed to be hard. We were being stretched to the very limit as part of a necessary process that had to be gone through before we could even be considered fit to join an operational unit. In the event, however, it was a surprise political development that was to bring our days at Schleissheim to an unexpected and slightly premature end.

When we heard the news that Hitler had ordered troops to occupy the demilitarized zone of the Rhineland there was more than a little unease among our ranks. This was in direct contravention of the Locarno Treaty. The *Führer* was clearly taking a gamble. And just how big a gamble quickly became apparent to us. The course was abruptly terminated. We trainees were divided up and posted to a number of different fighter units, some already well established, others only recently activated. Everything was done in such a mad rush that there was no time for lengthy goodbyes. We packed our kit and set off for our new stations without a moment's delay.

My destination was to be Döberitz, an airfield about 25km to the west of Berlin and home to I. Gruppe of JG 132 '*Richthofen*'.

Chapter 3
I./Jagdgeschwader 132 '*Richthofen*'

I arrived at Döberitz on 10 March 1936, just seventy-two hours after the re-occupation of the Rhineland. I./JG 132 was the oldest established fighter unit in Hermann Göring's new Reichsluftwaffe. It had been activated in the spring of 1934 under the cover title of the '*Reklamestaffel Mitteldeutschlands des DLV*' (Central German Publicity Squadron of the German Air-Sports Association). Command of the Staffel had been entrusted to Major Robert *Ritter* von Greim, a 25-victory ace of the Great War who, incidentally, would be selected to take over from the disgraced Göring as Commander-in-Chief of the Luftwaffe in the closing days of the Second World War.

I./JG 132, as the unit had been re-designated in March 1935, now consisted of three Staffeln. I was assigned to 3. Staffel, whose Kapitän was Oberleutnant Erich von Selle, until recently himself an instructor at Schleissheim.

Dating back to the very beginning of the (twentieth) century and the days of the airship, Döberitz was an even older airfield than Schleissheim. But I./JG 132 was housed in newly-built and very modern accommodation blocks. In fact, the entire area occupied by the Gruppe was extremely well laid out. Our hours of duty allowed us plenty of free time to make use of the sporting facilities provided. And the field's proximity to Berlin was another bonus. The attractions of the Reich's capital city acted like a magnet to us youngsters and broadened our view of the world in quite a wide – and often unexpected! – number of ways.

On the base, however, we found things a little difficult at first. We were fresh out of training school and, like anybody thrust into a new and unfamiliar environment, were conscious of the fact that we would have to make a special effort to integrate and be accepted by

27

our more experienced comrades. I was the youngest of all the pilots in 3. Staffel and consequently had to try just that little bit harder not to be found wanting in any way.

But thanks to the splendid spirit of camaraderie within the Staffel, and thanks also to its exemplary leadership, any personal or service problems that may have arisen from our changing from the rigid and rule-bound life of the training school to the far more relaxed atmosphere of an operational unit were quickly put behind us.

The Staffel's flying personnel were a mix of officer and NCO pilots. This resulted in one or two administrative absurdities in the day-to-day running of the unit. The effects of the rapid expansion which the Luftwaffe was undergoing at this time were also apparent in other ways; shortages of qualified technical personnel and the lack of certain items of equipment, to name but two. Nor should it be forgotten that before the Luftwaffe's emergence as a separate branch of the Wehrmacht, Germany's air arm had formed an integral part of the army. Much of the new service's organizational style and form still reflected that fact. The Luftwaffe's independence was slow to develop and, in reality, it never did manage to shake off its army roots entirely.

But none of this detracted in any way from my sense of achievement – after a grand total of 574 training flights – at finally becoming a member of an operational unit. My first flight at Döberitz took place on 12 March and was, to be honest, a bit of an anticlimax. It was a practice hop in an Arado Ar 76, a single-seat fighter trainer similar in many respects to the Fw 56 'Stösser'. This was followed by two longer flights in an Arado Ar 65, a type I had already flown at Schleissheim, which served to familiarize myself with my new base and its immediate surroundings. Only then was I allowed to get my hands on one of the Staffel's operational fighters, a red-nosed Heinkel He 51, on which I was ordered to perform two brief circuits of the field. Luckily all went well.

The He 51 was very different from the Ar 65, the type which had equipped the Döberitz Gruppe prior to the Heinkel's entry into service in the spring of 1935. The latter was smaller, lighter and aero-dynamically much improved. Consequently it was also faster; so fast, in fact, that it was fitted with wheel brakes to slow down its landing run – something I had not encountered before. Its flight characteristics were good, which made it easy to handle. The 750hp BMW VI liquid-cooled engine gave the He 51 a top speed of 320 km/h and its armament comprised two 7.92mm machine-guns.

The days that followed were spent in learning how to use these guns. But first we had to be taught how to make a controlled approach and line up our sights on a ground target. The practice targets were wood and canvas affairs measuring some 3m². An attack had to be made in a shallow dive starting from a height of 200m. It took quite a bit of practice to get the target in one's sights, and then even more to hold it there. It was no easy task, especially for complete novices like us.

Recovery from the dive before getting too close to the target also looked easier than it proved to be. This led to several pilots receiving severe reprimands for dangerous flying after they had failed to pull up in time and had come within an ace of crashing. Despite this, the more daredevil among us took great delight in flying so low over the target that it was to knocked over by their prop wash. The excuse was always the same: 'Beg to report, Herr Oberleutnant, I totally misjudged my height.'

Once it was felt that we had mastered the approach technique, weapons practice began in earnest. At first, however, the results were far less satisfactory than we ourselves imagined. It was not uncommon for a trainee to complete a firing run convinced he had left the canvas target in tatters, only to be informed at debriefing that there wasn't a mark on it. But here too, as in so many other walks of life, it was a case of 'Practice makes perfect'.

This was even more true when it came to aerial gunnery. The ground targets had at least stayed still (when they weren't being knocked over, that is), but now we found ourselves having to aim at a bundle of children's balloons released into the air. This was a primitive but extremely effective method of teaching us how to shoot at a moving target. Buffeted by the wind, the balloons bobbed about all over the place and proved very difficult to hit.

Together with this ground and air gunnery practice, the bulk of our daily flying programme at Döberitz was taken up with formation flying in battle order, air combat exercises and aerobatics. We did no night or blind flying; JG 132 was strictly a day-fighter unit. Nor were we required to carry out any practice flights above solid layers of cloud; an exercise that had played such a prominent part of our training at Schleissheim.

Some elements of our early practice and familiarization flights with 3./JG 132 at Döberitz were, however, very similar to procedures we had been accustomed to at Schleissheim. The exact sequence of manoeuvres to be carried out, for example, was always set out in a detailed briefing before every flight and our performance was watched intently by the more experienced pilots of the Staffel. As at Schleissheim, flight discipline was paramount. If mistakes were made, nobody – be he Gefreiter, Unteroffizier or Leutnant – was spared what could, at times, be some very harsh criticism at the post-exercise debriefings. Rank simply didn't come into it. The sole concerns were the individual's abilities as a pilot and his compliance, or otherwise, with the instructions issued for the exercise in question.

Nearly all our practice flights were restricted to the vicinity of the base. We didn't have to venture far afield, even when acting as aerial targets or towing drogues for our own anti-aircraft gunners – or for those of other units, as the latter were either stationed in the Greater Berlin area anyway, or were engaged in exercises on the Döberitz troop training grounds nearby.

But these limitations had a plus side. For although we had to remain close to the field during the working week, we were given the whole of the weekend to make good the cross-country hours we were missing. We were allowed to fly to any airfield of our choice at weekends, with return to Döberitz on the Monday morning, and we all made full use of this concession. The favourite destinations were either the pilot's home town or one of the Baltic Sea coastal resorts.

All in all, these weekend flights were a splendid idea. They constituted part of our overall flying programme and were open to everybody irrespective of rank or seniority. A perfect example of mixing business with pleasure.

There were just two provisos to these weekend jaunts: there was a set minimum distance that had to be flown and, more importantly, we were forbidden to enter any prohibited airspace close to the Reich's borders in case we lost our bearings and inadvertently violated an international frontier.

Based as we were well within Germany, this latter restriction did not worry us unduly. But back at the beginning of March a number of pilots from all three of the Gruppe's Staffeln had been sent on detachment to the Rhineland region. Here they were seconded to other fighter units to help bolster the Luftwaffe's 'show of strength' in support of Hitler's re-occupation of the area. (It was rumoured that the reason for our abrupt transfer from Schleissheim to Döberitz had been to make up, at least numerically, for their temporary absence.) And, almost inevitably, there had been an 'incident'.

Early one afternoon at Döberitz the entire Gruppe was suddenly ordered to fall in on parade. As was usual whenever this happened, we weren't told the reason why. The Gruppen-Adjutant, Hauptmann Axel von Blomberg – son of the then Defence Minister, and the later Feldmarschall Werner von Blomberg – called the parade to attention and reported all present and correct to Gruppenkommandeur Major Carl Vieck.

Major Vieck, our erstwhile course leader at Schleissheim who had been appointed to the command of I./JG 132 only days earlier, could be irascible at the best of times. Now, without mincing his words, he informed us that a very serious occurrence had just taken place over Strasbourg, an event that could have disastrous political consequences.

It transpired that a certain pilot, whom I happened to know from our time together at Magdeburg as a perfectly straightforward and happy-go-lucky kind of individual, had quite unintentionally flown across the Rhine. He didn't realize the seriousness of the situation he was in and had apparently welcomed the fighters that rose to intercept him as new playmates ready for a spot of mock dogfighting. It was only when he noticed the *tricouleur* roundels on their wings and grasped the fact that they were French that the truth sank in. He immediately turned tail and headed back eastwards at top speed. Lady Luck had always smiled upon him, and she did so again on this occasion. He managed to give his pursuers the slip and return to base all in one piece.

Because of the gravity of the situation, and the possible international repercussions, word of the incident quickly spread to higher quarters, as did the name of the pilot involved. The

Kommandeur's account of the event was couched in very colourful terms. And when it came to describing the human error involved he used expressions that are very seldom heard in polite society. We were all thinking to ourselves, poor old '*Schorsch*', they're going to throw the book at him this time. But, somehow, he got away with it again.

Quite by chance I bumped into him again during the war on a forward landing strip in Russia. I mentioned the Strasbourg incident to him, but he simply laughed it off. He seemed to regard the whole affair as a bit of a joke – still the same old '*Schorsch*'!

At Döberitz a considerable part of our daily routine was taken up with non-flying activities. Administrative duties, sport, rifle practice, clay-pigeon shooting, inspections and guard duties all ate into our working day. This did us no harm personally, of course, but neither did it do much – if anything – towards improving the operational efficiency of the Staffel. And therein lay the problem; a problem that those occupying the corridors of power were slow to recognize.

Other much more useful pursuits, such as further schooling in operational strategy, the conduct of aerial warfare, ground tactics, weaponry, communications and the like, were not dealt with in any depth – a common failing of those pre-war years that was to become all too apparent during the course of the subsequent conflict.

On the subject of communications, there was one important innovation that we *were* introduced to at Döberitz. Hitherto, the only means of communication between pilots in the air had been hand signals. An established set of hand signals had been introduced, each indicating a particular order or manoeuvre, but these of course only worked if the aircraft were in close visual contact. And, short of dropping a message container, there was no communication possible at all between air and ground.

In an attempt to rectify this situation, our He 51s were fitted with a primitive radio-telephony (R/T) set. But it was almost impossible to hear what was being said when using this equipment. For some reason which I can no longer recall, we were instructed not to make a pause between each individual word, but to deliver every message in one go without stopping to take a breath. This proved surprisingly difficult to do. And it was even more difficult for the intended recipient of the message to understand what was being gabbled at him.

Initial trials had been conducted in an enclosed workshop area in one of the Döberitz hangars. But the results were so disappointing that they were soon called off and we reverted to our familiar hand signals. Further tests with improved equipment would later lead to the installation and successful use of R/T sets in the unit's Heinkels, but by that time I was no longer with them.

For on 18 May 1936, little more than two months after joining 3./JG 132, I flew for the last time as a member of the Staffel. Flight No. 656 in my logbook was yet another gunnery exercise against ground targets. Altogether I had made eighty-one flights as a budding fighter pilot with the Jagdgeschwader 'Richthofen'. I had spent a total of exactly 28 hours and 34 minutes in the air and had flown six different types of aircraft: the Arados Ar 64 and Ar 76, the Focke-Wulfs Fw 44 and Fw 56, and the Heinkels He 51 and He 72. Of these, the Ar 76 and the He 51 had been new to me.

By now, however, Hitler's calculated gamble back in March of re-occupying the Rhineland was very much a *fait accompli*. A plebiscite held three weeks after the event showed overwhelming public support for the *Führer's* actions. The feared armed response by the British and French had failed to materialize, and many of the German troops that had been moved up into the area as a safeguard were being returned to their home bases. This included a number of I./JG 132's pilots, which meant that the Gruppe was now above establishment. And this, in turn, meant that – without our being aware of it – we trainees recently drafted in from Schleissheim were suddenly 'surplus to requirements'.

As a result I found myself posted to *Fliegerschule* Salzwedel, situated midway between Berlin and Bremen, where I was to be trained as a flying instructor.

Chapter 4
Fliegerschule Salzwedel

The posting to Salzwedel had come totally out of the blue. Neither I, nor any of the others who were to accompany me, had received any notification prior to being issued with our travel warrants.

The suddenness of our transfer was the main topic of conversation among our little group on that morning of Tuesday, 19 May 1936 as our train pulled out of Berlin for the 150km journey to Salzwedel. The only explanation we could come up with was that our hasty move had been brought about by the uncertain political climate. Hitler's Rhineland adventure had been a risk that had paid off. All that the British and French had been prepared to offer in response was some outraged bleating.

But the *Führer* could not rely on bluff working a second time. To back up any future territorial demands he would need a real military presence, not a sham 'show of arms' of the kind that had secured him the Rhineland. The Luftwaffe was therefore about to embark upon an even bigger wave of expansion than it had seen in 1935. New aircraft were coming off the production lines, new pilots were needed to fly them – and new instructors were needed to teach those pilots how to fly.

This was all pure speculation on our part, of course. It didn't alter our situation in the slightest. But it did help soften the blow at the abrupt termination of our fighter careers to think that we would be engaged in something useful and worthwhile. All we could do was accept our lot and make the best of it.

I didn't find it all that easy to say goodbye to Berlin. I had assumed that Döberitz was to be my permanent station for the foreseeable future and many of my personal plans were focussed around the many real opportunities offered by the capital. But I soon discovered that our new base made up for it in many ways.

Salzwedel was a typical garrison town. For the fifty years leading up to the end of the Great War it had been home to a famous regiment of Uhlans. So when the Luftwaffe set up a new training school some 5km to the east of the town in the autumn of 1935, the good citizens of Salzwedel looked upon the newcomers as the rightful successors to those cavalrymen of old. They, and we, were given a warm welcome which, in my case, was in sharp contrast to the sense of anonymity that I must admit to having felt in the big city of Berlin. The locals couldn't do enough for us and we soon felt at home as we got to know the town and the surrounding region.

The accommodation area of the newly-built school consisted of a row of red-brick buildings set into a park-like landscape that blended in well with the Saxon countryside. There was a sports ground within the camp, but unfortunately no swimming pool. Lake Arend was only 25km away, however, and was a popular bathing venue for the school's personnel and for locals alike.

The flying training facilities were less impressive. The field itself was too small, even for those days. It was of the standard circular layout, which allowed take-offs and landings to be made whatever the direction of the wind. Large asphalt aprons in front of the hangars and workshops provided ample space for the school's many and varied aircraft. Close by, the school commander and his staff, together with the instructing staff, flying control and meteorological office, were all housed in the usual type of ops building. Despite certain obvious limitations, the *Fliegerschule* Salzwedel was thus a typical example of a Luftwaffe flying training establishment of the time. To provide additional navigational and bad-weather approach assistance, there was a direction-finding (D/F) station situated on the flight base line (QMS) to the east of the field.

For the purposes of schooling there was a building containing a number of lecture rooms complete with all the necessary teaching aids. The ground teaching staff were mainly civil servants, although we trainee flying instructors were sometimes called upon to take classes in specialized subjects.

The school commander was a Major Rudolf Trautvetter. He was ably supported by chief instructor Oberleutnant Külbl. The flying instructors, as at Magdeburg, were partly military personnel and partly civilian. They all worked well together as a team, which made for a relaxed and friendly atmosphere within the school and contributed in no small part to its growing reputation.

My training as an instructor began on Friday, 22 May 1936. It was very much a case of back to square one as I puttered busily about in an Fw 44 '*Stieglitz*' doing circuits, carrying out precision landings and performing all the other stuff that was apparently required to establish my *bona fides*, including aerobatics, night flying and cross-country exercises.

Having to switch from the 750hp He 51 fighter back on to the little 150hp Fw 44 two-seat trainer was hard to take. It felt like being put back a year at school – only ten times worse – and it was quite a long time before we came to terms with it. In fact, it wasn't until the exercises we had to fly became more challenging, rather than merely routine, that I, together with the others who had had to leave Döberitz with me, began to have a change of heart.

And some of those exercises were challenging in the extreme; bordering more on stunt flying than military flying in the accepted sense. One, for example, involved stretching a rope at a height of some 3m just in front of the landing cross. The object was to clear the rope safely, but then to put the aircraft down as quickly as possible and as close to the landing cross as possible. Needless to say, there were many failed attempts. But this surprised nobody, and certainly not our instructors.

Another favourite was to order the trainee to perform a series of precision landings from various heights, the catch being that each attempt had to begin when the machine was directly above the landing cross ... with a dead propeller!

Here the pilot faced two problems. The most important, as with every precision landing, was of course to get the aircraft down as close to the cross as he could. But even if he managed this satisfactorily – and the permitted margin of error was very small – the test was only considered successful if the propeller had been absolutely motionless when he was above the landing cross at the start of his approach.

And this was problem number two; or, more accurately perhaps, number one, as this marked the beginning of the exercise. It was very easy to switch an engine off in flight. But it was another matter entirely to get the propeller to come to a dead stop. Unless the aircraft's speed was reduced to an absolute minimum, the propeller would continue to windmill in the airstream. It required careful judgement. Too great a reduction in speed and the machine would stall, as many a beginner found to his cost. There were frequent scares, but fortunately no-one actually crashed. Although this particular exercise was extremely difficult, it was ideal training for our future role as instructors. It gave us the confidence to be able to take over the controls at the very last moment should any pupil make a complete botch of his landing.

After completing the flying and theoretical training that gained us our A-2 instructor's licences, the next part of the Salzwedel course would take us on to our B-1 and B-2 instructor's licences. These would qualify us to teach on much larger and heavier aircraft: the B-1 for single-engined machines weighing in at up to 2,500kg and carrying a maximum of three people; the B-2 for single or twin-engined aircraft of up to 5,000kg in weight and for three or more passengers.

A lot of our time was also taken up by long cross-country flights, often with one or more intermediate landings at mostly unfamiliar airfields along the way. My logbook contains the names of more than thirty such fields that I visited during this period as I criss-crossed the length and breadth of Germany from Kiel in the north to Munich in the south, from Kassel in the west to Cottbus in the east.

In addition to these lengthy overland practice flights and all the other training I was undergoing to become an instructor, I also had to find the time to study for the exams that I would have to take, and pass, in order to further my own service career and gain promotion to Unteroffizier (corporal). These involved a lot of both theoretical and practical work, which had to be fitted in on Saturday mornings and on days when bad weather prevented flying. But I somehow managed it and on 1 August 1936 I was duly promoted to the rank of Unteroffizier. This was a significant step up for me, but it was only the very first rung on the ladder. There were still a lot of hurdles to clear before I could realize my ultimate ambition to become an officer.

While my training on larger aircraft continued apace, it was not long before I successfully completed the initial instructor's course. And on Monday, 23 September 1936, four months almost to the day since my arrival at Salzwedel, I took to the air for the first time as a newly fledged flying instructor. It was to be a 21-minute familiarization flight in an Fw 44 – almost an exact re-run of my very own maiden flight at Magdeburg on 27 April 1935, also in a '*Stieglitz*', when Feldwebel Bachmann first introduced me to the joy and magic of flying. Only now the roles were reversed and it was I who was occupying the rear seat, while a no doubt nervous but excited trainee sat in front of me.

And so began an almost three-year stint as a flying instructor, the job that would occupy the greater part of my time right up until 14 August 1939, only a matter of days before the outbreak of the Second World War. It proved to be an immensely rewarding job and gave me a lot of satisfaction, especially when I was able to tie those red 'first solo' pennants to the aircraft's wing struts to indicate to all and sundry that my trainee was about to go up for the first time on his own – and then to congratulate him on his safe return.

My cross-country flights were also paying dividends. With the B-Class licences securely under my belt, I was now aiming for my C-2 licence, which would allow me to fly multi-engined, multi-seat aircraft of more than 5,000kg. In effect, this meant any machine then in Luftwaffe service, which is probably why the C-2 was soon to become more popularly known as the Advanced Military Pilot's Licence.

The types used during this final phase of my own flying training were the Dornier Do 11 and Do 23 twin-engined bombers and the three-engined Junkers G 24 and Ju 52 transports. For me the course culminated on the afternoon of 9 October 1936 with three precision landings successfully carried out on the lumbering Do 11. These three short flights – Nos 989 to 991 in my logbook – had lasted a total of just thirty-one minutes.

After very nearly a thousand flights, my training as a Luftwaffe pilot was finally completed. On 24 October I was issued with Advanced Military Pilot's Licence No.13 by an officer of the local Luftwaffe area command, *Luftgaukommando* XI, Hannover. I was just six days short of my twenty-first birthday.

The overwhelming majority of my flight hours over the course of the next three years were to be spent not on multi-engined bombers or transports, however, but on small biplane trainers as I taught successive intakes of new Luftwaffe recruits the basics of flying.

The training programme remained virtually unchanged throughout this time. Each separate course was made up of carefully planned stages designed to take the pupil step by step through the training process. The course group leaders, or chief flying instructors, were usually highly-experienced NCOs, although there were one or two of Leutnant rank as well. Each group leader had some half-a-dozen instructors under his command and they, in turn, would each be responsible for about six trainees. A complete course, from beginning to B-2 licence stage, lasted approximately six months.

Collectively, the groups thus organized for each new intake of aspiring pilots were formed into a single trainee company, whose commander also held the post of head of training. Before each day's flying, the head of training's staff would assign the aircraft required for the day's programme to the various chief flying instructors. This would be followed by a briefing outlining each group's schedule for the day and the allocation of machines to the individual flying instructors. This procedure was common throughout the Luftwaffe's training command organization. In effect, this meant that the flying instructors were given full responsibility for ensuring that the training was carried out in a proper and methodical manner.

The initial stages of training placed particularly heavy demands on the instructors. It was during these early phases that the strengths and weaknesses of every trainee had to be established and assessed. This was arguably one of the most important parts of the entire programme, for it was nearly always possible to form an accurate judgement of a pupil's potential, to estimate how well – and how quickly – he would respond to training, and to decide to which type of unit his flying abilities were best suited.

In the beginning the main job of the instructor was to keep a close eye on his trainees in order to get to know them all as well as possible and to gain their trust. If a pupil clearly enjoyed flying and was also eager, prepared, and willing to carry out all the many other more mundane tasks associated with pilot training, the battle was half won. As a rule, the cheerful, friendly and extrovert types stood a much better chance of success than the quieter, more introverted individuals.

There was another way of distinguishing between the two main groups of hopefuls. The one group was keen, not to say fanatical, about flying, while the other was determined rather than passionate and had to work hard at learning to fly. Teaching the latter was not just more difficult, at times it could be downright dangerous for all involved.

For that reason new recruits were never coerced into volunteering for flying training. The expenditure in time and effort would simply be too great to make it a worthwhile proposition. There had to be at least a reasonable chance of a successful outcome. This was a dilemma frequently faced by instructors when having to decide whether there was justification for persevering with the training of a demonstrably poor pupil. It was not so much a matter of the many extra hours that would have to be devoted to additional flying tuition, but more of weighing up the risks involved to both pupil and instructor during those hours.

The six main qualities that the instructor was looking for when assessing a trainee's potential as a pilot could be itemized as follows:

a natural 'feel' for flying,
lightning-fast reactions,
physical toughness,
spatial awareness,
the ability to concentrate, and
mental flexibility.

It was the measure of one or more of these main qualities, together with individual traits such as character, temperament and intellect, which would determine each and every trainee's subsequent role as a pilot in the Luftwaffe. In short, the type of unit he would be posted to, and the type of aircraft he would fly after completing the Salzwedel course and being awarded his pilot's badge.

An even greater responsibility for the instructing staff came on those occasions when a pupil proved incapable of mastering the mechanics of flying and had to be washed off the course. This was a decision not taken lightly. But although every applicant for flying training had first to undergo a rigorous series of tests and examinations by doctors and psychiatrists to establish his suitability, it was estimated that some 5 per cent of all entrants would fail to finish the course.

On a more personal level, it was during my first year of instructing at Salzwedel that I took another step towards achieving my aim of becoming an officer. I had left school without sitting my *Abitur*, the exam that one needed to enter university. The *Abitur* was also pretty much a prerequisite for meaningful advancement in the Luftwaffe of the pre-war years and, thanks to the understanding and encouragement of my superior officers, I was provided with every facility to study for it during my off-duty hours.

I duly took and passed the *Abitur* as a mature student at a secondary modern school in Magdeburg in the autumn of 1937. This inspired me to continue studying in my free time. I concentrated on modern languages and natural sciences, little dreaming just how useful these would prove to be to me in the post-war years.

'Free time' was something of a misnomer, however, as I often found myself busier during my off-duty hours than when actually instructing. Early on in my days at Salzwedel I had discovered the joy of aerobatics. And that joy quickly developed into something of a passion as I began to seize every opportunity to study and practise this exhilarating form of flying. And, once again, I received the full support of my superiors, even to the extent of their now and again obtaining the use of a Bücker Bü 133 '*Jungmeister*', or 'Young Champion' – a specialized aerobatic trainer that had not yet entered service with the Luftwaffe – upon which I could hone my growing skills.

But before I got my hands on a '*Jungmeister*' I spent innumerable hours practising on the school's Fw 44s. In order to get special permission to fly below the regulatory minimum height of 1,000m, I would first have to show that I was able to perform all the set figures in the aerobatic repertoire – the loop, the bunt, the falling leaf, the stall turn, the slow roll, the barrel roll, and every other kind of roll – with absolute accuracy. I continued doggedly to practise whenever I had a few spare minutes, much to the amusement of my colleagues, some of whom pulled my leg unmercifully.

Ignoring my comrades' unkind witticisms, I was convinced that I was doing the right thing; precision flying demanded constant practice. But not even practice, however intensive, could guard against a moment's lapse of attention, as I was to find out – very nearly to my cost – a short time later.

It was a gloriously sunny day and I was using what was left of the lunchtime break to put in a little practice in an Fw 44 over the south-west corner of the field. Everything was proceeding normally. By this time I had been given official permission to fly below the minimum 1,000m mark. But fortunately I had begun this session a little higher than that and was only losing altitude in gradual stages as I went through my routine.

I was in the middle of performing a loop when I received a very nasty shock. Just as I reached the top of the loop the '*Stieglitz*' suddenly flipped over and pointed her nose towards the ground. What on earth had happened? I immediately realized what I had done wrong. I had obviously started the figure with too little speed and too close to the ground.

I eased the stick slowly back – too sharp a movement and the machine could easily flick roll – but there was no absolutely no response, no feeling of pressure pushing me down into the seat to indicate that she was coming out of what was now very nearly a vertical dive. The roof of the workshop hangar was hurtling up towards me at an unbelievable speed. I had no option but to pull harder on the stick, but it still had no effect whatsoever. For what must been several seconds – but to me seemed like an eternity – I stared transfixed at the hangar as it grew alarmingly in size directly below me.

With only metres to spare, the elevators finally started to respond. Throwing caution to the winds, I yanked the stick fully back. My mind registered the bare expanse of the hangar roof flashing past beneath my wings. I swear I could have reached out and touched it!

Terrifying as it had been, the experience did not put me off aerobatics for life. Quite the opposite, in fact. It prompted me to research into the flight characteristics of aircraft at, or very close to ground level; what today would be termed 'ground effect'. I later got the opportunity to participate in some very informative discussion groups with experts in this field.

But I would never forget this particular incident. There would be many other occasions during the course of my flying career when I would find myself in difficult, not to say critical situations. But I always managed to get myself out of trouble by taking some form of remedial action. Never again would I ever feel so helpless – the controls unresponsive, staring transfixed through the windscreen in sheer disbelief at that hangar roof – as I did for those few seconds at Salzwedel.

Once I felt I had mastered all the main aerobatic figures, from the relatively simple to the most difficult, I started trying to put them together into a programme that would enable me to take part in air shows and competitions. In this I received generous and unstinting help from Albert Falderbaum, one of the Reich's leading aerobatic pilots (he would win the German Aerobatic Championships in both 1938 and 1939), who was currently serving as a flying instructor at Kassel-Rothwesten. He let me into the secrets of advanced aerobatics, describing the best combinations of individual high-value figures – i.e. the most difficult to perform and therefore those earning the most points in competition – and explaining how to fly them in a programme, fluidly and without losing either speed or height while doing so.

The system of scoring at competitions was fairly straightforward. Each figure had a fixed difficulty rating, and this was multiplied by the number of points awarded for its execution by each of the four judges stationed at the four points of the compass around the field. A typical aerobatic programme lasted about five minutes and had to be flown directly above the field. There were many factors influencing the outcome; the weather, of course, but also the position of the sun in the sky, the aircraft itself – and a large helping, or otherwise, of luck on the day!

I had the good fortune to take part in many air shows, open days and competitions. They brought me one or two trophies and a host of lasting memories. I was twenty-two years old at the time, arguably the best age for such activities which called for dash, exuberance, daring and a disregard for danger all in equal measure.

43

Meanwhile, the instructing side of my career continued to provide me with plenty of variety as I got to fly a whole range of new and sometimes lesser known aircraft types. In addition to the venerable Focke-Wulf A 17 '*Möwe*' (Gull) and Junkers F 13, both single-engined transports dating back to the 1920s, I was introduced to several smaller trainer and liaison machines such as the Bücker Bü 131 '*Jungmann*' – the forerunner of the '*Jungmeister*' aerobatic aircraft – the Klemm Kl 26 and the Messerschmitt Bf 108 '*Taifun*' (Typhoon).

The real icing on the cake though was the special training I was given that allowed me to fly some of the most modern machines then in, or entering Luftwaffe first-line service. These included the Heinkel He 70 '*Blitz*' (Lightning) high-speed reconnaissance machine, the Heinkel He 111 bomber and – the most exciting of all – Messerschmitt's sleek new Bf 109 fighter.

But in the spring of 1938 my hectic schedule of instructing, familiarizing myself on new types and aerobatic flying was brought to a temporary halt. The political storm clouds were gathering over Europe once again. Hitler was planning his next major coup: the annexation of the land of his birth, Austria, into the Greater German Reich. And despite the Luftwaffe's massive expansion since his Rhineland gamble two years earlier, it was still nowhere near strong enough fully to support this latest venture.

One major concern was the shortage of air transport units needed to get the Wehrmacht's ground troops to key points within the newly-acquired territories as rapidly as possible. One of the measures taken to remedy this situation was the activation of several *ad hoc* transport units made up of personnel and aircraft gathered together from various training schools throughout the Reich.

Totally unaware of what was going on, a number of us at Salzwedel were suddenly ordered to get our kit together and fly a Junkers Ju 52 down to Memmingen in southern Bavaria. As usual, we were told nothing, but rumours abounded. In fact, we were to be placed under the temporary command of a *Lufttransportgruppe* '*Ziervogel*'. This unit, a motley collection of some thirty Ju 52s named after the officer appointed to command, Oberst Dr Maximilian Ziervogel, was one of two such Gruppen – the other being the much larger *Lufttransport-gruppe* '*Fleischhauer*' – that were tasked with transporting the paratroops of IV. Batallion, Regiment '*General Göring*', to Graz in Austria.

On Friday, 11 March 1938 we left Salzwedel for Memmingen, where we were finally let into the secret and briefed for the coming mission. The next day the Gruppe flew to Berlin-Staaken to pick up the '*General Göring*' paratroops. Once they had emplaned, we returned south to Schleissheim, where we were to stay overnight.

On 13 March, just twenty-four hours after the first German ground troops had crossed the border into Austria, we lifted off from Schleissheim for the flight to Graz. The first part of our route was to take us eastwards, along the northern edge of the Alps towards Vienna. Upon approaching the Austrian capital we would then alter course south-south-west and fly down the far side of the Alps to Graz.

The weather at take-off had been far from good and by the time we were nearing Vienna it had deteriorated to such an extent that the second leg down to Graz would only have been possible for crews with blind-flying experience. Few of us from the training schools had done any serious blind or night-flying and, as a consequence, the Gruppe was ordered to make an intermediate landing at Wiener Neustadt. Already crowded with Dornier Do 17 bombers, which had also been forced down by the adverse weather conditions, the field had a distinctly warlike air about it.

But at 15.15 hours, just fifty minutes after touching down, we were on our way again. Carefully keeping a safe distance from the mountains on our right, we battled on for a good three-quarters of an hour through poor visibility and low-scudding cloud before eventually reaching Graz. In those days Graz was an extremely small airfield. We were therefore ordered to land singly at short, spaced intervals and taxi separately across to the unloading areas that had already been marked out for us.

Everything went remarkably smoothly. Once the paratroops had deplaned and left the field, we aircrew were also loaded aboard trucks and driven into town where we joined the marching columns making their triumphal entry into Graz amidst scenes of wild jubilation from the local populace.

The celebrations in Graz may have been wild, but they were as nothing compared to what took place in Vienna two days later, on

15 March, when Hitler proclaimed to a cheering crowd, estimated to be a quarter of a million strong, packed into the city's *Heldenplatz* that the Ostmark – as Austria would henceforth be known – was the 'newest bulwark of the German nation and thus of the Greater German Reich'.

Later that same afternoon the *Führer* took the salute at a parade of mixed German and Austrian military units. Proceedings opened with a massed, low-level fly-past by nearly 400 Luftwaffe bombers and Stukas, the majority of which had flown in especially from their bases in neighbouring Bavaria. Symbolically, a group of Austrian Air Force Fiat CR 32 biplane fighters also took part. And bringing up the rear came the Ju 52s of the *Lufttransportgruppe 'Ziervogel'*! We had a number of passengers with us for the 300km round trip from Graz up to Vienna and back, including several officers from an Austrian mountain division who had joined us at the express invitation of our Gruppenkommandeur.

After two more very pleasant days at Graz it was mission accomplished; time for the *Lufttransportgruppe 'Ziervogel'* to return to Germany and time for its crews to return to their parent units. In the interim the weather had improved beyond all recognition. The sky was a cloudless vault of the deepest blue and visibility was perfect. In reward, or so we were led to believe, of a job well done – we later learned that this had been the first time that German paratroops had been airlifted operationally – we would not have to retrace the lengthy dogleg route via Vienna that had brought us to Graz. Instead, the flight back to Schleissheim would take us directly across the Alps.

Few of us had ever had the opportunity to experience a panoramic view of the Alps from above before. We were all excited at the prospect. And none more so than our Staffelkapitän, who was Munich born and bred and knew almost every single peak by name. His enthusiasm may have been a little too infectious, which is perhaps why we didn't pay the amount of attention to the pre-flight briefing that we should have done. We 'flatland flyers' from the north, in particular, ought to have heeded the note of caution sounded by the more experienced Alpine pilots.

We left Graz on 17 March, taking off singly commencing at 13.10

hours. In our unloaded state we quickly gained height and were very soon rewarded with the majestic vista of the snow-capped Alps stretching away before us. There were a few innocent-looking banks of cumulus in the far distance, but we didn't give them a second thought.

We continued to marvel at the spectacle of the searingly white brilliance of the serried ranks of mountains all around us. But the further we flew the more noticeable it became that the peaks in front of us were becoming larger, more massive and rearing higher into the sunlit sky. The first doubts began to creep in. Would the Ju 52, a machine not exactly noted for its high-altitude performance, be able to climb above them?

Without our realizing it, those distant little blobs of fair weather cumulus had also been slowly gathering strength and closing in on us until, suddenly, we found ourselves confronted by a solid wall of cloud seemingly intent on barring our way. The spectacular long-distance views that we had been enjoying had all but disappeared. And with nothing but a confusing jumble of glistening white peaks and deeply shadowed, almost black, ravines below us, it wasn't long before I began to lose my bearings.

To add to my woes the Ju 52's engines seemed to be feeling the effects of the constant climbing. It was only slowly and with much effort that I was able to coax her up to 4,000m. And even this didn't give us much of a safety margin as the *Grossglockner* – at close on 3,800m Austria's highest mountain – lay somewhere not far to the south of our intended route.

The jagged peaks were already getting uncomfortably close and soon we were being buffeted by very severe turbulence. It was high time I got us out of what was fast becoming a trap. My first thought was to establish radio contact with Schleissheim or some other airfield in the area. But this proved to be a non-starter. Unnoticed by me, the wireless-operator, who also happened to be named Kaufmann, had been struck down by a very bad case of air-sickness and was now slumped comatose in front of his set. The flight engineer, who was occupying the co-pilot's seat next to me, went back to see what he could do to help, but to little avail.

Our pleasure trip across the Alps was rapidly turning into the stuff of nightmares. Thank God I wasn't feeling the effects of air-sickness myself. I made a rough guess as to our approximate position and turned the Ju 52 hard to starboard. I was taking something of a gamble, but I wanted to have the highest peaks at my back and, with luck, emerge out into the open country to the north.

We were now flying through intermittent cloud and getting only occasional glimpses of the terrain below as I cautiously descended to 3,000m. Suddenly, and a little too close for comfort, the unmistakeable 2,962m high bulk of the *Zugspitze* loomed up out of the clouds to my left and I immediately knew where I was. I had almost overshot my destination, for the *Zugspitze*, Germany's highest peak, was not far from Garmisch and a matter of some 90km to the south-south-west of Munich. If I had remained on my original heading for much longer we would have found ourselves in Switzerland!

As it was, although the high wall of mountains behind us was still wreathed in cloud, the rolling Bavarian countryside stretching out in front of us was bathed in sunshine. We had made it. Both the wireless-operator and the Ju's engines also seemed to have recovered from their previous ailments as I opened the throttles and set course for Munich.

We put down at Schleissheim at 16.00 hours, just under three hours after setting out from Graz. The following day, 18 March, we bade farewell to the short-lived *Lufttransportgruppe 'Ziervogel'*. Taking off from Schleissheim at 10.00 hours, we finally landed back at our home base of Salzwedel exactly 2 hours and 38 minutes later. Our Austrian adventure was at an end. It had been a memorable week.

I soon got back into my familiar routine of instructing, inter-spersed with aerobatic practice and displays. The Luftwaffe's part in the annexation of Austria had been hailed as a success but, at the same time, it had brought to light several shortcomings. The most serious of these was perhaps the lack of adequate blind-flying experi-ence among aircrew. The adverse weather conditions that had prevented the deployment of the Dornier Do 17 bombers of KG 155 from Vienna down to Klagenfurt close to Austria's border with Yugoslavia, for example, may not have been of vital importance in itself. But it did serve to underline the urgent need for more blind-flying training.

At that time the Luftwaffe had just two dedicated blind-flying schools. The first of these had been established as far back as 1 July 1934 under the covert title of the *'Fliegerschule des DLV Celle'* (The German Sports Flying Association Training School, Celle), although it did not begin operating until the following year. In the summer of 1936 the cumbersome cover name was dropped and the school was re-designated simply as the *'Blindflugschule Celle'*. Nine months later, on 1 April 1937, it moved the 30km east from Celle to Wesendorf to become the *'Blindflugschule Wesendorf'*. And it was to Wesendorf that I was posted early in 1939 to commence my own blind-flying training.

As with almost every Luftwaffe flying school, the course at Wesendorf was divided into the theoretical and the practical. Both parts were highly intensive and demanded a great deal more effort and application than any of the other specialist courses I had attended in the past. Flying had entered the technological age. And although less than four years had elapsed, the days of my trundling about the sky in an open cockpit, stick-and-string biplane, communicating with my fellow trainees by hand signal, now seemed positively prehistoric.

The theoretical side of the training dealt first and foremost with radio navigation. This covered three areas: equipment, procedures and meteorology. A comprehensive understanding and good working knowledge of all three was essential if a pupil was to stand any chance of successfully completing the six-week course.

Radio navigation encompassed both self-bearing and ground direction-finding, together with air traffic control. The latter subject was not given quite as much attention as the other two, however, as this was regarded as more the domain of aircraft navigators, who would have attended their own specialist schools.

The ground direction-finding, or D/F, training taught the various procedures that had to be carried out between the ground station and the aircraft in the air to ensure the safe departure from, and approach to an airfield, as well as to fix the position or establish the course of a machine in flight. Each of these procedures had its own specific set of calibrated values, which allowed for quick and simple calculation of any information transmitted.

Air-to-ground communication was handled by the navigator using the Morse key. On-board communication between members of the crew was either verbal – in other words, shouting at each other above the noise of the engines – or by means of the so-called '*Printator*', which was nothing more than a wipe-clean slate similar to that found in any child's playroom. This may seem a little primitive now, but it did the job and worked remarkably well.

Of all the various D/F procedures taught at Wesendorf, perhaps the most important, and certainly the one we practised most frequently, was the ZZ-System. This enabled an aircraft to approach and land in bad weather and was based on a constant flow of signals from a ground transmitting station that was monitoring the machine's bearing, speed and height (in effect, a forerunner of the post-war ILS, or Instrument Landing System).

If a pilot had followed instructions carefully and was coming down in compliance with the signals received, he would get the letters 'ZZ' as he passed over the ground station. This meant; 'Approach correct; cleared to land'. If, however, he had misjudged his approach – coming in too fast perhaps, or too high – the ground station would send 'JJJ', which was the order to abort the landing. He would then have to decide whether to go round again for a second attempt, or seek another airfield altogether. Incidentally, the Berliners on the course insisted that, in their vernacular, the three 'Js' stood for '*Justav jib Jas*' – 'Step on the gas, Gustav'!

The second set of procedures that we had to master were the self-bearing systems, those that allowed pilots and crews to establish their position and check their course while in flight. They relied on a countrywide network of non-directional radio beacons (certain radio broadcasting stations could also be used in their place, but the readings from these latter had to be treated with some caution due to signal ambiguity). The aircraft involved needed to be equipped with an appropriate receiver and loop antenna. The navigator could then measure the angle between the machine's longitudinal axis and the radio beam. This he passed in the form of a 'p' value to the pilot, who converted it into a line of bearing which he could then mark on his flight map.

If a crew were engaged on a long cross-country flight they would normally progress from one beacon to the next while making use of other beacons to either side of their direct line of route to check their position and ground speed at intervals along the way.

For practical purposes, a pilot would sketch out his planned flight on a transparent overlay showing the route to be taken, together with the relevant radio beacons and base lines. To these he would then add the necessary values in large, clearly legible figures. Prepared beforehand, such maps could save an awful lot of work once airborne, especially during lengthy night or overwater flights.

As mentioned earlier, meteorology also played an important part in the Wesendorf course. An understanding of the weather and its behaviour was essential as we were often required to fly in extremely poor conditions. The limited power of aircraft engines in those days meant that we were seldom able to climb through really thick high cloud into the clear air above. And this, combined with an average top speed of only some 200–300km/h, often forced us to spend lengthy periods flying through areas of bad weather with all the risks – such as turbulence and icing – that this entailed.

We were therefore taught to 'read' the weather by using whatever meteorological charts we had been issued with, backed up by direct observation from the cockpit of the conditions encountered during the course of the flight. This was in no way intended to replace the invaluable work done by the meteorologists, but it did allow a pilot to make his own on-the-spot decisions. Armed with this knowledge, he could decide which was the best route to take and what was the best height at which to fly – he could even get some idea of the conditions he was likely to encounter on arrival at his destination.

All in all, it must be said that the *Blindflugschule Wesendorf* did a thoroughly good job. On 17 February 1939, after successfully completing the course there, I was duly qualified as a blind-flying instructor. This new role occupied much of my time after my return to Salzwedel. But I was also called upon to carry out a host of other special flying duties. These included weather reconnaissance flights, test and check flights, and urgent VIP and courier flights in the most adverse of weather conditions. On the strength of the flying experience I had amassed to date, I was also officially named as a *'militärische Luftfahrtsachverständiger'* – a 'recognized authority on military aviation'. This brought no promotion or other kudos with it. It was more of a cross between an honorary title and a job description. It did, however, broaden the scope of my activities even further. But even experts can be caught napping – quite literally!

Monday, 19 June 1939 had begun with another routine weather flight, on this occasion in a venerable Junkers W 34. Taking off at 06.51 hours, I was back on the ground again in less than twenty minutes. Next came a spell of blind-flying instructing. I was scheduled to give two lessons – one in the morning, another in the afternoon – together totalling exactly 2 hours and 8 minutes, and then I had a break until it was time to commence night-flying tuition.

After the usual preliminaries, preparing a flight map and checking the met report, we took off in a Ju 52 at 21.15 hours. It was to be a self-bearing training flight taking us on a 530-kilometre round trip to the Hamm radio beacon and back. The weather was good and we encountered no problems.

I hadn't lowered the central dividing curtain, which meant that I was able to keep a close eye on the trainee sitting in the pilot's seat to my left and could also monitor the instruments during the flight. The cockpit was well illuminated and I settled comfortably in the right-hand seat. It had been a long day, nearly fifteen hours since the morning's weather flight, and I began to doze. Now and again I would cast a glance at the instruments just to make sure that my pupil was keeping to the correct course and altitude. Almost subconsciously, I found myself growing more and more irritated by the untidy pattern of reflections from the instrument panel on the windscreen.

Then I looked more closely at the instruments themselves. There was something odd about them. I shouted at the trainee to pay attention to what he was doing. There was no response. A second and louder yell finally got a reaction. He had been fast asleep – as indeed had I only moments earlier!

And those reflections on the windscreen weren't reflections at all. They were the lights of some unknown little town towards which the Junkers was now quite happily diving at an alarming angle of bank. I hastily grabbed the stick, got the machine under control and lifted her nose to regain the altitude lost. A slight correction of course and we were back on track for Salzwedel. Our tiredness had completely vanished and we completed the exercise as fresh as a couple of daisies.

Over-tiredness nearly landed me in trouble again less than a fortnight later. The week beginning Monday, 2 July had got off to a quiet start. I was not scheduled to fly that day as I had spent the Sunday putting the still relatively unknown Bf 109 fighter through its paces in front of an enthusiastic crowd at an airshow at nearby Dedelstorf airfield.

But the Tuesday more than made up for my indolent Monday. It kicked off with the usual early morning reconnaissance flight in another of the school's trusty Ju W 34s. This was followed by a full morning's blind-flying instructing; three separate sessions, all on W 34s and each lasting well over an hour. These were quite exhausting in themselves, and I was more than glad when the last one ended at 13.10 hours.

I was able to enjoy a fairly relaxed afternoon attending to paperwork before night-flying training began with the setting of the sun. For the first few flights I played a purely supervisory role overseeing other instructors, and then fitted in two quick check flights on a Focke-Wulf Fw 58 '*Weihe*' (Kite) before taking up several trainees of my own. Flying finally came to an end in the early hours and I couldn't wait to get some sleep – it had been another eighteen-hour day – before starting all over again.

A cross-country blind-flying exercise in a Ju 52 was on the programme for the Wednesday morning. After the usual pre-flight preparations checking the route and the prevailing weather conditions, we walked out to the apron where our Ju was waiting. The chief mechanic reported everything in order, which we accepted without question – unwisely as it turned out.

At 10.07 hours we took off in good flying weather, climbed to an altitude of 800m and set course for the radio beacon on the Baltic island of Rügen. As was mandatory during daytime blind-flying exercises, the blackout curtains on the left-hand side of the cockpit were fully drawn, meaning that the trainee in the pilot's seat was completely cut off from the outside world and had to rely solely on instruments to fly the aircraft. We reached Rügen without incident and, after overflying the beacon, reversed course and set off back for Salzwedel.

About halfway through the return flight I noticed that the revs of the middle engine were dropping. Not long afterwards the two outer engines began running irregularly. We had not been in the air for much more than two hours, so the problem couldn't be shortage of fuel. The flight engineer had been sitting in the rear cabin throughout the flight. I beckoned him forward up into the cockpit and pointed at the engine rev gauges. For a moment or two he stood between the two pilot's seats looking perplexed. But when I asked him straight out if he had checked whether the machine actually *had* been refuelled before take-off, he immediately answered with a guilty 'No'.

So that was one problem solved. At least I knew what the trouble was. But now we were faced with another – what to do about it? An emergency landing due to lack of fuel seemed unavoidable. The blind-flying curtains were promptly rolled up and I hastily changed places with my trainee so that I now occupied the left-hand pilot's seat. I motioned for the flight engineer to return to the rear cabin. A quick glance at the externally mounted fuel contents gauges confirmed my suspicions – we were almost out of fuel.

But things could have been a lot worse. We were still at 600m, visibility was excellent, the wind was light and there were only a few small cumulus clouds in an otherwise clear blue sky. I wasn't at all sure of our exact position, but knew that we must be nearing the River Elbe. The countryside below was fairly open, just a few trees, but the ground looked a little soft, even boggy in places, and was criss-crossed by drainage ditches.

By this time we were running on empty. I would have to put her down somewhere in the next couple of minutes and a level expanse of meadow ahead seemed to offer the best chance. I throttled her back almost to stalling speed and carefully floated her in. I needn't have worried about running out of meadow. The soft ground brought us to a halt almost at once. Relieved, we jumped down from the machine and spent a moment or two taking stock.

We inspected the fuselage and undercarriage but could find no evidence of any damage. That left just two questions to answer. First and foremost, how was I going to lift the Junkers off from this soggy grass without standing her on her nose, or even flipping her over on to her back completely? And secondly, as there didn't seem to be a soul about, where were we going to find the aviation fuel to enable me to make the attempt?

We weren't even exactly sure where we were. But it wasn't long before a small group of *Reichsarbeitsdienst* (Reich Labour Service) men appeared. They had watched us land and had come to see if we needed any assistance. They informed us that we had come down near the Brahlstorf Estate a couple of kilometres to the east of Lake Schwerin. Their unit was working on a construction project nearby and they said we could count on their help and support.

Firstly, one of the men who knew the area well took me to the estate office where I was able to telephone our course leader back in Salzwedel to inform him of the situation. He acknowledged my report and gave me permission to take off again once I considered the conditions suitable. That was one worry less.

I next called the airfield at Hagenow, some 40km away, explaining our predicament and requesting that they send two drums of aviation fuel and a hand pump, to which they readily agreed. A small truck duly turned up during the course of the afternoon and the driver and his mate laboriously hand-pumped sufficient fuel into the Junkers' tanks for the short hop down to Hagenow.

By now the wheels of the machine had sunk deep into the boggy ground. The Labour Service men dug two trenches and laid a couple of thick baulks of timber in front of, and partly beneath each of the two wheels. This would, I hoped, at least provide me with a firm start for my take-off run.

To keep the weight to a minimum, I sent my two companions back with the truck to Hagenow. Then, with the throttle lock off – in other words, with the engines at full emergency power – I slowly climbed out of the shallow trench and gradually gathered speed, engines screaming in protest, across the marshy meadow. It was touch and go. For a moment I thought I wasn't going to make it. But at 18.30 hours, exactly six-and-a-quarter hours after our involuntary landing, the Junkers staggered reluctantly back into the air.

Fifteen minutes later I touched down at Hagenow. I had the Ju checked over and refuelled, thanked the airfield personnel for all their help, and waited for the arrival of the truck carrying my two comrades.

At 19.45 hours we lifted off for the 45-minute flight back to Salzwedel. The whole unhappy incident, entirely of our own making, had ended without serious mishap. We were reprimanded but not punished. For me it was a timely reminder of the old adage: 'Never rely on others, always check the condition of your aircraft yourself before even touching that throttle'. You could also add, '... and *never* fly unless fully rested' – which, after the previous day's marathon session in the air, was certainly not the case as far as I was concerned on this particular occasion.

Despite the high number of flying hours that I was putting in, I had not lost sight of my ultimate ambition of becoming an officer. During this time I attended several courses at the Berlin-Gatow and Fürstenfeldbruck *Luftkriegsschulen* (Air Warfare Academies). But political events were once again about to put my personal plans on hold. The carefree days of peacetime flying were rapidly drawing to a close.

Flight No. 3666 in my logbook, dated 15 August 1939, was to be a short check flight in a Ju 52 that had just undergone routine maintenance. Almost immediately after take-off from Salzwedel at 13.51 hours, however, the middle engine died on me. It was only with the greatest difficulty that I managed to scrape over the roofs of the buildings on the edge of the field. The check flight was reduced to a quick circuit and four minutes later I was back on the ground taxiing over to the workshop hangar for further repairs.

Although I didn't know it at the time, that 240-second hop had marked the end of a chapter in my flying career. And little did I suspect what awaited me on the morrow.

PART II: THE YEARS OF CONFLICT

Chapter 5
Kampfgruppe Z.B.V.9

On the afternoon of 16 August 1939 I was informed that I was to be posted for an indefinite period to a new transport unit being formed at Tutow in Pomerania. I was ordered to get my kit together, full marching order, and fly one of the school's Ju 52s to Tutow the next morning. My crew was to be made up of flight-engineer Rudi Lucas from Munich, a typical easy-going Bavarian, and wireless-operator Karl Badorrek, who hailed from Ortelsburg in East Prussia. Chalk and cheese, you might say, but we three knew each other well and had often flown together on training exercises and while instructing. This made the move into the unknown that much easier for all of us. We had not been told the reason for our posting, of course. Everything was top secret – as usual.

While we were going through our pre-flight checks the following morning the school commander, Major Trautvetter, came out to the aircraft to say goodbye and wish us well. It was an unusual gesture for a commanding officer, and therefore all the more appreciated, but it was typical of the Major's firm but solicitous style of leadership. He then bade farewell to the other crews who had also been posted to Tutow along with us. Clearly there must be a special mission of some sort in the offing.

After some delay we began taxiing out to the take-off line. And there was Major Trautvetter again, standing beside the runway, his hand lifted to the peak of his cap as if taking the salute at some ceremonial parade. His gaze followed each of the Junkers as one by one we trundled past him. I was close enough to see that his expression was serious, almost sombre – he presumably knew what lay ahead of us.

We eventually lifted off from Salzwedel at 13.15 hours. It was a glorious late summer's day and the north German countryside that unfolded before us was bathed in brilliant sunshine for the whole of the 66-minute, 210km flight.

Tutow was a hive of activity. Our new Gruppe was still in the process of being formed. Its four component Staffeln were made up primarily of experienced crews, like ourselves, drafted in from various schools and training establishments. Although officially designated a *Kampfgruppe zur besonderen Verwendung* (*KGr.z.b.V.*), or 'Special Purposes Bomber Wing', the unit was, in reality, a straightforward transport Gruppe. This nomenclature was not so much an attempt at deception, but more of a throwback to the earliest days of the Luftwaffe when the Ju 52 was classed as an auxiliary bomber (and had, in fact, served as such during the Spanish Civil War).

At Tutow we quickly became much more aware of the rising levels of tension between the governments of Poland and the German Reich. Every one of the increasingly frequent special news bulletins was listened to with rapt attention, and then discussed and dissected. We could clearly see the storm clouds gathering, but we all fervently hoped that a peaceful settlement could still be found. The whole atmosphere of the place was muted. There were no signs of enthusiasm or jubilation whatsoever.

Although *KGr.z.b.V.* 9's specific role was intended to be the transport of heavy weapons, equipment and supplies, we spent our first few days at Tutow flying a number of routine missions ferrying men and *matériel* to and from airfields both nearby – Schwerin and Wismar, for example – as well as to several others further afield, including Jüterbog and Göttingen. There was even time to drop in at Salzwedel on 26 and 28 August to sort out one or two personal matters that had been left undone in the initial rush to get to Tutow.

On the morning of 1 September 1939 we listened to the broadcast of Hitler's speech to the Reichstag. We were at war with Poland.

At 12.17 on that same day our Staffel was transferred south to Aslau, a forward landing ground in Lower Silesia situated roughly midway between Dresden and Breslau. We landed at 12.50 hours to find everybody there very nervy and tense. Reports of imminent enemy air raids meant that we were kept at constant cockpit readiness. But, although we remained on the alert for the rest of the day, absolutely nothing happened.

At 08.08 hours the following morning we took off from Aslau for the twenty-minute hop to nearby Görlitz, where we rejoined the rest of the Gruppe. We were to remain at Görlitz until the afternoon of 12 September, spending most of the ten days there practising flying in close formation. One of the exercises involved flying back to Aslau, touching down and then immediately returning to Görlitz. This gave us the opportunity to practise a massed take-off, as well as line-astern landings in quick succession, as might be required of us under combat conditions. Not a particularly exciting or warlike interval, it must be admitted, but it kept us busy and did wonders for our nerves during a period that was rife with rumour and uncertainty.

Our physical well-being was also more than adequately catered for. We had been billeted in a charming old inn in the village of Girbigsdorf, which was little more than a kilometre away from the field. The rooms were comfortable and homely, and the food was plentiful and delicious. The landlord and his wife couldn't do enough for us. They treated us as if we were their own sons. The news bulletins were full of nothing but German successes. Our vague feelings of unease and concern began to lift. There really did seem to be no cause for undue pessimism and the evenings spent in the company of the locals in Girbigsdorf were carefree and convivial.

The Wehrmacht's daily communiqués were not always telling the whole story, however, and consequently we did not realize just how critical the situation at the front sometimes was. We were not privy to any sensitive information at our lowly Gruppe level. But that was perhaps all to the good. We were totally unaware of the true course of events overall, and seeing them from a worm's-eye view would hardly have helped us to understand the bigger picture.

But things were about to change. Late in the afternoon of 12 September, suddenly and without any warning, we were ordered to move up to Sagan, some 60km to the north of Görlitz. After a hurried take-off and thirty-minute flight we touched down at Sagan at 18.15 hours.

The early morning of 13 September was then taken up by an extremely lengthy and thorough briefing on the mission we were about to carry out. It was clear that the operation was not going to be at all easy, but it was of critical importance to the infantrymen of Generaloberst Johannes Blaskowitz's 8. *Armee*, who were encountering fierce resistance from elements of the Polish '*Poznan*' Army as it fell back on Warsaw.

Our Staffelkapitän, Oberleutnant Trenck, explained the task that lay ahead of us. We were to transport troops of an air-landing unit to a forward landing ground north of the Polish town of Lódz. The mission had to be flown under strict radio silence.

The Oberleutnant's orders for the post-landing procedure were even more explicit. Once our wheels had touched the ground we were to taxi as quickly as possible in close line-astern to the far end of the field, where we were to draw up in a wide semi-circle to the left to allow the troops to deplane. Our engines had to be kept running the whole time and all machine-gun positions had to be manned throughout in case of possible enemy attack. Our superiors were obviously taking no chances as the military situation in this area was still very volatile.

We didn't spend too much time worrying about these implications for now. Our more immediate concern was how on earth we were going to find, let alone reach our intended landing ground under the prevailing conditions. Air operations over Poland had been bedevilled by poor weather from the very opening hours of the campaign. This morning, the visibility was down to just a few metres; in fact, it would be no exaggeration to describe it as 'zero visibility'.

In addition to the ground mist, a further complication that perhaps posed an even greater danger was the total absence of any wind. Given the heavy loads we were to be carrying, any take-off – even in perfect conditions – would have been problematical. As it was, the prospect was decidedly risky.

The troops hurriedly climbed on board. Their equipment was loaded with equal haste and lashed down in what can only be described as a very rudimentary manner. The time for take-off was rapidly approaching. We had practised blind take-offs often enough during our peacetime training days, but never under quite the same conditions as now – overloaded, no wind and zero visibility. But this was war. And each of us would have to cope with the situation as best he could.

At 07.35 hours, exactly to the minute as briefed, we began lifting off from Sagan. Keeping straight ahead, we were plunged almost instantly into thick grey cloud. After a painfully long and laborious climb we finally broke through into clearer air at an altitude of some 500m. Flying almost due east and squinting into the unaccustomed brightness of the early morning sun, we could soon make out a ragged collection of tiny black dots ahead of us. These were presumably the machines that had taken off before us, although it wasn't long before we lost sight of them again.

Plans for us to maintain some kind of formation, however loose, while *en route* to our destination had gone completely by the board. This was due mainly to the fact that, despite the ten days we had spent at Görlitz, there simply hadn't been enough time since the formation of the Gruppe for the crews, drawn as they were from a miscellany of different units, to gain the expertise required to enable them to form up after take-off and keep station on each other. This was a problem that would continue to plague the Luftwaffe's often *ad hoc* transport operations throughout the war.

We therefore quickly worked out a course of our own to follow and stuck rigidly to it. After about thirty minutes in the air the layer of solid cloud below us began to break up and very soon had disappeared altogether. But the countryside still lay hidden beneath a blanket of early morning mist and it was to take some little while before we were able to establish our exact position.

In the meantime we were kept more than busy fending off the constant barrage of questions from our passengers impatient to know precisely where we were. This finally proved too much for our flight engineer, who was sitting in the co-pilot's seat to my right. At the next enquiry as to our present position, Rudi's native Bavarian good humour deserted him. 'Exactly here', he snapped curtly, pointing down to the ground below. And you couldn't really argue with that. 'Here' is exactly where we were – flying over a dense patch of woodland. The only problem was, none of us knew where this particular wood happened to be. But we weren't yet too worried about our present predicament, as we still had a fair way to go before we were scheduled to reach our intended landing ground.

And reach it we did, despite a few further difficulties, and – even more surprisingly – right on time. The other crews had also made it and we touched down one after the other in rapid succession, just as we had been briefed to do. Once we were on the ground we taxied smartly to the far end of the field, again as per the pre-op briefing, where we were amazed to see the figure of General der Flieger Alexander Löhr, the AOC of *Luftflotte* 4, the air fleet responsible for all air operations in the southern half of Poland.

Even more astonishing, the General wasn't there simply to witness our arrival. He was busily engaged in marshalling and directing the incoming aircraft. As each Junkers bumped over the grass towards him, he would indicate where it was to execute its turn to the left and then point to the exact spot where he wanted it to come to a stop, engines still running. All the while he was gesturing and shouting orders to other officers going about their duties on the field and constantly looking at his watch. If any proof were needed, the General's presence and active involvement in the landing operation showed us just how urgent and important it must have been. Fortunately, he seemed satisfied that everything was going to plan.

Not a second was lost as the troops scrambled from the aircraft and quickly formed up. We weren't able to see what happened next as the moment each machine was unloaded it was immediately sent back up to the other end of the field close to where we had first touched down. Here we were finally permitted to switch off our engines, but the guns still had to remain manned.

We pilots left our machines and gathered round our respective Staffelkapitäne to receive further orders. Everybody was in high spirits. There had been no reaction whatsoever from the enemy and we hadn't suffered a single loss. The operation had been an unqualified success and nothing further was required of us. Perhaps it's worth pointing out that the successful outcome of the mission was due in no small measure to the fact that all the pilots taking part were highly-experienced instructors with many hours of flying under their belts. Coming from various schools, the majority were fully qualified in blind-flying, and many held the advanced 'C' Certificate as blind-flying instructors.

At 16.20 hours that same afternoon we took off for the return trip to Sagan. The entire 80-minute flight was made in perfect weather; a far cry from our early morning battle with the elements.

The Lódz operation was the only mission of its kind that we flew during the Polish campaign. The remainder of my time with *KGr.z.b.V.* 9 was taken up with routine cargo flights. One of them, however, promised to be something rather special. On 6 October three aircraft of our Staffel, under the command of Oberleutnant Otto-Heinrich Wildau, were to fly a mobile D/F station from Berlin-Tempelhof to Moscow. Having got to Berlin, we sat at Tempelhof for several hours on the evening of 5 October waiting for a briefing. But whatever deal had been struck between Germany and the Soviet Union must have fallen through at the last moment. So rather than setting off for Moscow the following morning, three very disappointed crews returned instead to the Gruppe's new base at Grossenhain, north-west of Dresden.

The fifty-one missions that I flew while serving with *KGr.z.b.V.* 9 from 17 August to 20 October 1939 – Nos. 3667 to 3717 in my logbook, totalling exactly 58 hours and 54 minutes in all – had brought me a host of new experiences. They had taken me to nearly a dozen previously unfamiliar airfields not only in eastern Germany, but also in occupied Poland. Landing at some of these fields, often in extremely poor weather and with a cloud base less than 50m off the ground, was sometimes touch and go, not to say downright dangerous on occasion.

And since the outbreak of hostilities any pilot flying over longer stretches, either blind, through thick cloud or at night, had a new navigational problem to contend with. The proliferation of defensive Flak belts around Germany's larger cities and certain vital industrial targets meant that there were an increasing number of no-fly zones and aircraft were restricted to flight lanes across many parts of the country.

Unlike the short-lived *Lufttransportgruppe 'Ziervogel'*, which had been disbanded immediately after the successful annexation of Austria, *KGr.z.b.V.* 9 remained in being long after the Polish campaign had been fought and won. In fact, the Gruppe continued to operate throughout the war, latterly as I./Transportgeschwader 3. But our crew was one of those earmarked for return to its parent unit and so for us it was a case of 'back to school'.

Back to school did not mean back to Salzwedel, however. Shortly after the beginning of the war the original *Fliegerschule* Salzwedel had been transferred to Prenzlau and re-designated as the *Flugzeug-führerschule* (Pilot Training School) A/B 120. And thus it was for Prenzlau, an airfield some 50km to the south-east of Neubrandenburg, that we set course when we said goodbye to *KGr.z.b.V.* 9 on 20 October 1939.

Chapter 6
Flugzeugführerschule A/B 120

Although I had only been away for a little over two months, my old unit had changed almost beyond recognition. Lots of new faces and very few from the pre-war days. Most of the regulars among the staff had been posted to front-line units and their places taken by reservists. This took a bit of getting used to as the whole nature and style of the training was now very different. There was far less off-duty time, the hours were much longer and free weekends just a distant memory.

Flying training had been organized into shifts in order to make maximum use of every single serviceable aircraft and increase the school's output of trained pilots. The new order wasn't exactly welcomed with wholehearted enthusiasm. But the school was now very much on a war footing. There was no longer any friendly rivalry between the instructors. Everybody simply buckled down and got on with the job in hand.

The school's training capacity had grown to such an extent that satellite fields had to be set up. Because of the personnel and technical support that these outstations required, they couldn't be located too far away from the main Prenzlau facility. And it was at one of these new satellite fields, Schönfeld, situated about 35km to the east of Prenzlau, that I resumed my instructing duties on 22 October.

The trainees were all reservists, called back into service and somewhat older than the average pupil I had previously been accustomed to teaching. But to their great credit they were eager to learn and made good progress right from the start. None of them tried to gain any unfair advantages by harping on about the ranks they had held during their earlier service days. All in all they proved an amenable and comradely bunch and were more than happy to fit in with each other.

The aircraft types employed at Schönfeld were all well known to me from my time at Salzwedel and before. They were a mixed lot and included the Arados Ar 66 and Ar 96, Bücker Bü 131, Focke-Wulf Fw 44, Gotha Go 145, Heinkel He 72 and Klemm Kl 35. After the trainees had gained their A-2 flying certificates, the course moved back to Prenzlau for further training on the heavier Heinkel He 46, the Junkers W 33 and W 34, and the twin-engined Focke-Wulf Fw 58.

During this period I was able to add two new types to my own logbook. These were the Arado Ar 79, a sporty little communications machine that had won a number of international speed records before the war, and the Avia B 534, a fighter biplane originally built for, and flown by, the Czechoslovakian Air Force.

Such was the increased tempo of the training programme at Schönfeld that I found few opportunities to indulge in my private passion for blind-flying. I had to content myself with taking one or other of the school's elderly Ju W 34s up for a weather-reconnaissance flight whenever I could. These flights had to be carried out however bad the conditions happened to be at the time. This meant that getting back down again could often be tricky. More than once I found myself having to make a sharp ZZ landing, which only added to the excitement. My second great love, aerobatic flying, was also severely curtailed, although I did manage to organize one or two short sessions on a Bücker Bü 133 'Jungmeister' just to keep my hand in.

This was the period of the 'Phoney War'. There were no land campaigns being fought in continental Europe at the present time. So after our all-too-brief taste of operational flying over Poland, we instructors didn't feel that we were missing out on too much. We accepted our training role with as good a grace as we could muster. It was, after all, an essential job and now that there was a war on every able-bodied man in the country had to do his bit, whatever that might be.

In March 1940 I was assigned to train a group of officers, both regular and reservist. Among them were the navigator and flight-engineer of a Heinkel He 111 bomber who had been offered the chance to retrain as pilots in recognition of a rather extraordinary feat. Their story had received wide coverage in the press and was well known to the public. The pilot of their Heinkel had been killed while they were on an operational mission and somehow the pair, Oberleutnant Münter and Leutnant Baden, had managed not only to fly the damaged machine back to base, but had also succeeded in landing it, thereby saving not only themselves, but also the two other members of the crew, from possible injury or worse. It was a real privilege to hear them describe the event at first-hand and everyone was full of admiration for what Münter and Baden had done.

The training of this officer-only group lasted from the end of March until mid-June 1940. A period of only some ten weeks in which to teach both the practical and theoretical aspects of flying was cutting things rather tight. But times were changing and needs must. The only real difficulty I faced was in keeping this motley collection of out-and-out individualists on the same track. There are a couple of lines of German doggerel to the effect that nothing is harder than keeping a bunch of officers under control – '*Nichts ist schwerer zu regieren, als ein Haufen von Offizieren*' – and yet everything went surprisingly smoothly.

I may have been outranked by my more illustrious pupils, but all of them were more than happy to defer to my greater experience when it came to flying. Many convivial evenings spent emptying a glass or two helped us relax after a gruelling day's schedule. There were no drop-outs from the course, and only in two cases did I have to put in that little bit of extra effort to keep the trainees up to the required level.

My combined activities as a group instructor and a recognized authority on military aviation provided me with many welcome opportunities to become involved in other areas of flying which, in turn, added considerably to my growing fund of knowledge on the many and varied aspects of the aeronautical world. They also enabled me to undertake some very enjoyable cross-country flights, my particular favourites being those spent piloting Heinkel's elegant He 70 '*Blitz*' high-speed communications machine. These flights took me to yet more airfields across a broad swathe of north-eastern and central Germany that I had rarely, if ever, visited before. Among the dozen or more new names to appear in my logbook during this period, two that spring readily to mind are the former free city of Danzig, and Königsberg, the capital of East Prussia.

But perhaps my most memorable flight of all while serving with A/B 120 was not exactly what one would call cross-country – in fact, it lasted no more than five minutes.

The winter of 1939/40 has been described by many as the worst in living memory. Temperatures plummeted, remaining below zero for weeks on end, and much of Germany, from the North Sea islands to the southern Alps, was blanketed in snow and ice. And it was in the very depths of that winter – on 25 January 1940, to be precise – that I was tasked, 'if at all possible', with retrieving one of the school's Ju W 33s, which had had to make an emergency landing in deep snow.

Presumably the school hoped to avoid having to send out a recovery team to dismantle the aircraft and bring it back in pieces by road. But it was left up to me, once I had inspected the site, to decide whether I should risk the attempt to fly the machine out, or veto the whole idea as being too dangerous.

The Junkers had just failed to make it back to Prenzlau and had put down on land belonging to the large government-run Marienhof farm estate. We drove out there to assess the situation. The first thing we did was to take a look at the immediate surroundings, checking that there were no wires or cables strung along the edges of the meadow in which the machine was sitting. Next we probed the snow, trying to establish exactly how deep it was and whether there were any obstacles or ditches concealed beneath its deceptively even surface.

Not surprisingly, our activities had attracted the attention of some locals, who told us that there were no obstacles of any kind and that the field was perfectly flat under the layer of snow. It was on the strength of these assurances, plus the fact that I was only too aware that the school needed every aircraft it could muster to cope with its busy training schedule, that I persuaded myself that the attempt to fly it out should be made.

There would be no need to do any taxiing. The field was large enough to allow me to take off in a straight line from where the aircraft had come to a stop. With the help of some of the estate workers we shovelled the snow free from in front of the Ju's wheels and for some 20 or 30m out along the intended line of take-off. This,

I hoped, would allow me to get her rolling and pick up a little speed before I started ploughing through the really thick stuff.

To keep the weight down I climbed aboard on my own. Settling into the pilot's seat, I ran the engine warm and opened the throttle. She began to move. After a few initial bumps and jolts the going got easier. I was now holding the engine at full power and could feel the 310 horses straining to keep up the forward momentum. Pulling back on the stick, I finally managed to get the gutsy old W 33 off the ground. With a feeling of relief I took her up to 150m and pointed her nose towards Prenzlau airfield which I could already see in front of me. In less than five minutes I was back down on the ground again. It may have been only the shortest of hops, but the sense of achievement was none the less for all that.

On 10 May 1940, in the middle of training my group of officers, came the news that Hitler had unleashed his *Blitzkrieg* in the West. All hopes of an early end to the war appeared to be dashed. Every radio bulletin was followed with keen interest. There was a definite feeling of apprehension, not to say concern, in the air at Prenzlau, although nobody expressed their misgivings out loud. We had already reached the stage where most of us were beginning to think it prudent to keep our views on current events to ourselves.

Despite any misgivings, training continued without let-up. Shortly after my officers had completed their course and moved on, I was given a batch of young airmen to train. This small group I took to Salzwedel where, from the end of June until mid-August 1940, we were to spend some six weeks of intensive and uninterrupted training.

My new group of pupils had been well selected. Their behaviour was exemplary and they all got on well together. When they were not in the air, their time was taken up with lessons on a wide range of aeronautical subjects, and by sport. But purely educational tuition and more traditional military duties – rifle practice, standing guard and the like – had disappeared from the curriculum due to lack of time. Flying training was all-important and the strict timetable had to be adhered to at all costs.

Under such circumstances it was not always easy to keep sight of the quality of the training being given. This placed an extra burden on the instructors. It was crucial to recognize the character traits and gauge the potential ability of every single pupil. While flying training was in progress out on the field there was ample opportunity to chat to those trainees gathered around the take-off line waiting for their turn to go up. This proved an ideal way of getting to know them collectively and as individuals. This particular group of youngsters impressed us all by their openness, their willingness to learn and their genuine sense of comradeship. I'm sure these qualities were of enormous help to them when it came to dealing with the pressures of the training course.

At this relatively early stage of the war flying training differed little, if at all, from the days of peace. There were no signs as yet of the increasingly drastic cuts in the training schedules brought about by the fuel shortages of the later war years. It was simply that everything had to be done in a much shorter time.

The Salzwedel course came to a close in mid-August with the awarding of the B-1 military pilot's licence. For the next stage of their training – the B-2 licence – I would have to take the group back to Prenzlau. By this time the campaign in the west had long been won. But any revived hopes that this would lead to a cessation of hostilities were again quickly dashed. The war had entered a new phase with the opening of the air offensive against Great Britain.

Then, on 5 September 1940, little more than a fortnight after returning to Prenzlau, I suddenly received a new posting. I was ordered to report to the Paris section of the *Chef AW* the following day. I managed to get a seat on the regular Berlin-Paris courier flight and as I was borne westward I could not help wondering what new assignment awaited me in the capital of occupied France.

Chapter 7

Chef Aw Le Bourget

On 6 September 1940 I reported to my new station as ordered. The recently established Paris section of the Luftwaffe's Director of Training Department – *Chef des Ausbildungswesens*, or *Chef AW* for short – was based at Le Bourget airport 12km to the north-east of the French capital.

No time was lost in informing me of my new duties. I was to be part of a small team, or *Kommando*, whose job was to collect captured aircraft from all over France and fly them back to Le Bourget, where we would then carry out all the necessary check and test flights to help establish their airworthiness and possible suitability for use by the Luftwaffe. It sounded a relatively simple and straightforward task, but it threw up some fiendishly awkward problems, as we were soon to discover.

The *Kommando* was headed by an elderly major, who presided over a small staff. Their offices, together with a couple of workshop spaces, were housed within one of Le Bourget's large hangars, which is still standing at the time of writing nearly fifty years later. The unit's flying personnel were quartered in nearby hotels – handy both for the airport and for the many legendary attractions that Paris had to offer.

We had a single Ju 52 on strength, which was used to ferry us pilots to wherever the ex-enemy aircraft were waiting to be picked up. On arrival we would take charge of the machine to be collected and be responsible for flying it back to Le Bourget. There was no question of a familiarization flight before setting off. And rarely were there any pilot's notes available. Each of us was left very much to his own devices. We were expected to deal with whatever problems that arose as we best saw fit.

Here it should perhaps be said that, despite our still somewhat tender years, all the *Kommando's* pilots were what could be termed '*alte Hasen*' – literally 'old hares', or 'old sweats' – Luftwaffe jargon for flyers with a great deal of experience. We had learnt to fly long before the war and belonged to that small band of early instructors that formed the backbone of the Luftwaffe's training organization. We had clearly been carefully chosen. There were no beginners among our ranks, and consequently the authorities knew that they could demand, and expect to receive, that much more from us.

On Saturday, 7 September, the day after my arrival at Le Bourget, I was handed my first assignment. A Morane-Saulnier MS.230 had to be collected from Bourges, some 180km to the south of Paris, and flown back to Le Bourget. The 230, a parasol-wing two-seater which had been the French *Armée de l'Air*'s mainstay elementary trainer throughout much of the 1930s was, as one might imagine, quite a robust machine with few vices and therefore relatively easy to fly. I must admit, though, that the left-handed propeller, the unfamiliar instrumentation and the aircraft's somewhat 'foreign' flight characteristics when it came to aileron response and stability, did give me some anxious moments at take-off and during the first thirty minutes of the flight. But after that all went well.

I had made a mental note of the Morane's speed at take-off and so tailored my approach and landing at Le Bourget accordingly. Touch-down was smooth and I taxied across to our hangar without any difficulty. Number one safely delivered.

I was to ferry so many Moranes back to Le Bourget in the weeks ahead that it soon became a matter of routine. After arriving at the various aircraft factories and airfields where machines were waiting to be picked up, I frequently had the opportunity to take a look inside the assembly or repair shops. The sheet metal workers employed in these places impressed me in particular. They were true craftsmen. It was little short of miraculous to watch as even the most complicated component slowly took shape and form under their skilled hands.

Quite often I would have to wait for longer periods while a particular aircraft was being prepared for collection and all the necessary paperwork completed. On these occasions I liked to have a good look around the works. As I had spent four-and-a half years as an apprentice in an aircraft factory myself before joining the

Luftwaffe, perhaps it was only natural that I should draw comparisons between the French methods of working and the way we did things back home in Germany. There were differences, of course, but they were so minor as to be hardly worth mentioning. As far as I could see, the quality of work on both sides was equally good and left nothing to choose between them.

Trainer aircraft of all shapes and sizes accounted for a large proportion of my early work with the *Chef AW* Le Bourget. But one particular type sticks out in my mind above all others: the North American NAA 57. My first encounter with this product of the transatlantic aviation industry left me totally in awe. The noise the engine made was indescribable. Luftwaffe pilots would later joke that a single NAA 57 could drown out the sound of a whole Staffel of Bf 109s. And the cockpit was so large and roomy that I felt somewhat lost, almost as if I could get up and have a stroll around in it!

France had ordered well over 200 NAA 57s from America, of which about half had been delivered prior to the Armistice of June 1940. We had to collect many of these aircraft direct from the French Atlantic port of St.Nazaire, where they had been unloaded from ships, uncrated and assembled ready for flight. This meant that they were brand new when we picked them up and ferried them back to Le Bourget.

The St.Nazaire run was always a popular assignment, and not only for the thrill of piloting a noisy but pristine NAA 57. These jobs frequently entailed a long wait while the machines were being made ready for us, and this gave us the opportunity to sample the offerings of the many fresh seafood restaurants in the area. The Le Bourget *Kommando* wasn't just about the risky business of flying unfamiliar and not always reliable foreign aircraft; it had its benefits too – what today might be called the 'perks of the job'.

Although originally designed as a six-passenger light transport aircraft, the twin-engined French Caudron C.445 'Goéland' (Seagull') was also to see extensive use as a Luftwaffe trainer. This was another machine that proved very popular as it was an absolute delight to fly – not that we had to fly it very far, as most examples were collected straight from the Caudron factory at Issy-les-Moulineaux, which was just the other side of Paris from Le Bourget. As an added bonus there were always works test pilots or engineers on hand at Issy who could show us the ropes and iron out any bugs for us.

The '*Goéland*' had one feature that I had not yet come across. This was the radio compass, or automatic direction-finder. While we were still having to use hand-cranked loop antennae in our aircraft to determine our bearings and fix our position, this was done automatically in the C.445. Although we weren't yet allowed to get our hands on this equipment, it was at least nice to know of its existence. It was something we 'old hares' of the blind-flying fraternity had been waiting for for a very long time.

While trainers such as the Morane-Saulnier MS.230, the North American NAA 57 and the Caudron C.445 '*Goéland*' were to prove useful additions to the Luftwaffe's inventory, the same could not be said of the many captured French fighters and bombers that we were dealing with. These latter could not be employed operationally as the technical and logistical problems involved were simply too difficult to overcome.

Moreover, despite the losses that we were currently suffering over Great Britain, the powers-that-be were obviously of the opinion that the output of our own aviation industry was more than adequate to fill the gaps. The official stance was that the Luftwaffe did not require augmenting by taking foreign aircraft into front-line service. As a consequence, many of the French operational types that we had captured were later either sold, presented, or otherwise made available to various friendly nations such as Romania, Croatia and Bulgaria.

My having to collect aircraft from all over France, from the Channel coast to the Bay of Biscay and the Mediterranean, meant that I was constantly visiting yet more new and unfamiliar airfields. Some I found myself returning to time and time again, and it wasn't long before I got to know all their good points and bad. Their accessibility, ease of approach, and the quality of the ground support services on offer ranged from excellent to the abysmal.

These ferry flights also allowed me to enjoy the beauty of much of the French countryside. And not just the countryside. Sometimes the flights out to the more distant airfields where machines were awaiting collection would take so long that there wouldn't be enough time for me to make the return flight on the same day. On these occasions I would spend my afternoons and evenings exploring the nearest town or city, all of which did wonders in helping to improve my schoolboy French.

But, now and again, even a routine ferry flight could spring a nasty surprise – such as the time when I was ordered to collect a Bloch 152 from Biarritz and fly it some 170km up the Biscay coast to Bordeaux. The Bloch 152 was one of France's newer fighters. The first examples had been delivered to the *Armée de l'Air* in the months leading up to the outbreak of war. Its powerful 1,000hp Gnome-Rhône GR 14N radial engine gave it a top speed in excess of 500km/h and the short hop up to Bordeaux should have posed no problems at all.

But the portents weren't good right from the start. Upon arrival at Biarritz I was told that on no account must I retract the Bloch's undercarriage. Nor was anybody quite sure just how the machine would behave once it was in the air. The engine had been ground tested and seemed to be running well enough. It would certainly get me as far as Bordeaux, I was assured. None of this exactly filled me with confidence, and to cap it all there was a report that bad weather was on the way.

In view of the circumstances, I was not given a direct order to make this flight; the decision whether to do so or not was left entirely up to me. To help me make up my mind I first walked round the aircraft with the chief mechanic, inspecting all external parts and ensuring that the control surfaces moved freely and easily. Then I checked the oil and fuel levels. I found nothing amiss and so, after some initial hesitation, and despite my never having been this close to a Bloch 152 in my life before, despite their being no pilot's notes whatsoever, and despite the absence of any French personnel to whom I could turn for advice – I decided to give it a go.

I carried out a brief taxiing test and made sure that the brakes were working properly before selecting a suitable spot to start my take-off run. The Biarritz field was only a few hundred metres inland from the coast and the wind direction on this particular day meant that I would have to take off towards the sea. After winding the engine up to full power, I released the brakes. The Bloch shot off like a startled hare. I lifted off without difficulty and immediately executed a sharp turn to starboard as I didn't want to head out over open water. So far, so good.

With map in hand I stooged off along the coast towards Bordeaux. Visibility was becoming poorer by the minute, however. The clouds were getting lower and, to add to my woes, it started to rain heavily. As instructed, I had not raised the undercarriage and, as a consequence, I was making only very slow progress. That engine really was in good shape, otherwise it would not have been able to cope with the additional drag. Up to this point luck had been on my side.

But then the rain became torrential and I was forced to sacrifice more and more height as the elements conspired against me. By now it was too late to turn back. There were no alternative fields along my route where I could put down and seek shelter. And soon I had totally lost my bearings. My only hope of establishing my position lay in the River Garonne. This flowed north-north-west into Bordeaux and out into the broad estuary of the Gironde. I couldn't fail to miss it, surely?

But this was not my main concern at the moment. My chief worry was the tall radio masts at Bordeaux. At my present altitude, and hemmed in by low cloud, these posed a real threat. I knew I couldn't clear them. The best I could hope for would be to fly around them – *if* I spotted them in time. From the landscape below, and the time that had elapsed since my leaving Biarritz, they should already have been visible. I certainly didn't relish the prospect of flying into one. That would be the end of me and the Bloch, no question – and it wouldn't do the mast much good either.

Suddenly the dim shapes of the masts loomed up out of the murk. And then, just a split-second later, they were gone again. I didn't even have time to be scared. The gods must have been smiling on me. My lucky escape had not been of my own making, but it had taught me another invaluable lesson: I should never have taken off in the first place.

My arrival at Bordeaux caused quite a stir. They hadn't expected anybody to turn up in this kind of weather. The Bloch was taken into the workshops, while I spent a quiet hour in the mess to calm my nerves. I didn't discuss the flight with anyone. Nor did I mention the close shave I had just had.

The following day I flew another Bloch 152 from Bordeaux back to Le Bourget, making an intermediate stop at Tours on the way. This time the flight, in a fully airworthy machine (with its wheels retracted!), was a pure joy. At Le Bourget I privately celebrated my safe return, feeling I had every right to do so and swearing to myself that I would never venture anywhere near Bordeaux's radio masts again.

November 28th 1940 found me back in the south-west of France. A whole group of us had been flown down to Mont-de-Marsan in the unit's Ju 52. Here we were to collect a batch of Caudron C.620 '*Simouns*' (Simooms) and ferry them back to Le Bourget. We arrived at Mont-de-Marsan in the early afternoon and got straight down to the hand-over formalities, hoping to take off again as soon as possible and get back at least as far as Bordeaux – giving the radio masts a wide berth! – before night fell.

The machines awaiting us were parked out on the perimeter of the field apparently abandoned and unguarded, which came as a bit of a shock. None of us had ever clapped eyes on a '*Simoun*' before. The personnel at Mont-de-Marsan themselves knew next to nothing about the type, and there was no-one around who could fill us in on the aircraft's technical details.

The '*Simoun*' was, in fact, quite a smart-looking little single-engined four-seat cabin touring monoplane dating from the mid-1930s. The pilot's seat was upholstered in red leather and was extremely comfortable. There was no provision for a parachute, however. Not that a parachute would have been of much use to anyone flying a '*Simoun*' who got into difficulties, as there was no way of bailing out directly from the cockpit. A pilot would have to leave his position and make his way between the rear seats of the passenger cabin to reach the tiny exit door at the back of the machine.

By no stretch of the imagination could the '*Simoun*' be classed as a military aircraft. In my view, it wasn't even suitable as a trainer. We wondered why the *Chef AW* was interested in the type at all, until someone pointed out that it would be ideal as a personal transport and for courier duties.

The original plan to leave Mont-de-Marsan on the same day as our arrival had had to be abandoned. There was simply too much involved in readying the machines for the flight back to Le Bourget. It was noon on 29 November before we finally departed Mont-de-Marsan and set course for Bordeaux. The weather was fine and we wasted little time at Bordeaux, preferring instead to take off again as quickly as possible and get started on the long haul up to Paris.

We were flying in very loose formation – more of an untidy gaggle, really – and when we reached Tours, the regular inter-mediate stop on the Bordeaux–Paris stretch, the leading aircraft flew a couple of wide circles, indicating that we land briefly to top up our fuel tanks. We followed him down but, anxious as we were to make good time, it was not long before we were on our way again. My engine was running sweetly and the flight was proving very pleasant. All I needed to do was cast the occasional glance at my map, for we had agreed among ourselves beforehand that we wouldn't simply tag along behind the machine in front of us, but rather that each of us would do his own navigating. It was becoming slightly more overcast and we could see some storm clouds gathering to the north-west of us, but not close enough to make a change of course necessary.

Soon we were approaching Paris. I was already over the south-western outskirts of the capital, flying at an altitude of about 600m, when I suddenly felt my engine cough a couple of times. A few seconds later and it had stopped altogether. I pulled the starter switch and it promptly sprang back into life. But it was only a moment or two before it started coughing and spluttering all over again. By this time I was no longer watching the instrument panel. My attention was focussed on the city of Paris spread out in all its glory just below me. I realized that I was going to have to make an emergency landing – but where?

I knew I wouldn't need a great deal of space to get the little 'Simoun' down safely and so I wasn't unduly worried about the situation I found myself in. But Le Bourget was too far away on the other side of the city. My salvation lay to the south and I immediately turned the machine's nose in that direction. I spotted a patch of green alongside a main road and made straight for it. Unfortunately, the open space was surrounded by tall apartment blocks. But I reckoned that if I made my approach in a series of tight spirals I could just about manage it.

The trouble was, the lower I got the bumpier the air became. I wrestled the '*Simoun*' down in ever-tighter turns, trying desperately not to scrape the walls of the buildings with one of my wingtips. By now I had forfeited so much speed that the machine was in imminent danger of stalling. But the lack of space meant that I had to keep on turning almost until the point of touchdown. I set her down hard and immediately slammed on the brakes. The aircraft came to a shuddering halt with its propeller almost touching one of the buildings.

Needless to say, my somewhat dramatic arrival from out of nowhere had not gone unnoticed and a large throng of excited Parisians came pouring out of the surrounding blocks curious to see what was going on. They were also eager to help and quickly led me to the nearest telephone.

I called Le Bourget and reported what had happened. They asked me if the aircraft could be flown out of its present location, to which my answer was an emphatic no. With the best will in the world, and even with a sound engine, it would be impossible for the machine to lift off from this enclosed space and gain sufficient height to clear the neighbouring buildings. It would have to be dismantled, the wings removed, and taken back to Le Bourget by truck.

At Le Bourget the cause of my involuntary landing was quickly established: I had run out of fuel. Apparently, I had been steadily losing fuel ever since leaving Tours. Another pilot in the group had noticed the thin banner of white vapour streaming from my machine but hadn't been sure what it was. Nor did he have any way of warning me. I had just been unlucky, or so I thought. Later examination revealed, however, that the screw-plug connecting the fuel line to the tank had been overtightened, causing it to leak. Whether this had been done deliberately or not it was impossible to say.

I may have got away with it, but this incident preyed on my mind for a long time. I vowed never again to fly over a large town or city without a good margin of height.

Although mishaps such as this did occasionally occur, the vast majority of the ferry flights bringing aircraft back to Le Bourget passed off without incident. The same could not be said of the test and check flights that we sometimes had to carry out once the machines had been delivered. It was then that we quickly learned to expect the unexpected.

Air tests of unfamiliar aircraft often presented us with problems. This was particularly true in the case of ex-*Armée de l'Air* bombers and fighters, as operational machines were constantly undergoing modification and improvement – much the same as the aircraft of our own Luftwaffe – and we were never quite sure what we were going to be faced with.

On 15 December 1940, for example, I was scheduled to air test a Potez 631. This was one of France's newer first-line aircraft, a twin-engined two–three-seat heavy fighter not dissimilar to the Messerschmitt Bf 110. I was taking my old friend and comrade Rudi Lukas up with me. Rudi had served with me before the war as my flight-engineer and had also been one of the crew aboard the Ju 52 during our brief stint in Poland.

We took off from Le Bourget at 10.40 hours. The wind was light and I headed west intending to skirt the northern edges of Paris. Even while taxiing I thought I had detected a certain sluggishness in the Gnome-Rhône engines; they seemed to lack any real punch. Without the benefit of pilot's notes of any kind I had absolutely no way of knowing if this was their normal behaviour or not. I didn't know the machine's specified take-off speed either, and so had to trust my own judgement. The acceleration was just enough to get the Potez off the ground before I reached the perimeter of the airfield. I had already left it far too late to abort the take-off, so the only way to go was up – retract undercarriage, raise flaps, ease off the throttle slightly, gradually build up speed and gain a little height – in fact, more than a little as the first houses were already getting dangerously close.

There was clearly something seriously wrong with the machine. The engines were running very irregularly and every now and again one or the other of them would 'spit', as we used to say. Slowly, much too slowly for my liking, I began to gain a little altitude. Even for a so-called 'heavy fighter' this state of affairs was far from normal. But what was the cause of it? It wasn't just the engines that were the problem. By constantly juggling the throttles and increasing speed bit by cautious bit, I finally got them running a little more evenly and so decided to carry on with the air test rather than follow my initial instinct, which had been to abort the flight and immediately return to base. I made sure, however, that I remained in sight of Le Bourget so that I could get down safely again in the event of an emergency – even if both engines died on me which, in my present state of mind, did not seem beyond the bounds of possibility.

By this time I had managed to climb to an altitude of about 2,000m. I began to carry out some basic load tests in various flight attitudes. The results were not exactly impressive. The Potez reacted far too slowly to normal control movements and was altogether too ready to start shaking and vibrating the moment I reduced speed; so much so that I was very wary of its suddenly going into an uncontrollable spin.

I did not feel at all comfortable during this flight. I was totally unused to the extraneous noises coming not only from the engines, but also from the airframe itself. I must admit that I had probably done a lot of things wrong, simply because I did not know any better. Nobody had been able to tell me anything about the Potez 631 before I took off. It was, quite literally, a flight into the unknown that all too easily could have gone disastrously wrong. So it was with no little relief that I landed again after just thirty minutes in the air, swearing to myself never to do anything so foolhardy again. The aircraft was parked in a quiet corner of the field and was, I presume, later scrapped.

In all fairness, I have to say that I subsequently air-tested a number of other Potez 631s. But I always made sure that I was given a thorough briefing from a works engineer beforehand, and every one of these flights went without a hitch.

Having learned my lesson on the rogue Potez, I was careful not to make the same mistakes again when called upon to fly two other ex-*Armée de l'Air* twin-engined machines, the Bloch 174 reconnaissance-bomber and the Breguet 693 ground-attack aircraft. Even so, this air testing of unfamiliar foreign aircraft remained a risky, not to say nerve-wracking business. All my comrades engaged on similar duties at Le Bourget were of the same opinion. Nonetheless, our endeavours must have served a purpose, if only to prove the unsuitability of most French operational types for service with the Luftwaffe. Germany's subsequent use of such captured types fell far below original expectations but, truth be told, there really was very little that could be done with them.

A few days after my unfortunate introduction to the Potez 631, just before Christmas 1940, I was handed another recovery job. A Morane-Saulnier MS.230 trainer had been put down in a field near Asnières-sur-Oise a few kilometres to the north of Paris and I was instructed to fly it out if possible and bring it back to Le Bourget.

When I got to the field in question I drove slowly along what I considered to be the best line of take-off in order to check the going and assess the chances of a successful lift-off. But the ground was very soft and I risked ending up with the aircraft standing on its nose. After searching around for a little while, however, I found a relatively dry and firm stretch of grass and decided to try my luck. The pilot of the Morane had got lost in bad weather but had managed to pull off a reasonably smooth emergency landing. Upon inspection, the machine appeared to be undamaged and I could foresee no technical reason preventing a successful take-off. And such proved to be the case. I got her off the ground with no problems whatsoever and landed safe and sound back at Le Bourget a mere fifteen minutes later.

Then, on 20 January 1941, after collecting yet another machine from the Potez works at les Mureaux on the other side of Paris for delivery back to Le Bourget, my time with the *Chef AW* came to an end.

Some weeks earlier I had been enjoying an evening off at the famous Lido cabaret in Paris when I happened to bump into an old trainee acquaintance from my Salzwedel days. We got to chatting and the now Oberleutnant Dr. Balfanz told me that he had since served as Adjutant to Major Werner Mölders, the Geschwaderkommodore of JG 51 and at that time the Luftwaffe's most celebrated and successful fighter pilot.

As a personal favour I asked Balfanz whether he could use his influence – by which I meant, of course, 'pull a few strings' – to help me obtain a posting to an operational unit. As varied and interesting as my present job at Le Bourget was, I couldn't help but feel that it was something of a backwater, especially in these turbulent times with the air offensive against Great Britain still not yet resolved. But then neither did I want to return to instructing at Prenzlau. That kind of duty was now better suited to a member of the reserve, I argued, than to a regular with well over five years' flying experience under his belt.

My reasoning must have struck a chord somewhere along the line, for it was not long before I was ordered to report to the *Zerstörerschule* Schleissheim for heavy-fighter training. Although I was being sent back to school, I was more than happy at this new direction my career was taking. Flying heavy-fighter operations meant learning new tactics and acquiring new skills. This was not something my service to date had prepared me for. But if I successfully completed the Schleissheim course my chances of being posted to a front-line unit were extremely good. My long-cherished desire for an operational role had just got one step closer.

I did not regret my time at Le Bourget for one minute. It had added enormously to my store of flying experience and knowledge, and had resulted in many new types gracing the pages of my logbook. I had learned to recognize and appreciate the different flight characteristics between our own aircraft and foreign machines. Each displayed its own particular set of traits and foibles which made it difficult to draw meaningful comparisons.

It required a certain amount of time to get to know an aircraft properly. A definitive evaluation was therefore not always possible. One could almost say that it was purely a matter of personal choice when it came to judging the merits of one machine against the other. The performance that could be got from an aircraft depended to a large extent on the pilot's familiarity with the type. This was particularly true when it came to load limits; exceeding these posed very real risks. I gained a lot of valuable expertise in this area, although I didn't realize at the time just how useful this knowledge was to prove in later years. From this standpoint alone, I owe the *Chef A*W a huge debt of thanks.

During my four-and-a-half months at Le Bourget I had carried out eighty ferry and test flights on no fewer than fourteen different types of foreign (predominantly French) aircraft. This meant I had spent a total of 82 hours and 35 minutes in the air. In addition, I had also piloted the unit's own Ju 52 on nine separate occasions; adding a further 11 hours and 55 minutes to my overall flying time.

I left Paris on the daily courier flight to Berlin. From there I made my way north to my old unit, A/B 120 at Prenzlau, where I reported my arrival and at the same time gave notice of my imminent departure for Schleissheim.

Despite an absence of little more than four months, I found much had changed at Prenzlau. I saw very few familiar faces. Most of my old friends and colleagues among the instructing staff had been posted away to operational units. Their places had been taken by younger newcomers, but training was still going on at the same frenetic pace as before. Apart from this, there were hardly any signs that there was a war on. Everyone seemed cheerful and full of optimism. The mood was buoyant. I said my final farewells to the unit I had first joined at Salzwedel back in the piping days of peace nearly five years earlier – five years full of happy memories and rich in unforgettable experiences.

I had to travel down to Schleissheim by train. This did me a power of good, for it gave me the opportunity to sit quietly and reflect on past events. I had suddenly been thrust back into my old world and I needed a little time to get used to it again. I didn't feel altogether at ease, everything around me seemed somehow to have become too narrow and restricted. But my arrival in Munich soon cheered me up. Bavaria's beautiful capital city was still untouched by the war and had lost none of its charm. I looked forward with pleasure to being able to revisit its many and varied attractions over the course of the next few months. This would more than make up for the rather lowly 'new boy' status that awaited me at the nearby *Zerstörer* school. So – off to Schleissheim!

Chapter 8

Zerstörerschule Schleissheim

My first posting to Schleissheim to train as a fighter pilot back in December 1935 had been brought to an abrupt close by Hitler's unexpected re-occupation of the demilitarized zone of the Rhineland. This had resulted in my brief deployment to the Jagdgeschwader '*Richthofen*' before then being re-assigned for future service as a flying instructor. Now, more than five years later, I was back at Schleissheim, back at school, and about to learn how to be a *Zerstörer* ('Destroyer') pilot.

I must admit that my feelings were a little ambivalent. Schleissheim, once the Luftwaffe's showpiece fighter training establishment, was no longer the same. The whole atmosphere of the place had become somehow cold and impersonal. It was wartime, of course, and the general mood was not exactly buoyant. There was a very definite sense of everybody's being under time pressure and this inevitably had a detrimental effect on the training. The instructors gave of their best but, at the same time, could not always conceal an underlying sense of irritability. If some part or other of the flying programme did not go entirely to their satisfaction, the offending pupil was quickly put right – in no uncertain terms and in a voice loud enough for everyone else to hear. There was little good humour or understanding and this affected the younger trainees in particular.

Outwardly, Schleissheim itself was little changed. The quarters were still comfortable and the surroundings pleasant enough. And then there was always Munich of course, with its many museums, galleries and other places of interest, which most of us visited as often as possible and which went a long way towards compensating us for the harsh realities of a trainee's lot.

The training programme was run along very rigid guidelines. For me it was almost a throwback to my earlier days in the Luftwaffe, for it began with the familiar Heinkel He 51. These now venerable biplanes were used for formation flying and air combat exercises, for teaching us how to operate in the standard battle formations of two (*Rotte*), four (*Schwarm*) or more aircraft, for high-altitude flying, and for aerial gunnery practice. While in the air we were under constant observation. Every manoeuvre was strictly monitored and controlled. The pressures upon us were enormous and any trainee who failed to come up to the required standards was summarily removed from the course.

By contrast, the navigational exercises on twin-engined Focke-Wulf Fw 58 '*Weihen*' were regarded almost as pleasure trips. I was required to carry out three such cross-countries during this period. At the start of the course we had been paired up into prospective crews. And the three navigational flights provided good practice for the young wireless-operator/navigator who had been assigned to me on a permanent basis. The first of these exercises took us from Schleissheim to Salzburg, Lechfeld and back, the second to Ingolstadt, Linz and Erding, and the third to Memmingen, Friedrichshafen and Kaufbeuren.

Although these cross-countries were little more than routine for me, I derived great pleasure from flying them, particularly as they helped enormously to boost my young wireless-operator/navigator's confidence. He had been instructed to make use of Schleissheim's ground direction-finding station during the take-off and landing approach phases of each flight, but for the remainder of our time in the air it was his responsibility to keep an accurate fix on our position by using the aircraft's own self-bearing D/F system.

As a combat crew we would have to be able to rely on one another totally, and this was an ideal way to begin that process. Unfortunately, only one of these cross-country navigational exercises was flown in a Bf 110 which, given the fact that this was the type we would be flying operationally, struck me as being a little short-sighted.

It was only after completing the first three weeks of the course on He 51s and Fw 58s that we finally began training on the Bf 110. Messerschmitt's twin-engined *Zerstörer* was what in those days we called a 'good natured' type of aircraft. Purely from a pilot's point of view it presented few difficulties. Its behaviour at take-off was perfectly normal, with no tendency to swing either to left or right, and landing was equally straightforward. Manoeuvrability was just about what one would expect from a machine of that size. Its acceleration and climb performance were nothing special. But for its time – the Bf 110 was very much a product of the mid-1930s – and given its intended role as a long-range heavy fighter, the machine more than fitted the bill.

We were given a very good introductory technical briefing on the Bf 110 and the flying training programme that followed had been carefully planned to give each of us ample opportunity to really get to know the machine. As with the initial exercises on the He 51, each one of our practice flights was carefully monitored to ensure that every single phase was carried out correctly. This attention was not always welcome, however, as it sometimes stretched our flying abilities to the limit. But this was no bad thing, as it turned out, for we later reaped the benefits when flying operationally.

Training progressed in consecutive stages from doing circuits and bumps, to making local flights, shooting at ground targets, and carrying out practice missions in combat formation. These latter invariably began with a formation take-off, usually followed by a '*Zirkus*', which involved getting into line-astern and performing a series of increasingly difficult aerobatic-like figures. More often than not the exercise would then degenerate into a wild free-for-all, which was always popular – show me a pilot who doesn't enjoy throwing his aircraft around all over the sky!

After about five minutes of this exhilarating near-mayhem we would be called back to order for the next, more serious, and potentially very risky part of the exercise. This was to teach us how to execute a sharp turn while flying in *Schwarm* (four-aircraft) or *Rotte* (two-aircraft) formation. It was vital that we master this manoeuvre, as it was considered essential for maintaining combat integrity during operational missions. A pilot who couldn't keep station on his leader and became separated from the formation – who 'burst out', in the jargon of the time – was easy meat for any prowling enemy fighter.

The manoeuvre itself was tricky to execute, and is even trickier to put down on paper. It was designed to ensure that the formation remained a cohesive fighting unit during and immediately after any sudden and unexpected tight turns.

In practice, it meant that whenever the formation leader – be it of a pair or a 'finger-four' – started a turn his wingman, or wingmen, had to slide across him – either above or below depending upon the direction of the turn – and then immediately re-formate on him on the new heading.

The formation thus remained intact, although the wingman was now on his leader's opposite side; in effect, the formation was a mirror image of what it had been before the turn.

Not surprisingly, this manoeuvre required a high degree of flying skill on the part of the wingmen and we practised it at every available opportunity, even if it meant having to use He 51s. The very real risk of a mid-air collision was ever present and there were, in fact, a number of near misses during our training. The formation leader would give no prior warning of a turn, but would suddenly break to one side or the other. A split second later, depending on which way he had turned, he might see a dark menacing shape flash low across the roof of his cockpit; so low that he would involuntarily duck his head. I speak from experience – in the months to come I found myself ducking my own head often enough.

Our practice flights also included mock air combat exercises and aerial gunnery against towed targets. At the end of each flight we would break formation and dive steeply away into line-astern. As we approached the field we would follow each other round in a series of steep turns, rapidly losing height before landing in quick succession, touching down close together in pairs. After taxiing in we would immediately gather around the formation leader/instructor's aircraft to hear his comments on the exercise we had just completed. Only very rarely did he have anything good to say. It was a constant learning process.

Almost all of our instructors had seen front-line service and so we listened attentively to everything they had to tell us. Now and again the knowledge they imparted, based on actual operational experience, was at odds with the official Schleissheim training programme. This was particularly so when it came to combat tactics and the advice they offered us 'off-the-cuff' was to prove invaluable in the months ahead.

Firing practice against ground targets posed no great problems in the Bf 110. The machine was a very stable gun platform and any necessary corrections could be easily made. The only thing to watch, as with any other aircraft type, was pulling up in time after the firing run. My early days of learning how to do this correctly were long behind me and so I had no difficulties. I greatly enjoyed these exercises. The massed firepower of the Bf 110's nose armament was a real eye-opener to me, used as I was to aircraft armed with two machine-guns at most. My one regret was that there were just six such practice sessions during the entire eleven weeks of the course.

In fact, for a specialized *Zerstörer* school, Schleissheim relied surprisingly heavily on the He 51. Of the ninety-nine training flights I made there, nearly two-thirds of them – fifty-eight in all, totalling 34 hours and 37 minutes flying time – were on the Heinkel biplane. In contrast, I clocked up just 14 hours and 58 minutes during thirty-seven flights in the Bf 110. The remaining four flights (amounting to 5 hours and 33 minutes in the air) were the cross-country navigational exercises, three of them flown in Fw 58s.

Furthermore, flying took place on only thirty-nine of the eighty calendar days that the course lasted. There was no flying at all on Sundays, except for 4 May 1941 (the reason for which I can no longer recall). During the week, non-flying days were spent in the classroom studying the usual range of subjects such as air tactics, airframe and engine technology, meteorology and navigation. There were also the usual lectures on 'actions to be taken in special circumstances' – put more plainly: 'how to deal with an emergency' – as well as instruction in general service matters.

As with all the other Luftwaffe schools I had attended, a great deal was demanded of every trainee. From the number of essential skills that had to be mastered, including fighter combat, attacking enemy bomber formations in the air, and engaging targets – both stationary and moving – on the ground, it was clear that the Bf 110 was regarded as something of a 'maid-of-all-work' and that any prospective pilot needed to have a wide range of flying abilities. But what was not so clear was whether the Schleissheim training programme could produce such an all-round, multi-functional pilot. Each of us had his own strengths and weaknesses in one discipline or the other. And this in turn raised the question of the *Zerstörer's* operational value and viability as a whole.

By the spring of 1941 the Bf 110's reputation had already lost some of its lustre. Its origins dated back to the years leading up to the start of the Second World War. This was the era when the perceived wisdom of every aerial strategist worth his salt was that the bomber would 'always get through'. And what better way to ease its passage than to provide it with a long-range escort fighter? This was to result in the Messerschmitt Bf 110 (and others of its ilk, such as France's Potez 631, the type that had given me so much trouble at Le Bourget).

Because of the distances it would be required to cover, the Bf 110 was, of necessity, a large machine powered by two engines. Lauded by Luftwaffe C-in-C Generalfeldmarschall Hermann Göring as his 'Ironsides of the air' when it first entered service, the Bf 110 seemed ideally suited to its long-range escort role. Its maximum range was, in fact, very nearly 1,000km, well over double that of its much shorter-legged Bf 109 stablemate.

The critical test for the Bf 110 had come with the opening of hostilities in September 1939. The three Gruppen of Bf 110Cs that took part in the Polish campaign performed well, if not spectacularly so. Just over six months later the *Zerstörer* more than proved their worth in Norway where the long distances separating the areas of ground fighting made it the ideal arena for the Bf 110's strengths. Then, in the *Blitzkrieg* in the west, the Bf 110 was fortunate to be faced by piecemeal and totally disorganized aerial opposition.

It was not until the Battle of Britain that the inherent flaw in the *Zerstörer* concept was finally exposed. The Bf 110 was unquestionably capable of escorting bombers over longer distances. But once they neared the target area they were always at risk of coming under attack from defending fighters – faster, more manoeuvrable single-engined fighters to which they had little effective answer.

And this is exactly what happened on a number of occasions during the early stages of the air offensive against Great Britain. On one disastrous day alone – 15 August 1940, or 'Black Thursday' as it became known in the Luftwaffe – a total of twenty-seven Bf 110s were lost or written off, with others being damaged. Among those failing to return were seven of the twenty-one machines that had dutifully escorted a formation of Heinkel bombers across the North Sea from Norway only to receive a savage mauling from RAF Spitfires and Hurricanes off the Northumberland coast.

We at Schleissheim were of course well aware of this historical background. There was no shortage of theories and opinions as to the best use to be made of the Bf 110. Some thought we should be given a thorough training for one specific role only. Others claimed that, with sufficient ability and experience, a pilot could become proficient at both air combat and ground attack.

While on the subject, it is perhaps worth pointing out that during our time at Schleissheim we received no instruction whatsoever on the tactics employed by army units in the field. In the light of our subsequent deployment – which the teaching staff must surely have been aware of – this strikes me as a very odd omission indeed. It later became all too evident that special tuition in this area was essential if effective ground-support operations were to be flown. And not just up to company level either; ground-support pilots needed to understand the workings of at least a division in order to be able to gain an overview, assess the situation on the battlefield below and respond accordingly.

But taken all round, I must say that I enjoyed my second posting to historic Schleissheim. Much had changed since my first arrival here more than five years earlier. Then, it had been to start my fighter training. Now, it was the final rung on the ladder towards achieving my ultimate goal of seeing front-line service. For once I had completed the Schleissheim course I could be almost certain of receiving a posting to an operational unit.

To call the Schleissheim establishment a *Zerstörerschule* was perhaps something of a misnomer, however, as I was not destined for the *Zerstörer*, or heavy-fighter arm. Instead, and together with most of my fellow trainees, I was to join an entirely new type of unit, the first of its kind in the Luftwaffe: a Schnellkampfgeschwader, or fast-bomber group.

Chapter 9

Schnellkampfgeschwader 210

Saturdays and Sundays were known as the Luftwaffe's travelling days. And so, true to form, my posting to Schnellkampfgeschwader 210, currently based at Merville in northern France, also took place on a weekend. After a long journey by rail from southern Bavaria we arrived in Brussels on Saturday, 10 May 1941. The following morning we took a local train across the border to Lille and from there travelled by road to our new base.

It was beautiful May weather as the Luftwaffe bus wended its way through a tranquil northern French countryside seemingly untouched by war. Our little group was made up entirely of two-man Bf 110 crews fresh from training at Schleissheim, just like Gefreiter Schmidt and myself. Upon arriving at Merville we were all temporarily billeted in a nearby boarding school.

Schnellkampfgeschwadser 210 – or SKG 210, for short – had its origins in a test unit that had been set up at the beginning of July 1940 to conduct operational trials with a brand new and as yet untried aircraft. As the numeric suffix in its designation indicates, *Erprobungsgruppe* (Test Wing) 210 was originally intended to operate the Messerschmitt Me 210, the machine designed as a successor to the Bf 110. But if the Bf 110 had proved something of a disappointment, its replacement was little short of a disaster, and *Erp.Gr* 210 had to be equipped instead with a mix of Bf 109s and Bf 110s.

Within two weeks of its activation at Cologne-Ostheim, *Erp.Gr* 210 found itself in action on the Channel Front, initially attacking shipping and later mounting fighter-bomber raids against coastal targets in southern England. After some early successes the Gruppe's losses began to escalate until, in October 1940, it was withdrawn for several weeks' rest and re-equipment. It resumed operations in the winter of 1940/41 and, weather permitting, carried out individual hit-and-run raids, reconnaissance flights and nocturnal bombing sorties over Great Britain.

Then, on 24 April 1941, the Gruppe was re-designated to form the nucleus of the new SKG 210. The Gruppenstab, 1. and 2. Staffeln, all equipped with the Bf 110, became the Gruppenstab, 1. and 2./SKG 210 respectively. The Bf 109s of 3./*Erp.Gr* 210 were incorporated into JG 51 and an entirely new 3./SKG 210 was formed from scratch. It was this which had brought my comrades and me to Merville to become members of the newly constituted 3. Staffel.

Command of the Geschwader, which initially comprised only two Gruppen – II./SKG 210 was to be created in June 1941 by the simple expedient of re-designating the existing III./ZG 1 – was entrusted to Major Walter Storp, while I./SKG 210 was headed by Hauptmann Karl-Heinz Stricker. Both Storp and Stricker were ex-bomber pilots of some distinction. The Kapitän of our 3. Staffel was Oberleutnant Heinz Forgatsch.

The Geschwader's role was to mount individual, all-weather pinpoint attacks on specific objectives both by day and by night. Depending on the given target, these attacks would be made with bombs, with the Bf 110's formidable array of forward-firing armament, or with both.

On Tuesday, 13 May 1941, we carried out our first familiarization flights as fledgling front-line pilots. These inevitably started with the usual circuits and bumps, of course, but we then quickly moved on to overland navigation exercises and practice bombing attacks on shipping targets. These latter, which involved dropping dummy cement bombs on shipwrecks along the French Channel coast, were something we had not been taught at Schleissheim and so special emphasis was placed on our mastering the technique properly now.

The book of rules stated that the target vessel had to be attacked from abeam, at high speed and in a shallow dive of approximately 30°. The bomb was aimed by means of the aircraft's normal reflector gunsight and released in accordance with a predetermined set of calculations based on the machine's speed and height. Once the bomb had been dropped, the pilot had to hold his course, fly over the ship at the lowest possible level, and not climb away until he was well beyond the range of the vessel's defensive fire.

It all sounded much easier than it really was. In actual fact, an attack of this kind required considerable flying skill and steady nerves. Our teachers had already scored some notable successes using this very method, however, and we hoped that we would soon be able to do the same.

Another glaring omission in the Schleissheim curriculum had been blind-flying the Bf 110 at night. This gap also had to be made good in the shortest time possible if we were to achieve operational status. On 18 May 1941, after a comprehensive briefing, I took off at 23.10 hours for a night exercise flight from Merville, along the Channel coast taking in two turning points, and then back to Merville. We flew at a height of about 3,000m, well above the near solid blanket of cloud covering the area, and the bright moonlight meant that we had good visibility.

We had been ordered to observe complete radio silence and to navigate by dead-reckoning alone. We had no navigational aids whatsoever and our course, altitude and speed all had to be maintained exactly as laid down in the pre-flight briefing if we were to get back to base again safe and sound.

Shortly before reaching the coast we caught a brief glimpse of the countryside below. Although dark, it enabled us to fix our position. We had also been instructed to keep an eye open for roving English night-fighters, but none appeared and we completed the exercise as planned and without incident. As we neared Merville we descended through the layer of cloud and flashed our identification letter to indicate that we wanted the airfield lighting switched on. There wasn't a lot of it, but it sufficed for the approach and landing.

Given my previous extensive experience of night and blind-flying, the exercise itself had presented no difficulties at all. But being so near to the front for the first time had added that extra dimension and made it somehow special. There was no civil flying activity in this area any more and the ground below was blacked out. We would have to get used to a whole lot of new restrictions.

Navigational exercises flown by day were far less affected by wartime limitations and these took us to a number of airfields including Calais, Le Bourget and Châteaudun in France, Ghent in Belgium and Mönchen-Gladbach and Paderborn in Germany.

By this time Staffelkapitän Oberleutnant Forgatsch had decided that we were ready to start flying on operations and we eagerly awaited notice of our first mission. But this wasn't to be on the Channel Front. We were briefed for missions on several occasions, but they were always scrubbed at the very last moment. Needless to say, we were never told the reason why.

This only served to heighten the air of tense expectancy that seemed to hang over the Geschwader. Rumours were flying around, fuelled not least by the recent and totally unexpected flight of Deputy *Führer* Rudolf Hess to Scotland. This event had been played down by the authorities. But was a secret peace settlement being brokered? Many hoped that this was the case, although it paid to keep such thoughts to oneself.

Had we but known it, it was not peace that was beckoning, but a dramatic escalation of the war that was looming. After just three weeks at Merville we were on the move again. At 16.25 hours on 31 May 1941 we took off for Lippstadt in Westphalia. The official order for our transfer gave the reason as: 'Replenishment and reinforcement of the Geschwader in the Homeland'. The 'replenishment' part no doubt referred to our I. Gruppe which, during the course of May – while we newcomers had been finding our feet at Merville – had lost several of its original members (from its days as *Erprobungsgruppe* 210) in action against the British, while the 'reinforcement' was presumably a reference to the imminent activation of II./SKG 210.

Eighty minutes after leaving Merville we put down at Lippstadt, the pre-war home of III./JG 134 *'Horst Wessel'*, whose quarters we occupied. During what was to be a very short stay at Lippstadt we spent two whole days, 3 and 6 June, practising a new method of attacking pinpoint targets: bombing in pairs during a steep 70° dive. On my very first attempt at this new technique I got quite a nasty shock, which could well have had even nastier, not to say fatal, consequences.

The dummy attack was to take place over the wooded slopes of the Teutoburg Forest, which lay less than 40km to the north of Lippstadt. We flew there in pairs led by Staffelkapitän Oberleutnant Forgatsch. Our orders were to commence the dive together from an altitude of about 2,000m, pull out at 800m, regain height and then repeat the manoeuvre.

The leader of each pair gave no hand signal or sign of any other kind to indicate that he was about to start his dive. It was up to the wingman to keep a constant eye on his number one and go over into his own dive the moment he saw his leader's nose begin to dip although, with no prior warning, there was inevitably always a fraction of a second's delay. The same applied at the end of the dive. The wingman could not initiate his own recovery until he saw his leader start to flatten out.

At first all went as intended. When my number one entered his dive I immediately followed suit. The engine revs and pitch of the propellers were both well within the prescribed limits. During the steep dive I kept a close watch on the leader's machine just in front of me. The instant I saw it start to level out I hauled back on my own stick which, to my absolute astonishment, had no effect whatsoever! It took several agonizing seconds before the machine finally started to respond and we came dangerously close to the treetops before her nose lifted and we were able to climb away to safety.

At a dive speed of some 550km/h, every second that passed meant another 150m of height lost. The ground came rushing up unbelievably quickly. It was a salutary lesson to me and one that was drummed into every new pilot from now on: the Bf 110 was no Stuka! It didn't have any dive brakes, nor was it equipped with an acoustic warning device coupled to an electric altimeter that could be set to the desired height for a safe recovery. But at first these shortcomings simply had to be accepted, even though they didn't just make the already difficult job of diving the Bf 110 that much harder, but actually resulted in a number of fatal accidents.

Nevertheless, we departed Lippstadt on 17 June 1941 and set course eastwards. We were not told our ultimate destination. This we only learned after touching down at Breslau at the end of the first leg of our transfer flight. The following day, 18 June, we arrived at our new base: the airfield of Radzyn, which was located some 80km west-south-west of Brest-Litovsk in that part of occupied Poland now known as the '*Generalgouvernement*'.

We landed there at 13.35 hours and lost no time in establishing ourselves on a full war footing. An advance party from our I. Gruppe had flown in earlier and they quickly guided us into the well-camouflaged dispersal areas hidden under the trees in the woods bordering the field. Also among the trees, but a little distance away, a hutted encampment served as accommodation.

Nobody knew the real reason for our transfer and so the rumours were soon flying thick and fast again. Oddly enough, most seemed to run along the same general lines and there was the nagging suspicion that they were being orchestrated from on high. The favoured theory was that we were to be part of a gigantic pincer movement designed to trap the British and Free French forces operating in the Middle East. The southern arm of the pincer was to be provided by the German and Italian troops in North Africa, who would advance across the Suez Canal and then wheel north through Palestine up into Syria. Meanwhile, the northern arm of the pincer – of which we were to be part – would sweep down through the Caucasus and Iraq for the link-up in Syria. All we were waiting for was for the Soviet authorities to grant us right of passage through their territory.

Strategically, this was plausible, if perhaps a mite overly ambitious. But we only had to look at everything that was going on around us here in Radzyn to see what the true situation was. Our Flak gunners were continually banging away at the Russian reconnaissance aircraft that came over the border at medium to high altitude and were clearly visible as they circled above us. The roads around the airfield were thick with troop movements and army units were encamped all over the surrounding areas. This all pointed to a very different scenario, and nobody really believed for an instant that we were preparing for a peaceful passage through southern Russia courtesy of the Soviets.

The afternoon of 21 June 1941 finally brought an end to the speculation. All flying personnel were assembled for a short address by Geschwaderkommodore Major Storp. It was he who revealed to us that hostilities against the Soviet Union could be expected to begin at any moment. We were ordered to full readiness and warned that, in all probability, we would be summoned to a briefing for our first mission of the new campaign sometime during the coming night.

The Kommodore went on to spell out a few rules of conduct that we were to observe in the war against the Soviets, and then briefly outlined the current military-political situation. He was very serious and quiet, and displayed no emotion whatsoever. Our trust in him was absolute.

When Major Storp had finished, an intelligence officer gave us some very useful information and advice on how best to deal with the sheer geographic size, climate and prevailing weather conditions in this totally new and unfamiliar theatre of war. But he made no mention of the ideological aspect of the coming conflict.

At about midnight we all re-assembled in a clearing close to the accommodation area. We were given yet another 'prior warning' of imminent action and started to get our things together for the mission. Flying clothing and equipment was laid out ready. Emergency rations were issued. We still hadn't been told of our intended target or targets; all we were given were large-scale maps covering the entire central sector of the front.

The rest of the night remained quiet. But none of us got a lot of sleep. There was too much uncertainty in the air to allow us to relax. It was not until close on 06.00 hours on the morning of 22 June 1941 – nearly three hours *after* the first German troops had crossed the Soviet border – that we finally got our operational orders, were given a briefing and began to prepare in earnest for our first mission against the Russians.

The invasion of the Soviet Union was the largest land offensive the world had ever seen. Hitler committed nearly 150 front-line divisions, about three million men in all. It is estimated that the Red Army fielded well over half that number again, organized into 139 divisions and 29 independent brigades.

The Eastern Front was divided into three main sectors – north, centre and south – each with its own army group. And each army group had its own *Luftflotte*, or air fleet, in support. Army Group Centre, in whose area we would be operating, was supported by Generalfeldmarschall Albert Kesselring's *Luftflotte* 2. This was made up of two *Fliegerkorps*: II. and VIII. Our SKG 210 formed part of General der Flieger Bruno Loerzer's II. *Fliegerkorps*, which also deployed five Kampfgruppen, three Stukagruppen, four Jagdgruppen and a single strategic reconnaissance Staffel.

These units all had their specific individual roles to perform, but our tasks in the coming campaign were fourfold:

Attack the enemy's airfields with the aim of neutralizing his air power;

Disrupt the enemy's lines of supply and block his attempts at withdrawal;

Provide immediate close-support for the ground units in the field; and

Carry out armed reconnaissance sweeps deep into the enemy's rear.

Our first operation was to be a maximum-effort raid on the Soviet airfield at Pinsk, over 150km inside enemy territory. After having waited all night, the briefing when it eventually came was a very hurried and sketchy affair. Although we were ordered to attack in separate *Schwärmen* (flights of four), we were not assigned specific objectives. We were simply told to find a suitable target ourselves, which wasn't a great deal of help under the circumstances.

We started taking off at 08.15 hours and then spent about 10–15 minutes getting into our individual *Schwärmen* and assembling in combat formation above the field before setting off on the 70km flight to the frontier. So far everything had gone without a hitch. It was almost as if we were on a training exercise. But when we crossed the border south of Brest-Litovsk the inferno of smoke and flames billowing up from below soon put paid to that illusion. We could only guess at what kind of hell our ground troops were going through as they forced a crossing of the River Bug, which marked the frontier at this point, and started to advance into enemy territory.

Now that we ourselves had crossed the front lines we were nervously searching the sky around us as we fully expected to be engaged by Soviet Flak and fighters at any moment. We hadn't been given any information as to the location and disposition of enemy forces in the area, but everything remained eerily quiet now that the frontier was behind us. Flying at an altitude of 2,000m, and with a cruising speed of some 340km/h, we reached our objective at 09.00 hours.

We had been carefully maintaining *Schwarm* formation all the way since assembling above Radzyn. This was one thing the pre-op briefing *had* been specific about. Each *Schwarm* formed a small combat unit in itself, but all were mutually supporting if the Gruppe came under attack as a whole. This sounded fine in theory, but theory quickly turned into confusion the moment we arrived over Pinsk. Pilots immediately began to jostle for position and get in each other's way as they sought a suitable target on the airfield below. Fortunately, everyone managed to sort themselves out as one aircraft after the other winged over into a steep 70° dive. Their bombs rained down in quick succession and bright explosions erupted all over the surface of the field. Fires and dark columns of smoke soon began to hamper visibility.

After releasing our bombs we continued diving, picking up speed until we were only some 300m off the ground. Then we flattened out and circled the field at low level before making several high-speed strafing runs along the lines of enemy aircraft standing unprotected around its perimeter. As there were no pens or blast walls between the parked machines we were able to attack at a very shallow angle, which increased the accuracy of our fire. We could line up individual aircraft in our sights, hold them steady, and then let fly with a devastating barrage from our 20mm nose cannon and machine-guns.

In fact, we were flying so low over our chosen targets that there was a very real danger of our own aircraft being caught up in the explosions. Also, there were so many of us making runs back and forth across the field, each intent on inflicting as much damage on the enemy as possible, that we had to be extra vigilant not to be hit by fire from one of our comrades or to collide with one another.

If aircraft returned to base with battle damage it was not always easy to establish beyond doubt whether the perpetrator had been friend or foe. The uncoordinated and chaotic type of attack we had just carried out needed desperately to be looked into and improved. But any such considerations were lost amidst all the euphoria and heady successes of this opening phase of the war against the Soviet Union. It was not until much later, when the enemy had begun to recover and our own losses started to escalate alarmingly, that serious thought was given to refining our tactics.

Unlike the outward flight, we did not return to base as a Gruppe. It had been left up to each pilot to decide when to break off his attack. Consequently, we straggled back to Radzyn in fours, pairs and even singly. Again, this was something that had not been adequately covered in the briefing.

I myself touched down at Radzyn at exactly 10.05 hours feeling both relieved and excited that I had my first operational mission as a Bf 110 pilot safely behind me. Of the 110 minutes I had been in the air, some twenty of them had been spent over the target area, first bombing and then strafing. Comparing notes with other pilots, we were fairly sure that the enemy aircraft based at Pinsk – the majority of them twin-engined types – had been almost completely destroyed. We couldn't be certain of the exact numbers, of course. Nor could we be absolutely sure about the amount of damage we had inflicted on the field's hangars, workshops, fuel and supply dumps. The reports and claims of the various crews involved differed widely. Perhaps the subsequent reconnaissance photos of the target area gave a clearer picture. But if they did, we never found out about it.

Late that same afternoon we were ordered to carry out an attack on another Soviet airfield, Volkovysk, to the north-north-east of Brest-Litovsk. As it was to be mounted by just a single *Schwarm*, it should have proved to be a far less complicated affair than the morning's maximum effort. But again the pre-op briefing left a lot to be desired. There was no mention of individual targets. The four of us were simply informed that the general aim was to help destroy the enemy's air force. Just how we went about it was left entirely up to us. Nobody seemed able to explain to us why this was. We had very little previous experience to fall back on and so, in the end, each decided on his own particular mode of attack which, surprisingly, was to prove a very effective way of getting the job done.

We took off at 16.26 hours, each machine carrying two 500kg HE bombs beneath its fuselage and with a full load of ammunition for the nose guns. These consisted of four 7.92mm machine-guns, each with 1,000 rounds, and a pair of 20mm cannon fed by drum magazines containing sixty shells apiece. The combined firepower from this battery of fixed forward-firing weapons was devastating and ideally suited to this type of operation. It was, however, important that one maintained strict fire discipline and made use of the nose guns only in very short, well-aimed bursts. Any pilot who failed to do this and sprayed his fire indiscriminately all over the place would not achieve any worthwhile results, would soon run out of ammunition, and would be nothing but a liability if we ran into enemy fighters on our way back to base.

Sitting behind the pilot was that other essential member of the Bf 110's two-man crew, the wireless-operator, who also acted as air-gunner and observer. Every Bf 110 pilot was totally dependent on his 'back-seat man', whose myriad duties included fending off enemy fighters, keeping a sharp watch on the surrounding airspace, confirming the results of a bombing attack – whether successful or not – and monitoring the situation on the ground below ... not all at once, of course, but a heavy responsibility all the same.

Communication between pilot and wireless-operator was by means of the on-board intercom. A good crew quickly reached a high level of mutual reliance on each other based on the understanding that the intercom was to be used only when there was something urgent to report. Otherwise strict radio silence was to be maintained at all times. In critical situations this was not always easy, but it too was something that we found improved with practice.

The rear cockpit armament initially consisted of a single 7.92mm MG 15 flexible machine-gun, but this was later replaced by a quick-firing twin MG 81Z installation. The Bf 110's twin tail unit meant that the wireless-operator had a good field of fire should an enemy fighter attack directly from astern.

The weather conditions for the raid on Volkovysk could not be described as exactly ideal. Scattered cloud at 1,500m would make dive-bombing difficult. In addition, visibility above the target area was poor, making accurate aiming against pinpoint targets well-nigh impossible.

We commenced our dives from about 2,500m and immediately followed these up with low-level strafing runs against the aircraft parked about the airfield. There were not many of them and consequently the results we achieved were not impressive. We managed to set a few enemy machines on fire and inflicted some damage to the runway and hangars, but the number of aircraft we were expecting to find at Volkovysk just weren't there. They had obviously been pulled back from the frontier zone, which is exactly what we had been trying to prevent.

Judging from the numerous explosions and puffs of white smoke that had begun to pockmark the sky above the field the moment we commenced our attack, however, Volkovysk's Flak defences were still very much *in situ*. But despite the hostile reception, none of our four machines sustained any damage and we all returned safely to Radzyn, where we landed at around 17.45 hours.

Our good fortune wasn't to last. During the Gruppe's opening attack on Pinsk on the morning of 22 June a 2. Staffel aircraft had been shot down by Soviet fighters, both crew members escaping with wounds, and other machines had been damaged. But our 3. Staffel had seen neither hide nor hair of the enemy. But all that was soon about to change. Our late afternoon raid on Volkovysk had been just a foretaste of things to come and it was to be a very different story on our next two missions: an attack on the airfield at Bialystok on 23 June, and a second strike against Pinsk on 24 June.

Both raids were mounted in the early morning hours under unfavourable weather conditions. Take-off for the attack on Bialystok was timed at 03.25 hours and for the following day's return visit to Pinsk we lifted off five minutes earlier at 03.20 hours. Because of the persistent poor visibility we were ordered to fly to the target area in loose Gruppe formation on both occasions. Once we had reached our objectives this enabled us to attack as individual Staffeln without having to worry about getting in each other's way. The attacks themselves were made in the usual two parts; first the dive-bombing and then the strafing. They both proved far more effective than our previous efforts. We had already gained sufficient experience to know exactly what was expected of us and now had the confidence to carry it out.

And yet, with the benefit of hindsight, I am now convinced that we could have achieved much more with far fewer aircraft. The pre-op preparations and briefing still had a lot of room for improvement. Not enough time had been allowed to do things properly. But perhaps the middle and lower levels of command really did lack the necessary expertise and were still feeling their way in this new and totally unfamiliar theatre of war, in which case it would be unfair to point the finger at any one person.

With the campaign in the east still little more than twenty-four hours old, the Russians were clearly starting to recover from the shock of our initial assault. The 23 and 24 June missions saw the Gruppe suffer its first combat fatalities. The unfortunate 2. Staffel lost another of its aircraft on 23 June, this time to enemy ground fire, with both crew members being killed. The following day it was the turn of 1. Staffel when one of their machines was brought down by Soviet fighters, again with both crew members losing their lives.

In terms of casualties, 3. Staffel's luck continued to hold. We suffered no losses, although several of our machines returned to base with obvious signs of battle damage, some with gaping, fist-sized holes in their fuselages and wings. My own aircraft was hit in the radiator during a low-level strafing run and I had to limp back from Pinsk to Radzyn on one engine. It was not a pleasant experience. I felt like the proverbial duck in a shooting gallery, but fortunately I ran into no enemy fighters and got back to base safe if not altogether sound.

The ground crews and mechanics immediately got to work and soon had all the damaged machines, mine included, repaired and fully serviceable again for whatever the following day might bring.

When not actually engaged in operations – by which I mean getting ready for them beforehand, flying them, and then analysing and discussing the results between ourselves afterwards (which latter invariably gave us plenty of food for thought) – we sat glued to the radio in the mess hut listening to the daily news bulletins reporting on the progress of the fighting on the ground. We were, of course, mostly interested in what was happening on our own central sector of the front, where the armoured spearheads of *Panzergruppen* 2 and 3 were advancing on either side of Bialystok in a gigantic pincer movement designed to entrap large numbers of the retreating Red Army.

Once we had neutralized the enemy's air power along the frontier zone, it would be our job to support the advance of these Panzer units as they raced towards Minsk where the two arms of the pincer – Generaloberst Hermann Hoth's *Panzergruppe* 3 in the north and Generaloberst Heinz Guderian's *Panzergruppe* 2 to the south – were to meet up and close the jaws of the trap.

And, in fact, I was to fly my first direct ground-support mission the very next day. At 07.00 hours on the morning of 25 June 1941 we assembled in the ops hut for a briefing on the current situation on the ground.

The intelligence officer produced a map and showed us the routes our armoured units had taken since breaking through the Russian frontier defences. He also indicated the points reached by the spearheads of the two *Panzergruppen* as they advanced in parallel east-north-east towards Minsk. He followed this with the latest information available on the enemy's known strengths and dispositions, in particular those areas where the Red Army was putting up the fiercest resistance. Our task would be to support the ground forces in their efforts to eliminate any such stubborn strongpoints.

It was not all that easy to make sense of the operations map. For one thing our Panzers were constantly on the move, making the situation on the ground both fluid and complicated. Another problem was the sheer size of the developing pocket of encircled enemy troops. It stretched all the way from Bialystok to Minsk, a distance of over 300km – roughly the equivalent of the distance from Hamburg to Berlin!

There were also strong enemy forces on the outer flanks of both *Panzergruppen* 2 and 3. Some of these Red Army units were offering more determined resistance than others. The Soviets' rate of retreat was therefore uneven, which only added yet more confusion to an already disorganized picture. The nature of the terrain beyond Bialystok, rolling densely wooded hills, was a further hindrance to finding and engaging the enemy.

In the light of the above, it is hardly surprising that we weren't allocated specific targets. The maps issued to us at briefing simply showed the regions where the heaviest fighting was taking place. It was our responsibility, we were told, to reconnoitre the indicated areas and identify any targets we might find beyond all reasonable doubt – in other words, make sure they were enemy units and not our own! – before launching an attack. We were also instructed to engage any other targets we could positively identify as hostile in the general Bialystok-Slonim areas.

This was going to pose quite a problem for us. Even with the help of the maps, we had found it extremely difficult to grasp the situation on the ground as it was at the moment, let alone how it might develop in the next few hours. We simply lacked sufficient knowledge of ground tactics and had little understanding of the workings of operational cooperation between the services. Nor did we have the benefit of a specialist *Fliegerverbindungsoffizier,* or air liaison officer – '*Flivo*' for short – whose job was to coordinate joint Army/ Luftwaffe operations from the ground. This meant that our effectiveness for such missions was impaired from the very outset.

After a short briefing on purely flying matters, we took off from Radzyn at 09.10 hours. We had been ordered to fly to the target area in individual *Schwärmen,* each *Schwarm* of four Bf 110s being made up of two pairs. In our *Schwarm* I was flying as leader of the second pair. From our altitude of some 800m visibility was almost unlimited and there wasn't a trace of cloud in the clear blue summer sky. Our approach route to the Slonim area was the best part of 200km. Given our cruising speed of about 350km/h, we could expect to reach the target area in a little over half-an-hour.

But after just twenty minutes in the air we could already see the huge columns of dust being churned up by our armoured units as they advanced along the unmade Russian roads below us, while the clouds of black smoke darkening the horizon ahead were a sure sign that we were rapidly approaching the scene of the fighting. The nearer we got to the battlefield, the more intense and confused the activity on the ground became. Tanks and armoured personnel carriers were milling about seemingly haphazardly in all directions. It was for all the world as if someone had disturbed a giant ants' nest.

We were expecting some kind of reaction from the enemy, either fighters or Flak, at any second. I could feel the tension mounting. But we had to focus our minds on the job we had been sent out to do. While my wireless-operator scoured the skies for the first sign of Russian fighters, I concentrated on navigating and reconnoitring the ground below. I also had to keep a constant eye on the leading pair of our *Schwarm* to make sure that we didn't become separated. Although it was imperative that we didn't lose sight of each other entirely, I nevertheless maintained a respectable distance between us. We were flying slightly higher than the two machines ahead of us. There were three good reasons for doing this. We didn't want to get in each other's way when it came time to dive. It enabled one pair to go to the aid of the other if either was attacked by enemy fighters. And it meant that we didn't offer too bunched and tempting a target to the Soviet Flak gunners, who were already starting to bang away at us with some vigour.

At first the spot that we had been ordered to dive-bomb presented a totally chaotic and confusing picture. So we circled the area a few times desperately trying to sort out friend from foe. This spurred the enemy gunners to even greater efforts. They were letting fly with everything they had by now. But their aim did not match their enthusiasm. We suffered no damage and their wild firing merely served to betray their positions to us.

Once we had got the situation on the ground firmly established in our minds, we opened out and started to climb in preparation for the attack. After a brief exchange over the R/T with our *Schwarmführer*, we positioned ourselves ready to dive on what we had identified as the leading group of enemy tanks. We followed each other down in rapid succession. I hardly had time to register the explosions from the leading pair before releasing my own bombs. If the mushrooms of black smoke and flames were anything to go by, our aim must have been spot on.

Pulling out of our dives at around 500m, we immediately got into line-astern formation – each machine some 300m behind the one in front – and executed a wide, flat turn ready to go in and strafe the area we had just bombed.

Now that we could see for ourselves exactly what was happening on the ground, we carried out a series of low-level strafing runs. These demanded the utmost concentration on the part of the pilot, and a high degree of teamwork between pilot and wireless-operator. During the initial dive-bombing phase of the attack we had spoken hardly a word. But now two pairs of eyes were needed to scan the ground racing past below us in order to spot the carefully camouflaged troops, vehicles and defensive positions concealed about the battlefield. There was thus a constant exchange of information between the wireless-operator and myself as potential targets were glimpsed and their locations reported.

Such low-level strafing attacks were, by their very nature, always very risky – but not necessarily always successful. If an aircraft was seriously damaged this close to the ground its crew stood very little chance of survival. A botched strafing run could also alert the enemy to an attacker's intentions. Even this early in the campaign it was already becoming all too clear that – unlike most other troops, who very sensibly took cover when attacked from the air – the rank and file of the Red Army had the annoying habit of standing their ground and firing back with every weapon they could lay their hands on. So if a pilot was foolish enough to repeat the same run twice, he would be faced with a veritable curtain of lead as the enemy troops let loose with everything they had at their disposal, from pistols to heavy machine-guns.

This is why we had been given strict orders to remain at low level after completing our first run and continue flying on the same heading until out of sight of the enemy. Only then could we turn and come in again from a different, and hopefully unexpected, angle. The obvious disadvantage to this, of course, was that it was extremely difficult to find the same camouflaged target again a second time without wasting too much time searching – especially in this hilly wooded terrain that stretched for many kilometres in every direction.

We would therefore decide upon a different angle of approach, climb to about 300m and start a new run, making course corrections as we did so. With the element of surprise gone, jinking about at low level trying to line up our sights on the target, and flying through an absolute hail of fire – the likes of which only someone who has actually experienced it could possibly imagine – it was little wonder that we collected innumerable holes in the fuselages and wings of our aircraft.

In all we spent a good forty minutes over the target area, from the time of locating and identifying the enemy's positions until breaking off the attack and returning to Radzyn.

When we got back we reported to the ops room for debriefing. As we hadn't had the opportunity to take any photographs while over the target area, we had to rely solely on our own impressions and observations to describe the attack. The *Schwarmführer* made his report first, after which the remaining three crews, pilots and wireless-operators, added theirs. What the debriefing officer needed to know was the nature and exact location of each target attacked, plus the damage inflicted.

Equally important were the results of our brief reconnaissance sweeps prior to the launch of the actual attack. These helped to establish the whereabouts of the enemy and the positions of our own troops, but could at times lead to a certain amount of disagreement between crews as our maps weren't all that accurate and it wasn't always easy in the heat of the moment to decide whether it was this or that particular landmark that was shown on the map. It was the intelligence officer's job to take all this down in writing, collate the information provided, and pass it on up to the next highest level in the chain of command.

We weren't the only ones engaged in operations, of course, and the ops room was a hive of activity with crews constantly coming and going. The mission we had just flown had lasted 135 minutes, from 09.00 hours to 11.15 hours. And at 12.45 hours we were back in the air again for a second strike in the same area.

This time we were assigned specific targets – presumably based on our earlier reports – and so we didn't have to spend too long on prior reconnaissance. Our task was to prevent the enemy troops encircled near Slonim from breaking out and escaping to the east. The attacks had to be carried out very close to our own forces. This called for absolute precision when bombing which, in turn, meant a quick sweep of the area at an altitude of about 500m to establish the exact situation on the ground. Once we had done this, we lost no time in beginning the climb up to 1,500m ready to start dive-bombing.

But, brief as it had been, our opening low-level pass over the heads of the enemy had stirred up a veritable hornets' nest of ground fire. The Soviets continued to hammer away at us furiously as we clawed for height. This always seemed to take an eternity. Weighed down with a drag-inducing external bomb load, the Bf 110 was not a natural climber.

In his post-war autobiography Adolf Galland famously described climbing in the twin-jet Messerschmitt Me 262 as like being 'pushed by an angel'. He should have tried it in a bomb-laden Bf 110! To us it felt more as if the devil himself was holding us back by the tail. In real terms, our rate of climb was little more than 250m per minute. And the six minutes or so that it took us to get up to dive-bombing height were a nightmare. At times it seemed as if we were standing still. But finally we were high enough to commence our attack. Our targets were once again enemy tanks, after which we carried out a series of short strafing runs. With these completed, we flew additional reconnaissance sweeps of the Bialystok, Slonim and Volkovysk areas before returning to base.

Although this had been only our second ground-support mission of the campaign, the little experience we had gained was already beginning to pay dividends in terms of correctly identifying and attacking worthwhile targets. There was a marked reduction in the hesitancy and uncertainty we had displayed earlier.

By this time the first of the great 'cauldron' battles of the Eastern Front was approaching its climax and the two Gruppen of our Geschwader were flying mission after mission in support of our advancing Panzers. My wireless-operator and I were very much part of it. At 17.45 hours we took off for our third mission of the day. It was to be a straightforward in-and-out dive-bombing attack on a reported concentration of Soviet armour. There was no need for any prior reconnaissance, or for any ground-strafing afterwards. Consequently it was a much shorter affair than our previous two missions, lasting just eighty minutes in all.

It was very different from the day's first operation when we had had to find the target for ourselves. But the information gathered and evaluated from the numerous missions flown during the course of the day, particularly our reconnaissance sweeps of the battlefield, meant that our briefings could now be much more precise with specific targets being assigned. There may have been a significant improvement in our performance as the day progressed, but it had come at a price. A II. Gruppe crew had lost their lives when their machine was shot down near Volkovysk. Fortunately, our I. Gruppe suffered no casualties, but two machines were written off in emergency landings, one near Bialystok, and the other in the Slonim area.

I was lucky, collecting just a few holes from machine-gun fire and Flak splinters in the fuselage and wings of my Bf 110. These didn't affect the aircraft's handling in the slightest and the damage was quickly patched up on my return to base.

It had been a long, eventful and exhausting day. But that didn't prevent us from getting together for a lengthy session in the mess that evening to swap experiences and discuss ways and means of making our ground-support missions even more effective. How could we increase the element of surprise, for example, so that the enemy wasn't alerted and didn't have his defences ready and waiting for us. Our opening reconnaissance passes before carrying out the actual attack were the stumbling block. They could not fail to give the enemy advance warning of our intentions. Surely it would be better – and certainly far less of a giveaway – for a single reconnaissance machine to fly a sweep over the area beforehand?

The ideas and suggestions tossed back and forth were purely our own points of view, of course. It could hardly be otherwise at this early stage in a new campaign and in a new and altogether unfamiliar country. But in the weeks to come the results of our experiences were gradually assimilated and accepted by the powers-that-be and put into practice.

On the following day, 26 June, I was ordered to fly another mission in the same area. Once again the Gruppe was split into separate *Schwärmen* and we all carried the same bomb loads as before. The results we had achieved to date seemed to suggest that we had hit upon the right tactic of mounting continual shuttle attacks by small individual formations. They were keeping the enemy off balance. And this was confirmed by the first messages from our ground troops describing the effectiveness of our attacks and thanking us for our valuable support. These were passed on to us by the Gruppe's operations officer and it was very gratifying to hear that the army appreciated our efforts on their behalf.

Our briefing for this particular mission called for us to dive-bomb specific targets near Volkovysk close to the southern edge of the Bialystok–Minsk cauldron, and then to follow this up with ground strafing pockets of resistance reported in the same general area. This normally meant troop concentrations, field defences or artillery emplacements. The latter were invariably very well hidden and almost the only way we could pinpoint their position was by the muzzle flashes when the guns were actually firing.

We carried out our attacks in the usual manner. The enemy threw up a massive amount of ground fire, but this was only to be expected given the numbers of Soviet troops crammed into this part of the cauldron. After dive-bombing we split into pairs and spent a good twenty minutes ground-strafing various targets in the vicinity. In between our firing runs we carried out a few dummy passes. These were intended not so much to keep the enemy's heads down, as rather to divert their fire away from other attacking Bf 110s. At the same time they gave us the opportunity for some really low-level battlefield reconnaissance in our search for fresh targets.

I had just commenced another run when there was an almighty bang and my machine shook violently. Just stay calm, I told myself as I fought to keep her level – and stay low, I added as an after-thought. If I attempted to gain any height every enemy gun within range would swing in my direction eager to deliver the *coup-de-grâce* to my obviously wounded bird.

From the cockpit I could see a large number of small jagged holes in the upper surfaces of both my wings. A Flak shell must have exploded directly beneath us, sending splinters up into the Bf 110. That would explain the loud bang and the aircraft's violent shuddering. The next question was, had it suffered any serious damage? A quick glance down at the instrument panel confirmed the worst. The needle of one of the coolant temperature gauges was rising at an alarming rate.

I hadn't yet said a word to my wireless-operator. Resisting the urge to break away, I held my course for a good minute – never have sixty seconds passed so agonizingly slowly – until I was out of the area of immediate danger. Only then did I risk a wide, flat turn in the direction of our own lines. Once I was pointed towards home I cautiously gained a little height and switched off the overheating engine. Then the usual drill: feather the propeller, trim the machine so that the wing with the damaged engine was raised a little higher to counter the torque, and remember what had been drummed into us during multi-engined training: *never* – under any circumstances – turn into the direction of the dead engine.

These were the thoughts chasing through my mind. In purely flying terms, the situation we were in was nothing to be unduly worried about. The real fear lay in the fact that, for what seemed like an eternity, we would be flying over enemy territory. We knew only too well what our fate was likely to be if we had to force-land or bail out behind enemy lines and fell into the hands of the Soviets. Whenever this subject came up we all pictured the Leutnant who had been one of the first members of our Gruppe to be brought down over enemy territory. Our rapidly-advancing ground troops had found him shortly afterwards, his hideously-mutilated body lying stretched out beside his neatly belly-landed Bf 110.

Pray to God nothing like that ever happens to me, we all thought, as we remembered the short talk our Geschwaderkommodore had given at the start of the war against the Soviets. He had closed by suggesting that we should seriously consider saving the last bullet in our service pistol for ourselves, rather than face an horrific end in the event of our falling alive into the hands of the Red Army. How right he was, and yet how reluctant we had at first been to face up to this unpalatable truth. It wasn't long, however, before the majority of the crews began to accept the fact that such atrocities were being committed. But, of course, it would *never* happen to them – the young Leutnant from Mannheim had probably thought the same.

In fact, another 2. Staffel machine was reported missing on this very day. Apparently it had crash-landed not far from us, just inside the pocket on the other side of Slonim. The crew came under fire from Soviet troops as they tried to escape on foot. The pilot was lucky enough to make it. His wireless-operator was never seen again.

I was determined that we weren't going to suffer the same fate. It was only after I had switched off the damaged engine that my unflappable wireless-operator casually enquired over the intercom what the trouble was. I was able to reassure him that we were now back over our 'own' territory and that otherwise everything else was all in order, except for the fact that we were returning from a mission on one engine and completely alone. I had no idea where the other three members of the *Schwarm* had got to. We only met up again at debriefing in the ops room. My flying back to base on one engine caused little comment from the others. It was the sort of thing that we were coming to accept as part of our daily life by now.

The Volkovysk operation had been my eighth combat mission of the war. It also proved to be the last I would fly from Radzyn. My Bf

110 had to go into the workshops for extensive repairs and an engine change. This meant that I had a break from ops for the next few days. I filled my time mostly by helping out with check flights and studying the situation maps. Unfortunately it was during this period, on 5 July, that the Staffel suffered its first combat fatalities when Leutnant Erich Disper and his wireless-operator were shot down by Soviet fighters south of Orsha.

The two arms of Army Group Centre's first great pincer movement had snapped shut at Minsk on 28 June, trapping some forty Red Army divisions. Leaving follow-up troops to reduce the gigantic Bialystok-Minsk pocket, *Panzergruppen* 2 and 3 continued to forge eastwards. Their objective was Smolensk, the next strategically important step on the road to Moscow. At the same time the 18. 'Chemnitz' *Panzerdivision* had bypassed Minsk to the south and was headed for the River Berezina (the scene, incidentally, of an epic battle during Napoleon's 1812 retreat from Moscow). By 3 July German troops had crossed the Berezina at a number of points between Bobruisk and Borisov. But ahead of them lay an even more formidable water barrier, the River Dnieper.

The rapid advance of the ground forces meant that our Radzyn base was now something like 500km behind the fighting front. As a consequence, and in order to reduce the distances we had to fly to reach our objectives, we began preparing for our first move of the campaign. On 7 July 1941 we transferred forward to a field just outside recently captured Minsk.

And so began our nomadic existence under canvas. From now on there would be no more permanent quarters for us. Barrack blocks and wooden huts had been replaced by tents. Day-to-day living became much more basic. Our new surroundings took a little while to get used to, but there was an undoubted plus: they brought us all much closer together as a Staffel.

Our tented 'village' was situated in the woods bordering the field and was thus very well camouflaged. Each of the Gruppe's three Staffeln had its own tent lines and so we didn't have to live too cheek-by-jowl with each other. Being kept separate also offered a certain element of safety in the unlikely event of an enemy bombing raid.

Also situated under the trees not too far away from us was that one indispensable item of equipment: the field kitchen. The *'Gulaschkanone'*, as it was universally known, bubbled away all day long without pause and there was always hot food and drink available for the asking. Our unit cook, Bellinghausen, was a marvel. It was an education and a pleasure to watch him at work – except, that is, when he was butchering the carcass of some poor animal. Then the scenes of blood and gore were simply too much, even for the most battle-hardened of pilots.

The ops room and all the other necessary admin offices were also under canvas, as were the sick quarters, although the latter were some distance away from us as they had to serve the entire Gruppe. The medical officer was a very professional but understanding type. He looked after our health in exemplary fashion and we all had the highest regard and respect for him.

Our aircraft were dispersed among the trees close to our tent lines so that we could get to them quickly if an emergency arose, or if an unplanned mission suddenly had to be flown in a hurry. This was happening more and more frequently and soon became almost the rule rather than the exception. It didn't create any great problems however, for we were, to all intents and purposes, permanently at readiness as we never left the camp. We were given no opportunity to venture far afield and so had no contact with the local populace. The Soviet Union and its people remained a closed book to us.

Our working day began at sunrise and ended at sunset. In some ways it was a very primitive existence, but everything seemed to run perfectly well. Comradeship and discipline within the Staffel couldn't have been better. Despite the basic living conditions, the health of the unit remained good. Nobody wanted to risk contracting any contagious diseases and so cleanliness was the strict order of the day. The medical officer played no small part in keeping us all fit and well with his numerous injections and frequent snap hygiene inspections of the camp.

We received letters and parcels from home on a regular basis. The *Feldpost*, or forces' postal service, did an excellent job and to get news from family and friends did wonders for our morale. It helped enormously to overcome the uncertainties of what lay ahead of us.

During off-duty hours there was seldom time for boredom to set in. There was always more to learn about our operations. Every crew returning from a mission was quizzed about how it had gone. Every last detail of their sortie was discussed and digested, and in this way every newly-won experience was quickly passed on to all the other crews in the Staffel.

There were plenty of other things besides to occupy us. We could lend a hand in keeping the camp clean and tidy, indulge our passion for sports of all kinds, read, write letters and, of course, sleep. Every now and again the Staffelkapitän would give a talk on the present situation on the fighting fronts, or lead a discussion on current political events. And yet, despite all this, there was always a slight feeling of tension in the air; tension from knowing that one could be called upon to fly a mission at any moment – a mission from which one might not return. The secret of our existence in those days was in learning to keep those tensions, and our fears, within acceptable limits.

It was all a very far cry from the permanent bases I had been stationed on before the war – comfortable barrack blocks, well-equipped sports facilities, a camp cinema, swimming pool, weekend passes – but such was now to be our daily lot in the Soviet Union.

At 10.05 hours on the morning of 8 July we took off for our first mission out of Minsk. The target area lay somewhere along the 100km stretch of front between Mogilev and Senno. These two towns were both some 180km away from Minsk, so the approach flight would take us a good thirty minutes.

On this occasion we had been given specific and very precise targets: the Russian armoured units that were mounting a major counter-attack on our forces in this sector. After a brief search in this new and hitherto unfamiliar area, we found the enemy near Senno, only to be met by a ferocious storm of fire for our pains. It was all we could do to maintain formation and carry out our mission as ordered. We attacked in the same way that had proved so effective back in the Bialystok–Minsk regions, but in the face of much more determined and better-directed defensive fire from the Soviets.

After completing our dive-bombing, we immediately began ground-strafing targets of opportunity in the same general area. To do this the Schwärme split up into their individual pairs. The battle raging below called for quick decisions and rapid action as each pair roared low over the enemy seeking suitable targets.

In marked contrast to the often confusing and hard-to-follow ground fighting that had typified the earlier engagements around the edges of the Bialystok-Minsk cauldron, the action here at Senno was a set-piece tank battle with the opposing forces clashing head on. This made it far easier – even for us with our limited knowledge of battlefield tactics – to distinguish friend from foe. Nonetheless, given the type of missions we were being required to fly, we were still very conscious of the fact that there was always the possibility of hitting our own troops. This was a constant worry to us. We were always prepared to expose ourselves to enemy fire for that little bit longer in order to be absolutely certain of our target, rather than carry out a hasty attack and run the risk of causing damage, or worse, to our own side.

But we were left in no doubt as to our targets today. The entire Gruppe, more than a dozen pairs of Bf 110s in all, weaved back and forth across the scene of the fighting in a non-stop series of low-level strafing runs, forcing the enemy on to the defensive and inflicting considerable losses. Even if the results of a particular run were not always immediately apparent, the cumulative effect of our attacks could be seen from the growing numbers of burning vehicles and immobile or abandoned tanks littering the battlefield below.

This first mission of the day ended at 11.50 hours. It was followed by a second at 14.20 hours. Our orders were the same: ground support for our armoured units engaged in the tank battle of Senno. And the outcome was the same, with yet more enemy vehicles knocked out or disabled. We landed back at Minsk at 16.10 hours. It had been an exhausting day and considering the amount of fire we had been subjected to throughout the course of it, we were extremely lucky to have escaped with just one machine damaged in an emergency landing after being hit by Flak.

The following day, 9 July, I was not called upon to fly until well into the afternoon. We finally took off at 15.45 hours and made straight for Senno, where the tank battle was still being fought. We began in our customary fashion by dive-bombing a packed group of enemy armour but this time, just as we were pulling out of our dives, we were bounced by a large gaggle of Russian fighters. Abandoning all thoughts of strafing runs, we prepared to defend ourselves. Despite being caught completely by surprise, and despite being heavily outnumbered – there must have been a whole squadron of enemy machines attacking our *Schwarm* alone – we gave a good account of ourselves.

It was the first time I had encountered the enemy in the air. I managed to get in a quick burst at one of the Russian fighters as it shot past me only metres away. But I couldn't see any results as he immediately sheared off and I was having enough problems of my own. I had taken a number of hits, whether from my assailant of a moment before I couldn't be sure, and was once again wrestling with an overheating engine. This is becoming too much of a habit, I thought to myself as I switched the engine off and carefully turned for home. This time, however, I didn't have to make the journey on my own. Noticing my predicament, several other Bf 110s formed up around me and escorted me back.

The Gruppe had escaped lightly from this latest brush with Red Air Force fighters. A 1. Staffel machine had received superficial damage during the brief engagement and had been forced to make a wheels-up landing in open country. Otherwise we had all returned to base more or less intact.

Although I had flown only three missions out of Minsk, there wasn't to be a fourth. The headlong advance of our armoured units was showing no signs of slowing down. Spearheads of Generaloberst Guderian's *Panzergruppe* 2 had already reached the banks of the River Dnieper and on 10 July they forced crossings at three thinly-defended points between the heavily fortified towns of Orsha and Rogachev. The ground forces were outstripping us again. From Minsk we were unable to offer Guderian's Panzers effective support. The fighting front was simply too far ahead of us. And so on 12 July, after just five days at Minsk, we leapfrogged forward a further 200km or so to newly-captured Orsha, the next important town along the Minsk-Moscow highway.

With the campaign in the east now exactly three weeks old, the two arms of *Panzergruppen* 2 and 3, which had smashed shoulder to-shoulder through the Soviets' frontier defences, had by this stage split into nearly a dozen separate armoured thrusts, each facing stiffening Russian resistance along a broad front that stretched some 250km from Vitebsk down to Rogachev.

Our first mission out of Orsha, flown on the evening of 13 July and which lasted from 18.15 hours until 20.25 hours, took us to Kopys, the northernmost of the three bridgeheads across the River Dnieper. Here the ground forces, including our old friends of the 18. 'Chemnitz' *Panzerdivision*, were being threatened by a major enemy counter-attack. Soviet Marshal Timoshenko had regrouped his Southern Front and on 11 July had begun to advance north-west towards the Upper Dnieper with close on twenty divisions. They had to be stopped at all costs, and our Geschwader was just one of the many Luftwaffe units supporting our ground troops as they fought desperately to do so.

We were given two tasks to perform. Not only were we to provide direct support above the battlefield and surrounding areas by attacking the enemy's armour, artillery positions, troop concentrations and airfields, but we were also ordered to help cut – or at least disrupt – the Soviets' rear-area supply lines. These latter played a vital role in bringing up the reinforcements and equipment from the Kiev region to sustain Timoshenko's massive drive towards Smolensk, where he planned to link up with elements of Marshal Yeremenko's three armies pushing down from the north.

The direct ground-support missions differed little from the operations we had been flying for the past couple of weeks, although they were now against a less demoralized and far better equipped enemy. The enormous amount of ground fire that greeted our every appearance was ample proof of that. But the attacks on the supply routes were a very different story. Firstly, we had to find our targets for ourselves. This was far from easy in the vast tracts of territory that needed to be searched. And the more time we had to spend looking for the enemy, the less we had to carry out our attacks.

And when we did manage to find a worthwhile target, we were not always carrying the right kind of bomb load for the job: anti-personnel bombs were of little use against a column of tanks, while armour-piercing bombs were wasted on a supply convoy of soft-skinned vehicles. The success, or otherwise, of these sorties deep into the enemy's hinterland was very much a matter of luck. The outcome could also be influenced by the decisions taken by individual crews. After a lengthy and often frustrating search, it was all too tempting, when a suitable target was eventually found, to go straight into the attack without first weighing up the risks involved. Many crews lost their lives in this way.

Once again, greater emphasis on prior reconnaissance – either visual or photographic – of a given area would undoubtedly have been much more effective and far less costly in terms of casualties incurred. But the Luftwaffe simply didn't have the necessary aircraft available. At the start of '*Barbarossa*' for example, our *Fliegerkorps'* fourteen Gruppen of bombers, dive-bombers and fighters – some 500 aircraft in all – were backed by just one single long-range reconnaissance Staffel of less than a dozen machines.

This was totally inadequate, of course. But in fairness nobody, not even the most omniscient of prophets, could possibly have foretold with any degree of accuracy just how the war against the Soviet Union was going to develop. The sheer scale of the fighting was almost unimaginable: the millions of troops involved, the vast areas being fought over, the tough determination and stubborn dogged-ness shown by both sides – simply the enormity of it all.

The situation on the ground remained extremely fluid; changing by the day, if not the hour. The inevitable delays before reports of the latest developments from the fighting fronts reached the various rear-area command HQs caused the planning staffs all sorts of headaches as they tried to ensure that the urgently needed reinforcements and supplies were sent to the right places at the right times.

Fortunately, we in the Geschwader didn't have to contend with such problems. Despite the recent transfers, the numerous missions we were flying, the damage to machines and the casualties suffered, we were still able to maintain our combat readiness as a unit and fulfil all the operational demands being made upon us.

This was thanks in no small part to our own efforts. Everyone pulled their weight, even under the most primitive and trying of conditions, to keep our aircraft and their weapons fully serviceable. All maintenance work was done in the open air along the edge of the airstrip and in the broiling heat of the sun. Shifts were measured not in hours, but by the physical endurance of the ground crews. They didn't just replace worn or damaged propellers and mainwheels, but carried out major repairs such as complete engine changes using little more than block and tackle.

At first we air crews would watch in awe as an entire engine was deftly stripped down and removed, and a replacement was uncrated and fitted in its place. Such sights soon became part of everyday life, however. But our admiration for the 'black men' – as the aircraft mechanics were universally known on account of the black overalls they wore – never lessened. It was their dedication and untiring work that kept our aircraft in the air.

Despite their every effort, however, a machine would occasionally develop some fault or other shortly after taking off for a mission that would require the crew to abort and return to base prematurely. This was always a most unpleasant experience and a pilot would not make such a decision unless *in extremis*, and then only with the greatest reluctance. Nobody wanted to be accused of turning back without very good reason and leaving his comrades to carry on alone or, worst of all, being charged with cowardice in the face of the enemy. That was unthinkable. Death would be preferable.

My turn to be faced with just such a dilemma came on 16 July, when I had an engine quit on me some fifteen minutes after taking off from Orsha. The engine had misfired once or twice as I was taxiing out to the start line, but I had lifted off without any difficulty and was able to remain in visual contact with the other aircraft that had taken off ahead of me. Raising the undercarriage and retracting the flaps also went perfectly normally. I therefore simply adjusted the pitch of the propellers manually in order to coax the maximum performance out of the machine.

At first I assumed that my delayed take-off had been at the root of the problem. The length of time that I had had to wait for clearance with the engines ticking over at low revs must have sooted up the spark plugs. Running the faulty engine at full power would quickly clear them – or so I thought. But unfortunately this didn't happen. The misfiring grew worse and the needle of the engine rev counter began to jump about wildly. I could no longer keep up with the rest of the formation. I had no alternative but to abandon the mission and return to base.

I had taken off from Orsha at 14.30 hours and landed back again just thirty minutes later. As I had not jettisoned the two 250kg bombs that I was carrying on the belly rack, I was very careful to make the landing as smooth and gentle as possible. All went well and I taxied across to my usual dispersal point where my unexpected appearance came as a total surprise. I handed the aircraft over to my crew chief, giving him a full account of what had happened. Then I made my way over to the ops room to report the reasons for my early return. My actions were deemed fully justified and accepted without further question. It was nonetheless with no small sense of relief that I resumed my normal duties for the rest of the day.

The engine fault was traced and put right that same afternoon and at 10.05 hours the following morning, 17 July, I took off on another mission. The briefing on this occasion again called for an armed-reconnaissance sweep far in the enemy's rear to locate and attack his lines of supply. After an uneventful outward flight and some desultory Flak when crossing the fighting front, we began the search for suitable targets. A railway line threading through some thick woods looked promising. We followed this and soon found a small station with a couple stationary goods trains under steam on sidings nearby.

We immediately went into the attack, first climbing to plaster the track and rolling stock with our 250kg bombs and then making several low-level passes dropping smaller HE and fragmentation bombs, before finally turning our attention to the locomotives, which we liberally sprayed with our 20mm nose cannon. During the low-level attacks with bombs and guns we flew to within a few metres of our chosen targets in order to maximise our accuracy and be able to observe the results at close range.

And, satisfying as it was to see the numerous thin jets of white steam spouting from the perforated locomotives, it was clear that in this, our first 'train-busting' mission, we were not doing the sort of damage we should be doing. We still had a lot to learn. For one thing, we had not taken the wind strength and direction into account.

This was an important factor in low-level precision attacks of this kind. Any pilot attempting a bombing or strafing run when there was a strong cross wind blowing would generally miss his target. And rather than repeat the attempt, he would then naturally alter his angle of approach and come in from a different direction. But this could also pose problems when there were several of us all attacking the same target. It was almost impossible for a pilot to convey a split-second decision to change direction to those around him. Our air-to-air communications simply weren't up to the job and the risks of confusion and possible mid-air collisions were very real.

Fortunately there hadn't been the slightest sign of any ground fire in the target area on this occasion and we all returned to base unscathed. The results of our first mission to cut the enemy off from his rear-area supply lines hadn't been particularly impressive, but the experience had taught us further valuable lessons for the future.

As usual, we all got together to discuss the tactics employed and the amount of damage we had inflicted. We all agreed that a series of low-level passes wasn't the ideal way to achieve the results we wanted. It was obvious that dive-bombing with heavier 500kg bombs would be a far more effective method of disrupting the enemy's rail traffic.

This had been my fifteenth combat mission since the start of the campaign and it was followed by a welcome break which took me to Warsaw, where I was to pick up a new Bf 110 for ferrying back to Orsha.

The flight to Warsaw as a passenger aboard a transport Ju was an absolute tonic and the perfect way to unwind from the stress of recent operations. We landed at Warsaw-Okecie, the Polish capital's main civil airport in pre-war days, and, after going through the usual formalities, I was driven to my quarters. Although I had been at the front for less than a month, the comfortable civilian surroundings of my hotel and the tranquil atmosphere of Warsaw felt totally alien to me. It wasn't just the white bed linen, the general air of peace and quiet, and the carefree couples strolling along the wide city streets, it was the sudden release of the tension that had been my constant companion for the best part of the last four weeks.

It was simply knowing that here I wasn't suddenly going to be summoned to an urgent briefing for a mission that could very well be my last. It might strike an outsider as banal even to mention these few unimportant and uneventful hours far removed from the battlefield, but this brief interlude is a reminder of the yawning chasm between the uncertainty of daily life at the front and the normality of everyday life in the rear areas.

On Saturday, 20 July 1941, I carried out a check flight on the Bf 110 which I was to fly back to Orsha, only to discover that there were a number of technical problems. These took several hours to put right and it was 11.45 hours on the Sunday morning before I was finally able to take off.

I was flying on my own, without a wireless-operator in the back seat, and had been ordered to make an intermediate landing at Radzyn, which was only some 120km away. Radzyn had been the Geschwader's jumping-off point for Operation '*Barbarossa*' and elements of our unit were still based there. I was not detained long at Radzyn and was soon back in the air again, reaching Orsha later that same day. It had been an enjoyable if all too short a break from the front, but now it was back to business as usual.

Except that things at Orsha were no longer 'as usual'. In fact, the situation had changed dramatically during my week's absence. The rapid advance of our ground forces, which had resulted in such immense territorial gains at the start of the campaign, was showing signs of slowing down in the face of ever-growing Soviet resistance and ferocious counter-attacks by the Red Army. Our airfield was now within range of heavy Russian artillery and we were being subjected to constant bombardment throughout the hours of darkness.

Thanks to the precautions that had been taken to ensure that our aircraft and all the Gruppe's equipment and stores had been well dispersed, this shelling caused little material damage. But it was wearing on the nerves to lay awake at night waiting for the screech of the next incoming round.

The countryside around the camp was also still full of Russian stragglers, remnants of Red Army units that had been cut off during the recent retreats. They were now becoming more active and we were no longer able to move about quite as freely as before. We also had to be particularly careful when taking off or landing as our aircraft could be vulnerable to even a single rifle bullet from a hidden marksman if hit in a vital spot such as a radiator.

On 23 July I flew my first mission since returning from Warsaw. I had a new wireless-operator/gunner with me, Oberfeldwebel Helmut Lindau, who hailed from Lyck in East Prussia. We took off in good weather at 17.20 hours with orders to attack Soviet infantry and artillery positions near Zhdanovo. It proved extremely difficult to find any targets however, for here, as in previous instances where the ground fighting had been in a similar state of turmoil and confusion, the Russians were employing their masterly camouflage skills to the full.

At first we could see no signs whatsoever of the enemy. Despite our obvious intentions, the Soviets were lying low and keeping very quiet. We separated into *Schwärmen* and continued the search, circling above the general area we had been briefed to attack. Not a thing. Then suddenly someone spotted muzzle flashes from one of the many small clearings dotted about the thickly wooded terrain below.

We tried hard to keep the approximate location of the enemy fire fixed in our minds as we looked for some kind of prominent landmark nearby that would enable us to get our bearings and launch an effective attack. I winged over into a steep dive and went down to have a closer look at the suspect patch of open ground among the trees. But even from a height of just 50m there was nothing to be seen. The other three members of the *Schwarm* had now joined me in the low-level search, but with equally little success. It seemed a waste to drop our bombs at random into the dense green carpet of foliage beneath us, and so we decided to make several passes, loosing off brief bursts of machine-gun fire as we did so, in the hope of provoking the enemy into revealing his positions.

The area we were concentrating on was about a kilometre square and we weaved back and forth across it at altitudes ranging from 800m down to very nearly treetop height. This had absolutely no effect at first. But eventually some trigger-happy Soviet gunner could resist it no longer and risked taking a pot-shot at us. That was all that was needed. Once the first shot had been fired, all the other guns opened up as well. At last we were able to pinpoint the enemy batteries, and once we had their positions established it didn't take us long to silence them with a combination of bombs and cannon fire. Columns of thick black smoke were rising from the trees as we turned for home with a feeling of a job well done.

We touched down back at Orsha at 19.10 hours. But at debriefing we were faced with the same old problem – where exactly *was* the target we had just destroyed? There were very few built-up areas or even any distinctive topographical features in this thickly wooded region and trying to match the terrain we had flown over with the maps then available to us was problematical to say the least. It was a situation that would continue to make life difficult for us throughout our time in the East.

Back on 16 July, the day I had been forced to abort and return early to Orsha due to an engine malfunction, the spearheads of Generaloberst Guderian's *Panzergruppe* 2 had reached the outskirts of Smolensk. But here they ran into resistance such as they had not encountered before. Until now they had swept all aside, encircling large bodies of Soviet troops and overrunning the many smaller units that had chosen to make heroic and often suicidal last-ditch stands. But at Smolensk, for the first time, Guderian's Panzers and motorized infantry met with firm resistance on a coherent and relatively wide front. It would be three weeks before they finally succeeded in taking the city.

Meanwhile, another of *Panzergruppe* 2's three component *Armeekorps* had managed to punch a hole deep in the Red Army's lines to the south-east of Smolensk, with 10. *Panzerdivision* capturing the town of Yelnya on 19 July. The Yelnya salient became the easternmost point yet reached by our forces on the central sector and, as such, provided a valuable springboard for the coming offensive against Moscow.

All too aware of the threat this posed to their capital, the Soviets fought desperately to eliminate the Yelnya salient. Our hard-pressed ground troops were in urgent need of air support. And so, for the third time in little over a month, we again found ourselves being transferred closer to the fighting front. Our new base was to be Shatalovka, a further 150km or so to the east of Orsha.

This time I was personally involved in the preparations for the transfer. At 10.05 hours on the morning of 25 July I took off from Orsha in a Junkers W 34 to ferry an advance party to Shatalovka.

The flight in such a slow machine – the W 34 couldn't be coaxed to do much more than 250km/h – over territory partly occupied by our own forces and partly by those of the enemy, was nerve-wracking to put it mildly. We could have been fired on at any moment and the Junkers' thin metal skin offered scant protection against even the smallest calibre bullet. It was also possible that, by the time we got there, Shatalovka had been retaken by the enemy. We had to be prepared for any eventuality, for the Red Army was no longer in headlong retreat, but fighting fiercely for every metre of Russian soil.

I had been briefed not to make directly for Shatalovka, but to head first in the direction of Smolensk before then turning south-east towards our final destination. This was in order to keep us over friendly territory for as long as possible. It also gave us the opportunity to spy out the land and note the position of our own troops. In the event, the flight passed off without incident and we landed safe and sound at Shatalovka where everyone immediately got down to the job of preparing the field for the arrival of the Gruppe. My orders called for me to fly the W 34 back to Orsha that same day, but the following morning I carried out a similar mission, albeit this time in a slightly faster Focke-Wulf Fw 58 'Weihe'. And on 27 July we flew our Bf 110s in to our new base.

With their spectacular earlier advances effectively checked, the troops of Army Group Centre now found themselves, for the first time in the war against the Soviet Union, having to fight a defensive battle. Our primary tasks in their support would be to undertake armed reconnaissance sweeps of the enemy's rear areas and to disrupt his lines of communication and supply. Our first two missions out of Shatalovka were flown on 28 July, the day after our arrival there, and our targets were the troop convoys and freight trains making their way down from the Moscow region towards the scene of the fighting around Yelnya.

The importance that the Soviets placed upon maintaining a constant flow of fresh supplies and reinforcements to the Yelnya front became immediately apparent to us. Every single target that we found and attacked was heavily defended. Never had we encountered such volumes of Flak. The nature of our operations – low-level bombing and strafing runs through seemingly impenetrable curtains of enemy ground fire – meant that we were suffering damage on almost every sortie.

The Gruppe's serviceability figures plummeted. Our ground crews and mechanics worked tirelessly around the clock to carry out what repairs they could on the spot. Improvisation, even cannibalization, was the order of the day. But some losses were beyond making good. By the end of that first day at Shatalovka 1. Staffel had reported two crews missing, while our own Leutnant Ernst Hackbeil and his wireless-operator had been brought down by Flak near Yermolino and another of our machines was totally written-off in an emergency landing, also as a result of Russian ground fire.

The general atmosphere on the base was noticeably more subdued than it had been of late and there was a palpable air of nervousness. This was not due solely to our own losses, either. The current uncertainties about the situation on the ground, and the bogging down of the offensive that had been crowned with such incredible success at the start of the campaign did little for the unit's collective peace of mind. We were virtually marking time at the moment, and the frequent talk of the possibility of Shatalovka's being overrun by a Soviet counter-attack was not exactly reassuring.

To add to our problems, now that we were nearly 700km inside enemy territory, our own lines of communication were starting to show the strain. Deliveries of supplies and spare parts were becoming increasingly irregular, and this too had its effect on our morale.

But, despite all these worries, each and every one of us was giving of his best to support and aid our troops in the field as efficiently and effectively as humanly possible. The fighting on the ground was murderous; the overall situation ominous.

While it was undeniably true that it was the army that was bearing the major brunt of the Soviet counter-offensive at Yelnya, we felt that we were doing our bit too. Every Red Army troop convoy that we prevented from reaching the front, every supply train that we destroyed, and every artillery emplacement that we knocked out helped to relieve the pressure on our comrades on the ground just that little bit more.

Although we were suffering considerable losses in terms of machines written-off or damaged, there was no let-up and missions continued to be flown as long as there was light in the sky. The ops room was a scene of constant activity, as was every other section throughout the Gruppe. On 7 August I flew two armed-reconnaissance sweeps to the south of the Yelnya salient. Three days later I took part in a dive-bombing raid on the airfield at Vyazma, one of the Red Air Force's main fighter bases in the area, and on 12 August I carried out two further missions in direct support of our ground troops who were coming under heavy attack at Churavichi. The next morning's raid on another enemy airfield was my twenty-fifth mission of the war. It earned me the Iron Cross First Class, and an Operational Flight Clasp in Bronze.

This latter mission, which had lasted from 04.32 hours until 05.25 hours, was followed by a much needed break. For later on that same 13 August a whole group of us were sent back to Warsaw to pick up some urgently-needed replacement aircraft.

In Warsaw it took a whole two days for us to carry out the necessary check flights and for all the various faults found on the aircraft to be put right. It was thus not until Sunday, 16 August that we took off for the flight back to Shatalovka. We staged via Minsk, where we landed briefly to refuel, before setting out on the second and final leg to Shatalovka. The total distance between our rear area support base and our front-line field was close on 900km which meant a flying time of 2 hours and 25 minutes in all.

With the Gruppe very nearly up to full establishment again, it was straight back into action. During the course of the next two days, 17 and 18 August, I flew three more missions over and around the Yelnya salient. My main focus of attention was on the rail traffic east of Klintsy, a small township on the Gomel-Bryansk line that ran to the south of the salient, but I also carried out several direct ground-support attacks in aid of our troops who were coming under heavy pressure from the Red Army in the Dorogobush area.

These ground-support sorties around the fringes of the salient were very reminiscent of our initial operations against the Bialystok–Minsk pocket. If anything, they were in fact harder as the situation on the ground was now even more fluid and chaotic than it had been in the opening weeks and months of the campaign. The two sides had become inextricably mixed and it was very difficult for us to establish the exact whereabouts of our own troops and those of the enemy without a thorough low-level search of the battlefield. And with every Russian unit, however small, now seemingly abundantly equipped with its own Flak defences, this could be – and often was – a perilous undertaking.

We therefore decided on occasion to split our *Schwarm* up and attack singly; each aircraft coming in from a different direction in rapid succession one after the other. This, we hoped, would confuse the enemy, divide his return fire and bring some relief, if only temporarily, to our own forces. There was no communication between the individual members of the *Schwarm*. Each pilot sought out his own target. Close cooperation between pilot and wireless-operator/gunner was therefore absolutely essential. The rear-seat man provided an extra pair of eyes in the search for suitable targets. He was also better placed to observe and report on the results of any attack carried out and would frequently fire off short bursts from his machine-gun at the end of the strafing run as the pilot jinked away at low level from the target area.

These tactics of ours obviously had a devastating effect on those enemy troops coming under direct attack from us, but there was no disguising the fact that our efforts were just a drop in the ocean. During our usual post-op sessions we had long come to the conclusion that missions of this kind were totally inadequate. Each could only be judged on its own merit. But none of them, successful or otherwise, made any real difference against the growing pressure being exerted by the Red Army.

And it was not only the central sector that was beginning to feel that pressure. Army Group North's advance on Leningrad was being seriously threatened by a strong Soviet counter-offensive at Staraya-Russa to the south of Lake Ilmen. If it succeeded, the spearheads of Generaloberst Erich Hoepner's *Panzergruppe* 4 were in acute danger of being cut off.

On 20 August 1941, as part of the response to this crisis looming to the north, we were suddenly ordered to transfer some 180km north-westwards to Vitebsk, an airfield closer to the boundary between Army Group Centre and Army Group North.

This latest transfer was carried out in even more of a hurry than those that had gone before. The situation was very volatile and confused, and we were told next to nothing about the actual conditions that awaited us in our new area of operations. We struck our tents with what was fast becoming practised ease and hastily stuffed all our kit and equipment into our *Gepäckbomben* – 'luggage-bombs' – as we called the cylindrical metal supply containers that accompanied us on our every move. At 08.15 hours all was ready and we took off from Shatalovka for the thirty-minute flight up to Vitebsk.

We had hardly touched down before I was sent straight back to Shatalovka, this time as a passenger aboard a Ju 52, to pick up another of the Staffel's Bf 110s that had had to be left behind. Our lost and damaged aircraft may have been replaced, but now it was the shortage of air crews that was becoming a problem. The costly operations of recent weeks had left their mark on the unit.

I landed back at Vitebsk at 16.50 hours and lost no time in pitching my tent and getting myself organized. That evening we sat around discussing developments. Our new situation gave us plenty to talk about, especially as we had been warned to take all kinds of precautions to ensure our personal safety. The area around Vitebsk, like so much of the newly-acquired territory in the East, was still full of Red Army stragglers cut off from their units and there was more than a possibility that the airfield could be attacked, or even overrun, at any time. Perhaps understandably, it was very late before we finally climbed into our beds for the night, trusting to luck – and the vigilance of our sentries – that we would live to see the morning.

We weren't able to fly any operational missions the next day as not all of the unit's technical support equipment had yet arrived. We spent the time instead studying maps to familiarize ourselves with the local area and trying to piece together what information there was on the current situation on the ground. There was a lot to take in, including the enemy's road and rail supply routes in this new region. We also did our best to memorize all the salient features of the local terrain in order to be able to make it back to friendly territory if the worst came to the worst. We didn't want to fall into the hands of the Soviets by mistake.

We took off for our first mission over the northern sector at 10.20 hours on the morning of 22 August. We had been briefed to attack any troop or supply movements we could find on the road and rail networks to the east of Velikiye Luki, a town about 130km to the north of Vitebsk.

Lacking any precise target details, we had to rely on our own devices once again and, as so often in the past few weeks, carry out our own reconnaissance. Splitting into *Schwärmen*, we searched the given area until we spotted the first signs of ground fighting and then spread out to gain at least a rough idea of the general situation. To the enemy's rear we came across only two targets worth attacking: a fairly large railway station occupied by a number of troop or supply trains, and another lengthy goods train on the move not far away.

We adopted our usual tactics of first dive-bombing and then strafing the trains standing in the station. Once these had been successfully dealt with we went after the moving train, which we quickly overhauled and attacked with cannon and machine-gun fire. The locomotive was put out of action in our very first pass. Almost hidden by the clouds of steam escaping from its boiler, it slowed to a stop, allowing us to concentrate all our attention on the now stationary line of wagons. By the time we had expended most of our ammunition many of these were burning fiercely. We had encountered very little ground fire and all four of our machines returned intact to Vitebsk, where we landed after a mission that had lasted exactly eighty minutes.

Despite our 'reconnaissance' activities, we were unable to add very much to the intelligence officer's meagre store of knowledge when it came to debriefing. The area was still totally unfamiliar to us and we had not recognized any distinctive landmarks that could be used as points of reference to identify the station we had attacked. We could only hope that those crews yet to return would be able to fill in a few more details.

That afternoon we were sent out on another mission to the same area; again targeting the enemy's rail traffic. Our tactics remained the same and this time proved even more successful. A number of trains were destroyed, a lot of rolling stock damaged, and several lengths of track torn up by our bombs.

This mission had lasted the best part of two hours and after touching down back at Vitebsk at 16.36 hours we finally learned at debriefing just how critical the situation around the Lake Ilmen area really was. Apparently the advance on Leningrad was in danger of coming to a complete halt unless General der Infanterie Erich von Manstein's motorized LVI. *Armeekorps* could block the Soviet counter-offensive south of the lake. Our Gruppe was being urged to provide maximum support for the troops on the ground, and the unit responded by giving of its utmost. There was no grousing at the extra effort being demanded of us, just a determination to get the job done. We all helped each other, constantly improvising to overcome the many difficulties that we faced.

The next day, 23 August, thus found us freed from rear area train-busting duties and despatched instead to give direct support to von Manstein's motorized infantry divisions which were engaged in heavy fighting against the Soviets to the north of Velikiye Luki. We took off at 04.50 hours – our mission: to prevent the enemy from regrouping and striking back at our troops.

With a full load of bombs and ammunition it took us some little while to reach the scene of the fighting. After a brief reconnaissance of the area we split into pairs and launched a series of individual attacks, dive-bombing the enemy's armour and artillery positions, and strafing his troops and soft-skinned vehicles. Unlike the trains we had been attacking for the last couple of days, the Red Army units north of Velikiye Luki were well defended by Flak. Each pass was met with massed, well-directed fire and nearly every one of the Staffel's aircraft, ours included, suffered damage to some degree. Fortunately there were no losses and we all got back safely to Vitebsk, where one pilot had to make a wheels-up landing.

At debriefing after this two-hour mission the news was much more positive. Apparently the Soviet counter-offensive had been repulsed and the situation in the Lake Ilmen area had stabilized. There was also a message of thanks from Manstein himself expressing his appreciation for the part we had played in support of his troops.

With no further missions scheduled, we were stood down for the rest of the day. It was a very welcome break after our recent hectic round of operations and we took full advantage of it, lazing in the sun outside our tents – almost all the Staffel's activities still took place in the open air, by the way – leisurely checking and cleaning our kit and equipment.

Around midday, however, I was given orders to fly back to the repair depot in Warsaw. It appeared that, on closer inspection, my machine had been more seriously damaged than at first thought. I duly flew back to Warsaw, with an intermediate stop at Minsk, and, after a day's wait, returned to Vitebsk via the same route on 25 August.

As my aircraft required extensive work, I had been given a replacement machine. This was powered by a very healthy-sounding pair of engines, which meant that my wireless-operator and I could look forward to our future missions with some degree of confidence. This last comment might again strike the reader as hardly worthy of mention. But to a pilot the condition of his engines was of the utmost importance.

There were some aircraft that you really couldn't do a lot with, but which were nonetheless classified as fit for front-line service. Nobody in authority was in the least interested in how you managed to cope with these tired old crates. As long as the engines didn't fall out of their mounts and the propellers continued to turn, the rest could look after itself – that was the official attitude. But only we knew how many other things could go wrong, and how the slightest problem could quickly escalate and land you in all sorts of hellishly tricky, not to say life-threatening, situations.

Any faults we reported were looked into, of course, but all too often a lack of a spare part or some other essential item of equipment made it impossible to effect a repair. But operations had to continue. And if a machine wasn't 100 per cent serviceable, we simply had to be aware of, and accept, its limitations. This was not a pleasant feeling when flying a combat mission and must have been particularly hard on our newer and less experienced crews. Just how many machines were lost as a result of minor technical faults during this period it is impossible to say.

I had returned from Warsaw only to discover that our deployment in support of Army Group North had come to an end. On that same 25 August we were transferred back south-eastwards some 270km to Sechinskaya. Here we were re-joined by those elements of the

Gruppe that had not accompanied us to Vitebsk but which had remained at Shatalovka. Having already seen action on the central and northern sectors of the front, the reunited I./SKG 210 was now about to find itself supporting the units of Generalfeldmarschall Gerd von Rundstedt's Army Group South.

After the phenomenal successes of the 'cauldron' battles in the opening days and weeks of the war against the Soviet Union and the subsequent capture of Smolensk in the first week of August, everyone naturally assumed that Army Group Centre's two *Panzergruppen* would continue their drive eastwards towards Moscow, which now lay only a matter of some 400km away.

But Hitler had other ideas, and his order of 21 August had thus come as a complete bombshell: 'The most important objective before the onset of winter is not the capture of Moscow, but the conquest of the Crimea ...'

This fundamental and totally unexpected shift of the main offensive southwards resulted in a major redisposition of the armoured forces on the Eastern Front. *Panzergruppe* 4 remained intact on the northern sector, but on the central sector the five *Armeekorps* that had hitherto made up *Panzergruppen* 2 and 3 were reduced to just two. This pair continued to operate under Army Group Centre, but were forbidden to advance any further eastwards and ordered instead to go over on to the defensive.

Of the remaining three central-sector *Armeekorps*, one had already been attached to *Panzergruppe* 4 in the north to assist in the siege of Leningrad. The other two were redirected southwards to reinforce Generaloberst Ewald Kleist's *Panzergruppe* 1 in the attack on Kiev. And it was to the south that we were being sent to provide additional support for the ground forces already engaged in the initial stages of the five-week 'cauldron' battle of Kiev.

I took off from Sechinskaya at 09.52 hours on the morning of 30 August 1941. It was my thirty-second mission of the war and our targets were trains and railway installations in the area east of Konotop, a town about 200km to the north-east of Kiev.

The bloody struggle for the Ukrainian capital, where over a million Soviet troops were fighting desperately to avoid encirclement, was already nine days old. We were given a foretaste of what awaited us in the days ahead before we even reached the target area. The moment we crossed over into enemy territory medium Flak opened up on us. It steadily grew in intensity until bursts seemed to fill the whole sky and we were forced to break formation in order not to make ourselves too closely bunched and easy a target for the Russian gunners.

As if that were not enough, the Red Air Force then decided to put in one of its rare appearances. But this particular gaggle of enemy fighters did not seem to be overly aggressive and even though we were still in fairly loose formation we managed to fend them off without too much bother. One of the attackers selected our machine as a likely-looking victim. But my wireless-operator/gunner held his nerve and his fire, letting the Russian pilot get to within 150m of us before giving him two brief bursts from his machine-gun. This was more than enough for our assailant, who immediately veered away and disappeared in a steep dive earthwards. We didn't see what became of him.

After successfully completing our mission, which we managed to do despite the intense opposition from the enemy, we did not return to Sechinskaya, but put down instead at Novgorod. This was to be our base for our future operations in the Kiev area.

But these could not begin straightaway. The intensity of the missions recently flown over the central and northern sectors, plus the frequent transfers from one airfield to the next, had had a disastrous effect on our serviceability figures. And it was not just the aircraft that were giving cause for concern. Wherever one looked within the Gruppe the shortages and deficiencies were all too apparent.

The situation had become so bad, in fact, that we were taken off ops entirely for several days. But this did not mean that there was time to relax. Everybody – mechanics, ground crews, storemen – was kept busy undertaking urgent repairs or trying to obtain replacement parts. We pilots were responsible for carrying out check flights of the aircraft that our own unit workshops had been able to repair. We also had to ferry those machines that needed more extensive work back to the base depot in Warsaw. Perhaps understandably, it was the older and more experienced air crews who were usually detailed for these jobs. Many of the aircraft that had to be got back to Warsaw had so many things wrong with them that they could hardly be called airworthy.

The 800km flight back to the depot in a faulty machine was chancy enough in itself, and bad weather *en route* could often pose additional problems. The briefings for these ferry flights were invariably sketchy. Weather reports were rarely available. Nor were there any ground navigational aids to fall back on if conditions worsened along the way. This is where experience came in. A pilot was completely on his own and had to rely on his own good judgement when deciding whether he had sufficient time and fuel to circumvent any bad weather front he might encounter, or whether he needed to find an intermediate landing ground and get down in a hurry.

On 31 August 1941 I was sent up to Sechinskaya to pick up one of these lame birds for ferrying back to Warsaw. My first stop was at Orsha. There I was asked to do a couple of works test flights. But no further complications were found and so I was able to continue on to Warsaw the next day. The Warsaw depot was too busy to handle my machine, however, and I was ordered to continue on the extra 100km down to Deblin-Irena, where it was taken in for a major overhaul.

For the next two weeks I thoroughly enjoyed the relative peace of life in the rear area far from the fighting front. During this time I was called upon to carry out several check flights of machines that had been repaired at Deblin. I also made a couple of ferry flights, which took me to Warsaw and to Schneidemühl, a town just over the Polish border in West Prussia. In the event, my machine wasn't returned to me after its overhaul. Instead, I was again entrusted with another brand new Bf 110 to take back to Novgorod.

Staging via Warsaw, Minsk and Sechinskaya, I touched down at Novgorod at 08.40 hours on the morning of 17 September and was immediately ordered to report to the ops room for a briefing. Here I was told of the loss four days earlier of our Gruppenkommandeur, Hauptmann Karl-Heinz Stricker. Apparently he had had both engines knocked out during a low-level train-busting sortie and had been killed in the ensuing crash. His wireless-operator/gunner Oberfeldwebel Karl Reiche had survived the impact, but was in a critical condition. However, this was not the time to dwell on such matters. I had just spent a relaxing couple of weeks far to the rear. I was in good shape. And I had a mission to fly.

At 10.05 hours, just eighty-five minutes after landing back at Novgorod, I took off again and headed for the area to the east of Kiev. It was here, in the early evening of 14 September, that the spearheads of *Panzergruppen* 2 and 1 – the former pushing down from the central sector, the latter circling around Kiev to the south – had made contact. This was the final stage of a gigantic pincer movement, the largest and most ambitious of the campaign to date, which had surrounded the Ukrainian capital and trapped the greater part of fifty Red Army divisions. The Soviets were now trying desperately to force a way into the Kiev 'cauldron' from the east to give those divisions an escape route out of the trap.

Elements of three Soviet armies were battering the exposed 25km-long eastern flank of *Panzergruppe* 2 at a number of points in their attempts to force open a breach in the ring of steel encircling Kiev. At Romny they had even got to within 800m of Generaloberst Guderian's forward observation post before being repulsed.

Our immediate task, therefore, was to provide direct support to relieve the pressure on our thinly-stretched Panzer divisions forming the eastern wall of the cauldron. We had been ordered to concentrate our attacks on the enemy's armour and artillery. But, as usual, the situation on the ground was one of total confusion and our initial exploratory reconnaissance sweeps stirred up an absolute maelstrom of Flak. It required an awful lot of determination to grit one's teeth and dive down into that almost solid cloud of exploding Flak shells. And even more luck to emerge still in one piece below it.

Then came the strafing runs. Here the watchwords were: show no signs of hesitation – think and act quickly – short bursts of fire to keep the enemy's heads down (although this didn't always work!) and keep jinking and weaving to spoil his aim. While at low level the wireless-operator/gunner was arguably the more important member of the crew. He had to keep his eyes open and his wits about him to report everything that was going on around us. My own wireless-operator/gunner was the perfect example. Rarely showing any excitement, his matter-of-fact voice kept up a kind of running commentary in my headphones as we thundered back and forth across the battlefield. Finally, with our magazines almost empty, we broke off and turned for home, landing back at Novgorod at the end of a mission that had lasted all of 100 minutes.

After debriefing and a hurried bite to eat, we were back in the air by 15.20 hours and ready to do it all over again. There was no shortage of targets. The Red Army may have been masters of camouflage, but even they were finding it impossible to hide the mass of men and material they were throwing into the battle for Kiev. Despite being faced by yet more heavy Flak, we successfully completed our mission before returning to Novgorod at 17.15 hours. It had been a gruelling day and the Staffel was lucky to have survived it without casualties and at the cost of just one battle-damaged aircraft being effectively written-off in a belly landing.

My next mission was on the morning of 19 September. Lasting from 06.40 hours until 08.25 hours, it was again in direct support of our ground forces to the east of Kiev. It may have been a rerun of the two sorties flown forty-eight hours earlier, but the tension was none the less for all that. Everyone seemed to have realized just how important these present missions were. The outcome of the battle for Kiev was clearly going to play a decisive part in the war against the Soviet Union. Its capture was of paramount importance if the Red Army's strength in the south was to be broken.

In fact, Kiev itself fell on that same 19 September, although the mass of enemy units trapped in the huge pocket to the east of the city continued to offer resistance for another seven days.

We flew two further ops on the day of Kiev's capture. The first was again in support of our troops in the field and the second against the enemy's rail network to the east of Novgorod. Between the two we had just eighty-five minutes to get our aircraft refuelled – by hand – rearmed and have a fresh bomb load attached to the belly and wing racks. The engines and fuselage also had to be checked for any evidence of damage.

Leaving these tasks in the capable hands of our ground crews, we then had to get over to the ops tent to give a full report on the mission just flown and receive a briefing for the next one. This left little time for the inner man. There was rarely time for a proper meal. We were lucky if we were able to snatch a hurried mouthful between all the other jobs that needed our attention. This must have had a detrimental effect on our well-being, but this was war and we all had to make the best of it. Everyone was in the same boat – indeed, many were far worse off than we were. So it was a case of stop griping and get on with it.

On 20 September we were given orders to move the 95km due south from Novgorod to Konotop. It was at Konotop, back on 7 September, that 3. *Panzerdivision* had broken through the Soviet front to launch the final drive which had closed the ring around the Kiev pocket. And even now, thirteen days later, the area was still not fully secure. As in nearly all newly won Russian territory numerous groups of Red Army stragglers, separated from their units, were roaming at large with the potential to cause a great deal of damage.

We had landed at Konotop at 15.52 hours. Unlike our recent bases, where we had lived and worked under canvas, Konotop was an established airfield. We lost little time in exploring it. From the well-equipped lecture rooms and the amount of illustrative teaching material lying scattered around – drawings of component parts, aircraft recognition charts, and the like – it was obvious that Konotop had been home to a Red Air Force flight training school. Everything was on a large scale, spacious and well organized. But we were not destined to enjoy the many amenities Konotop had to offer for long.

I flew my next mission the following day, 21 September. The target was once again the Soviet units trapped to the east of Kiev. It was little more than a repetition of our earlier sorties against the Kiev pocket, but now that we were based that much closer to the scene of the action it took only half the time from take-off to landing. Twenty-four hours later we were briefed for what would prove to be our final operation of the year on the Eastern Front.

The objective was Lebedin, a Soviet airfield only some 120km to the south-east of Konotop. The relatively short approach flight allowed us plenty of time over the target area. In a neat twist, our first period of operations against the Soviet Union would end as they had begun. For the attack itself was carried out in much the same way as those we had made against the enemy's frontier airfields at the start of the campaign. First we dive-bombed the hangars and technical sites, and then went in low to strafe the few aircraft dispersed about the field. At 12.50 hours on 22 September, after just sixty-five minutes in the air, I landed back at Konotop to complete my thirty-ninth mission of the war to date.

There had been rumours in the air for some time, but now it was official. The news that we were to return to Germany for conversion on to the Messerschmitt Me 210 was greeted with understandable relief. Truth be told, the past three months' campaigning on the Eastern Front had taken more of a toll on us all both physically and mentally than many of us would care to admit. Luckily, we didn't yet know what awaited us in the homeland!

The Messerschmitt Me 210 was the reason our Gruppe had been set up in the first place. It had been activated in the summer of 1940 to serve as a kind of operational trials unit to test the new Me 210's capabilities under combat conditions. But those capabilities were sadly deficient in almost every respect. Designed as a successor to the Bf 110, great hopes had been pinned on the Me 210. But it proved to be a disaster. And although our unit had at first retained its original designation as the *Erprobungsgruppe* (Test Wing) 210, it saw service in the Battle of Britain equipped solely with Bf 110s and Bf 109s.

Since that time, however, the Messerschmitt works had carried out an extensive programme of modifications and a new experimental unit – *Versuchsstaffel* 210, commanded by our erstwhile Staffelkapitän Oberleutnant Heinz Forgatsch – had been set up at the Rechlin test centre to determine whether the Me 210 was now fit for operational service. The signs were not good, however. Oberleutnant Forgatsch and his wireless-operator/gunner had both lost their lives when their Me 210 crashed during a training flight at Rechlin on 23 September.

But we were not bound for Rechlin. Our destination was Landsberg am Lech, an airfield about 50km to the west of Munich, where, despite the unsettling news from Rechlin, we were to start conversion training on the Me 210.

My own journey to Landsberg turned into quite a lengthy undertaking. We left Konotop on 25 September 1941 and headed north for Sechinskaya. The field at Sechinskaya had been greatly expanded in recent weeks and now served as our main forward supply depot. Its engineering shops also serviced and repaired our

Gruppe's aircraft, many of which had been showing distinct signs of wear and tear, not just from enemy action, but also from the rigours of hard use. Our own machine was in no worse shape than any of the others. Or so we thought. But the authorities at Sechinskaya had other ideas and flatly refused to let us continue on our way. We had to kick our heels for a whole week until a suitable replacement aircraft – in other words, one that was considered at least halfway airworthy – could be found for us.

Nobody bothered us very much during the seven days we were forced to spend at Sechinskaya. We used the time getting our personal kit into order. It too had suffered during our recent nomadic life under canvas and had been unceremoniously bundled into our Bf 110 for the transfer flight home. While on the subject, it was surprising just how quickly we had adapted to our open-air existence. We had not merely developed the ability to survive under the most basic of conditions, we had actually seemed to thrive on them.

Finally everything was ready. At 12.35 hours on Thursday 2 October we happily bade farewell to Sechinskaya as we lifted off on the next leg of our flight back to Germany. This was to take us to Deblin in Poland. After eighty-five minutes and with 490km already behind us, we put down at Minsk for a 45-minute refuelling break. But we couldn't wait to get back into the air again. We were in a great hurry and wanted nothing more than to get home as fast as possible.

But at Deblin we suffered another delay and it wasn't until 14.40 hours on the following afternoon, 3 October, that we were able to take off again. Because of this late start we only managed to make it as far as Guben, where we landed at 16.20 hours. It was still another 500km or so to Werl, the airfield near Osnabrück where we were to hand over our aircraft, but at least we were in Germany. And while the accommodation available to crews in transit through Guben was not what you'd call palatial, the prospect of an undisturbed night's sleep filled us with almost indescribable joy.

The next day saw us reach Werl without any further difficulties. Having surrendered our machine, we shouldered our kit and completed the rest of the journey down to Landsberg am Lech by rail, which provided us with another very comfortable and relaxing few hours.

Although we were now more than two years into the war, the airfield at Landsberg still retained much of its peacetime atmosphere. We immediately felt at home, and after a brief period of settling in, got down to our conversion training with a will.

The Messerschmitt Me 210 impressed us mightily. Our introduction to the machine was, however, somewhat basic as there were few qualified instructors or training staff serving at Landsberg. But one thing *was* drummed into us: we would need to treat our new mounts with a certain amount of caution until we could handle them properly and fully appreciate the improvements the Me 210 had to offer over the Bf 110.

The aircraft was a good 60km/h faster than its predecessor for a start. The bomb load was stowed internally rather than being carried on drag-inducing ventral racks. Its rate of climb was much more impressive and its dive capabilities far better suited to our operational requirements. The armament was harder-hitting and more effective, and the machine's navigational and radio equipment had undergone major improvement. It was also fitted with a tri-axial control system which, unfortunately, we were not yet entrusted to use. All in all, the consensus was that the Me 210 was a very sleek-looking bird, seemingly with a great deal of promise, and we were all looking forward eagerly to taking it up for the first time.

For me that time came on 14 November. I proceeded with great care, as one of the things we had been warned about was the Me 210's very nasty habit of swinging during take-off. Constant minor adjustments to the rudder and throttle settings were required to keep the aircraft on the straight and narrow. I got her off the ground without any undue difficulty, however, and performed a perfectly normal circuit lasting all of seven minutes.

With one under my belt and now knowing what to expect, my second take-off was a lot smoother. I remained aloft for nearly half-an-hour in order to get the feel of this new machine. I soon discovered that its flight characteristics were good and a definite step up from the Bf 110s that I had been used to of late. The two things that struck me in particular were the aircraft's manoeuvrability and rapid acceleration, neither of which had been terribly good on the Bf 110. The approach and landing seemed straightforward enough.

They differed from those of the Bf 110, of course, but not in any negative respect.

Once training got underway we practised bombing, aerial gunnery, dive-bombing and formation flying. We soon became used to the Me 210's little foibles and faced the future with a fair degree of optimism.

The first problems began to appear among the newer replacement crews. A spate of minor take-off and landing accidents resulted in the Gruppe's transfer to nearby Lechfeld, an airfield with longer runways and better technical facilities. Unfortunately, however, the winter of 1941/42 brought with it heavy snowfalls to southern Germany and we were to remain at Lechfeld for little more than six weeks, under ever worsening conditions, before being transferred again – this time to Tours in central France – on 2 March 1942.

Having staged via Regensburg-Obertraubling, where I had been ordered to pick up a new aircraft, I arrived at Tours on 3 March 1942. The sight that greeted me as I touched down was unexpected, to say the very least. A number of damaged machines littered the field. They were all Me 210s which had clearly come to grief on landing. That was all that registered for the moment, but when I went across to flying control to report my arrival, I was soon put in the picture.

Apparently things at Tours had not got off to a good start. The transfer flight from Lechfeld had been something of a disaster. One crew had already been killed, and many others had experienced problems when trying to land. A number of machines had suffered superficial damage and at least three would require more extensive repair.

But it didn't end there. Another aircraft would be damaged in a wheels-up landing after a training flight on 5 March, two more came to grief three days later, and on 9 March yet another pair sustained damage in forced landings, while a botched belly-landing wounded one crew and a crash killed another. Thus, in the space of just one week, the Gruppe had had four crew members killed and two wounded, and had suffered the loss of nearly a dozen aircraft – the equivalent of an entire Staffel – destroyed, written-off or damaged.

Apparently the incidents, without exception, had all involved our younger and less experienced crews. It was obvious that the Me 210's unstable behaviour in the air – not least its tendency to spin at the slightest provocation, especially at high angles of attack – were more than simply 'little foibles'. In fact, they were deadly vices that the Messerschmitt factory, despite numerous modifications, had been unable to eradicate.

The Me 210 had thus failed in its second attempt to be taken into service. A new decision about the machine's future needed to be made. It was not long in coming. In April 1942 production was finally brought to a halt. Those examples already serving with the Luftwaffe were withdrawn. We weren't allowed to keep ours, but had to convert back on to the old Bf 110 as we began preparing for the 1942 summer offensive on the Eastern Front. The Me 210 may have been deeply flawed, but it was nonetheless a bitter blow.

Altogether I had logged 31 hours and 14 minutes flying time on the Me 210. All but nine of the ninety-one flights that made up this total were basic circuits and bumps. The others comprised three bombing exercises, three aerial gunnery exercises, one dive-bombing practice flight and two ferry flights.

But the saga of the Me 210 was far from over. It underwent yet further modification and redesign to emerge at the end of 1942 as the Messerschmitt Me 410 'Hornisse' (Hornet), which finally entered service in the early summer of 1943. In all, a total of over one thousand Me 410s were built, and they went on to serve in a variety of roles, but not with our Gruppe.

And what of our Gruppe? I was not involved in the final chapter of its history as I./SKG 210. From Tours I was posted to the Luftkriegsschule (Air Warfare Academy) at Fürstenfeldbruck. And it was not until I had successfully completed the course there that I returned to my unit which, in the interim, had been redesignated to become I. Gruppe of a new and re-formed Zerstörergeschwader 1.

Chapter 10

Zerstörergeschwader 1

The course I attended at *Luftkriegsschule* (Air Warfare Academy) 4 at Fürstenfeldbruck helped to broaden my knowledge quite considerably over a wide range of subjects. But, not unnaturally, my main field of study was ground tactics. This was hardly surprising given my sometimes unpleasant experiences while flying ground-support operations on the Eastern Front the previous summer. But I felt I still had a lot more to learn and a lot of catching up to do.

I studied all the available files in minute detail and kept finding new questions to ask myself in my efforts to gain a better grasp and understanding of how the army conducted its operations. My task was made a whole lot easier by the help I received from an army major, who was an excellent teacher and expert in ground tactics. He was clearly pleased at my keen interest in the subject and took great pains to answer my many questions in a most thorough and comprehensive manner.

I had ample opportunity to explain and discuss with him my own views, gained from personal experience, on how the Luftwaffe carried out its direct ground-support missions. His comments and observations were a great help in preparing me for any such future operations and enabled me to work out in my own mind how missions of this kind could best be conducted.

The whole course was a very profitable and informative experience. The teaching staff did wonders in covering what was a very full curriculum in the short time available. The atmosphere was extremely relaxed throughout, with a mutual spirit of trust and comradeship between pupils and staff the whole time. The officer in charge of our group was an Oberleutnant Pawlik, whose straight-talking approach and keen intelligence commanded our total respect.

Towards the end of the course we were taken to the *Sportpalast* in Berlin to hear a speech given by Hitler to officers and officer-cadets on the developing political and military situation. Seated near the front of the hall, I was able experience the whole impressive spectacle from close quarters. Hitler spoke for nearly three hours and I listened in rapt attention as he described the events leading up to the war, the course it had taken to date, and his aims for the future. On the subject of the campaign against the Soviet Union, he said that the battles fought in the East thus far should be regarded as merely a prelude to what was to come in the months ahead.

It was not long before I found out for myself what was meant by that last remark. Shortly after our visit to Berlin, the Fürstenfeld-bruck course came to an end. Together with four others, I was immediately ordered to proceed by rail to Kharkov. We travelled via Berlin and Warsaw and the journey took several days in all. At Kharkov we were collected by truck and driven to the Gruppe's present base at Byelgorod, some 70km to the north.

A lot had changed since I had left Novgorod the previous September. For a start, Schnellkampfgeschwader 210 was no more. While our I. Gruppe had returned to Germany for its ultimately abortive attempt to convert on to the Me 210, II./SKG 210 had remained operational on the Eastern Front throughout the winter of 1941/42. Early in 1942 the two Gruppen had then been redesignated to become I. and II. Gruppe respectively of a new and reactivated Zerstörergeschwader 1 (the original Zerstörergeschwader 1 of the early war years having long since ceased to exist).

At the same time, an entirely new III./ZG 1 had been formed from three separate *Heeresaufklärungsstaffeln* (army tactical recon-naissance squadrons). But unlike I. and II./ZG 1, which were currently in the process of re-equipping with Me 110Fs – a marginally improved version of their earlier Me 110Es – III./ZG 1 was to fly single-engined Bf 109E fighter-bombers.

The change of identity from SKG 210 to ZG 1 had also brought with it a new Geschwader emblem. Hitherto our Bf 110s had carried a small shield depicting a map of the British Isles seen through a gunsight. This dated back to the days of the original *Erprobungsgruppe* 210 and was no doubt a very apt motif during the

147

Battle of Britain. But it had seemed rather out of place once we began operating over the Soviet Union. Now, however, the unassuming and anachronistic little shield was gradually being replaced by one of the most distinctive and flamboyant emblems ever to adorn a Luftwaffe aircraft: a huge, stylized wasp carried on both sides of our Bf 110s (and the Bf 109s!) noses. There was no mistaking our identity now. Soon we would be known to one and all, friend and foe alike, as the '*Wespengeschwader*' – the 'Wasp Group'.

The unit's recent history had not been an altogether happy one. In the last three days of May 1942 our 3. Staffel alone had lost three machines in crashes while *en route* to the front. In addition to its normal complement of pilot and wireless-operator/gunner, each Bf 110 had also been carrying its crew chief. In all, nine lives were lost, including that of Oberleutnant Georg Boxhammer, who had taken over as Staffelkapitän after Oberleutnant Heinz Forgatsch's appointment to the command of *Versuchsstaffel* 210 back in August 1941.

Much may have changed, but one thing had stayed the same: the type of operations we were required to fly. My first mission as a member of ZG 1 – and my fortieth overall – was on 6 July 1942. It was a combined dive-bombing and ground-strafing sortie in support of our troops fighting in the Nikolayev region, a good 200km to the south-east, and was very similar to the many such operations we had carried out the previous year. The following day I flew another mission to the same area.

The situation on the ground in this sector seemed very unclear to me at first and it took me some time to get my bearings and gain at least some understanding of the enemy's positions. I wasn't at all familiar with the local topography and had to make quite an effort to ensure that I was pulling my weight with the rest of the Staffel. The ops room personnel gave me a lot of support and slowly any feelings of uncertainty on my part began to fade; hesitancy was the last thing you needed when flying a combat mission.

The familiar evening get-togethers to discuss the day's events also proved a great help in getting acclimatized to the front all over again, although the circle was now much smaller and there were quite a number of new faces whose acquaintance I had yet to make.

The Eastern Front in the summer of 1942 was very different to what it had been twelve months earlier. In 1941 all eyes had been focussed on Moscow. But now the major emphasis was to the south. Hitler had spelled it out very clearly in his *Führer* Directive No.41 of 5 April 1942:

The winter battle in Russia is nearing its end. Thanks to the unparalleled courage and self-sacrificing devotion of our soldiers on the Eastern Front, German arms have achieved a great defensive success ...

... As soon as the weather and the state of the terrain allow, we must seize the initiative again, and through the superiority of German leadership and the German soldier impose our will upon the enemy ...

... In pursuit of the original plan for the eastern campaign, the armies of the central sector will stand fast, those in the north will capture Leningrad and link up with the Finns, while those on the southern flank will break through down into the Caucasus.

In view of the conditions prevailing at the end of winter, the availability of troops and resources, and transport difficulties, these aims can only be achieved one at a time.

First, therefore, all available forces will be concentrated on the main operations in the southern sector, with the aim of destroying the enemy before the Don, in order then to secure the Caucasian oilfields and the passes through the Caucasus Mountains.

The opening phase of the 1942 summer offensive, code-named Operation '*Blau*' ('Blue'), was to be another giant pincer movement. The northern arm of this pincer, comprising the 6. *Armee* and the 4. *Panzerarmee*, was to advance eastwards from the Kursk and Kharkov areas to the River Don, where it was to take the town of Voronezh and then follow the line of the Don southwards to link up with the southern arm of the pincer, consisting of the 17. *Armee* and 1. *Panzerarmee*, pushing up from the lower Don. This would effectively trap the bulk of the Soviet Southern Front in the Great Don Bend to the west of Stalingrad.

The Russians, however, had learned the lessons of the previous summer. They were no longer willing to cling stubbornly to every major town and sacrifice countless thousands of troops to encirclement and capture in the process. Instead, Marshal Timoshenko pulled his forces back across the Don, leaving the arms of Army Group South's gigantic pincer manoeuvre to clang shut on an almost empty pocket.

Hitler completely misread the situation. He failed to recognize that the Soviet withdrawal was part of a deliberate plan of 'trading territory for time'. He believed that the Russians were at the end of their strength and saw the enemy's retreat across the Don as little more than disorganized flight. And so, in just the same way as he had overruled his generals the previous year by ordering a halt to the advance on Moscow, he now made another of his 'intuitive' strategic decisions. But this one would have even more disastrous consequences.

The *Führer* ordered 4. *Panzerarmee* to wheel due south and join forces with 1. *Panzerarmee* in a massive armoured drive down into the Caucasus, leaving 6. *Armee* to march on alone towards Stalingrad – and into history.

The southern sector was thus split irrevocably in two, with the two parts on totally separate and ever diverging paths: the one leading due east to Stalingrad, and the other, larger force heading south into the Caucasus. Such a division of strength, which was entirely Hitler's doing, was a recipe for disaster. And disaster is what followed.

This then, in the very broadest of strokes, was the background against which we would be operating in the weeks and months to come.

Our reconnaissance had picked up heavy Soviet traffic moving south-eastwards on the rail and road networks to the south of Millerovo. This was presumably part of the enemy's general withdrawal back across the Don. But at Byelgorod, which was a good 325km distant, we were too far away from the target area to be able effectively to intervene. And so on 8 July, just three days after my arrival at Byelgorod, the Gruppe was ordered to transfer the 240km down to Konstantinovka.

I flew my first mission out of Konstantinovka the very next morning. It was now little more than 70km to the scene of the action around the town of Lissichansk on the River Donets, where we were ordered first to dive-bomb enemy artillery positions and then carry out ground-strafing in support of our own troops.

As usual, the pre-op briefing offered very few details as to the current situation on the ground. This meant we would have to be extremely careful not to attack our own troops. Unfortunately, it also meant that the extra time we thus needed to spend reconnoitring the battlefield would again give the enemy ample opportunity to let fly at us with every gun he could bring to bear. In situations such as this, success very much depended on just how quickly we could spy out the land, and what sort of dummy manoeuvres we could make to disguise our true intentions from the Russians.

I flew a second mission to the same area later in the day. We were met with heavy fire on both occasions. And this particular Soviet Flak was not only heavy, it was also unusually well directed, which made dive-bombing with any accuracy that much more difficult.

Just before reaching friendly territory while returning from this second operation, the Red Air Force quite suddenly and un-expectedly decided to put in an appearance and we found ourselves under attack from a group of about fifteen to twenty Polikarpov I-153s. These agile little biplanes were almost impossible to get to grips with as our Bf 110s were simply too sluggish to indulge in dogfighting of the classic kind.

I was nonetheless able to shoot one of them down a minute or two into the encounter although, to be perfectly honest, it was more a matter of luck than skill. My 'opponent' popped up out of nowhere right in front of my nose. He was so close I almost rammed him, and it was sheer reflex that made me jab the gun button. At that range I couldn't miss, and the I-153 tipped over and went down shedding pieces. To this day I haven't the slightest idea where he came from. The *melée* didn't last long and the enemy machines disappeared as quickly as they had come. Fortunately we returned to Konstantinovka without loss, albeit all a little shaken by the suddenness of the attack and with two pilots slightly wounded.

The two missions I flew on 10 July – my forty-fourth and forty-fifth of the war – were identical to those of the day before. The Flak over the target area was still as fierce, but at least we now knew what to expect. The terrain was more familiar and we had a good idea of where we would find the enemy. We had discussed all these points the previous evening and had decided to alter our tactics accordingly.

We therefore reduced our initial circling of the battlefield to an absolute minimum and instead bored straight into the attack almost at once, following our usual procedure of first dive-bombing and then strafing the enemy. It seemed to pay dividends, for we all got back to base with far fewer holes in our aircraft.

But there was still room for improvement. The Staffel usually flew and attacked in individual *Schwärmen*, tactical units of four machines made up of two pairs. But this posed problems of its own, particularly in the opening dive-bombing phase of our attacks. The tactics we now employed were for the two sections of the *Schwarm* to dive separately, but as close behind one another as possible. In practice, however, this meant that the second pair had to wait until the two aircraft in front of them were pulling out of their dives before they could follow. This interval between dives might be brief, but it was long enough for the target often to be obscured by the rising clouds of black smoke from the leading pair's bombs.

Communications caused further problems. It could on occasion be very difficult for the *Schwarmführer* accurately to describe the specific target he had selected to attack. As a result, the second pair sometimes didn't just miss the intended target, they attacked a different one entirely!

This could lead to recriminations back at base. Post-op debriefings frequently became quite heated, but nobody could come up with a suitable solution until, in the end, it was decided to reduce the size of the tactical unit even further. In future we would no longer normally fly in *Schwärmen*, but in separate pairs.

The final stages of most of our operational missions, the strafing runs, could also be problematical at times. One of our main concerns – apart from any reaction on the part of the enemy, of course – was the matter of identification. With both sides employing such large numbers of troops, and with the situation on the ground still extremely fluid, any intelligence regarding positions and locations we might be given at briefing could well be out of date by the time we arrived over the target area.

Our own forces used white flares as a means of identification and to indicate their whereabouts. But the Soviets quickly caught on to this and also began firing white flares as well in an attempt to deceive us. We very soon realized what they were up to and took great care whenever flares were directed up at us from the ground. Unlike ours, the Russian flares were not pure white, but had a faint yellowish tinge to them. This subtle difference, however, was not always easy to spot in the heat of battle, and especially not in bright sunlight.

Another means of identification were the so-called '*Fliegertücher*', literally 'flying cloths'. These were large panels of brightly-coloured fabric – more often than not the national flag would be used – which could be laid out on the ground or draped across vehicles to indicate the position of friendly forces. But this system was by no means infallible. The enemy would frequently display large strips of red cloth in front of his own positions and so, in the end, it all came down again to our own powers of observation.

The local terrain and the weather conditions also had a direct bearing on the measure of success achieved during the operations we were currently engaged in. Due to our troops' rapid advances, and the constantly changing areas we were being required to target, it was simply not always possible to familiarize ourselves with the local topography beforehand. This made navigation all the harder – if indeed you could call it navigation. There were no radio beacons or any other kind of ground navigational aids within our immediate area of operations. All we had were our maps, and these were sometimes more of a hindrance than a help.

In most cases the time available to prepare for our missions was so limited that we were rarely given a pre-op briefing in the true sense of the word. Everything had to be done in a hurry. But at least the weather was usually on our side. Day after day the midsummer sun blazed down out of a clear blue sky. We used this to our advantage, setting up our attacks so that we had the sun at our backs whenever possible. This impaired the enemy's vision and his aim, and was particularly effective during early morning and late evening missions when we would come in low and be almost invisible against the glare of the rising or setting sun.

The countryside had been baked hard by the unremitting summer heat. Any significant troop or convoy movements were easily spotted from the clouds of dust they threw up. Panzers and other tracked vehicles were the worst culprits for creating dust storms. After a while we found ourselves able to judge from quite some distance away what kind of target lay ahead of us simply from the amount of dust hanging in the air. The bare landscape also made retiring from the scene of battle that much easier. We didn't have to worry about any major obstacles *en route*, although we still had to be careful when navigating our way back to base as many of the water courses shown on our maps had dried up and were no longer visible.

Between 12 and 16 July I flew five more missions of a similar nature, together with one that was directed primarily against rail traffic. Reflecting the enemy's continuing withdrawal, our target areas were constantly shifting southwards and soon we found ourselves attacking objectives along the line of the Lower Don itself.

By this time I was flying most of my missions either in the role of *Schwarmführer*, or as the number one of a pair. My newly acquired knowledge of ground tactics gained from the recent course at Fürstenfeldbruck was clearly paying off and I felt a new degree of confidence. Our normal daily routine differed little from that of the previous summer. We were back under canvas and adjusted our way of life accordingly. There was the same healthy spirit of unity and comradeship. We were all in the same boat and we all faced the same risks when flying ops. There was no sense of apathy among us, although now and again a certain sense of weariness would become apparent. But this was only to be expected given the nature and the frequency of the operations we were being called upon to carry out.

Despite the sometimes oppressive heat we all had surprisingly hearty appetites and, with our cook continuing to work wonders, we were very well fed. We suffered few illnesses as the medical officer kept a close check on us. We were given regular injections against a variety of contagious diseases and so had little to fear in that direction. At the end of the day's labours we all slept soundly. In fact, with no outside distractions or temptations of any kind, we led remarkably simple and healthy lives.

This was no bad thing, for we were all very well aware of the dangers and privations that we would face if we were unlucky enough to be brought down over enemy territory and had to try to make it back to our own lines on foot. We had all heard and read first-hand accounts of pilots who had undergone that experience and knew that the fitter we were, and the greater our own powers of endurance, the better our chances of survival should we find ourselves in a similar situation.

As the fighting fronts moved steadily southwards, so too did we. By the middle of the month Konstantinovka was already too far from the battlefields to allow us to provide effective ground-support. On 17 July we therefore transferred the 90km south to Kuteinikovo.

By this stage heavy fighting was raging around the Don crossings as units of 17. *Armee* began their push down into the Caucasus. On 19 July I flew two missions in the Rostov-Bataisk area. Our tasks were threefold: to provide air cover above the bridgeheads across the Don, to attack the Soviet forces defending them, and to support our troops as they sought to expand their toeholds on the far side of the river. We were engaged mostly in low-level bombing and strafing runs. The fighting on the ground was clearly visible and the scenes that flashed past close beneath our wings as we hunted for suitable targets were gruesome to behold. Even the effects of our own cannon and machine-gun fire were plain to see as we cut bloody swathes through the massed enemy below.

On 20 July we turned our attention to enemy troops holding out at Konstantinovsk and Nikolayevskaya, two villages on the Don upriver from Rostov. And on 23 and 24 July I took part in five further missions in the Rostov area, all in direct support of our ground forces. The action was now concentrated mainly around the bridges at Bataisk, which were only taken after heavy fighting. Twenty-four hours later, on 25 July, I logged my sixtieth operational mission of the war, again in support of the Don crossings. Later that same day, after barely more than a week at Kuteinikovo, we moved south yet again, this time to Lakademenovka on the shores of the Sea of Azov.

After the broiling heat of the steppe, it made a very welcome change to be this close to a large body of water. We set up camp in the usual fashion, excited as a bunch of schoolboys on a trip to the seaside and determined to make the most of our good fortune, for we knew full well that our stay here wasn't likely to last long either.

The Caucasus offensive was beginning to make good progress and we continued to support the advance of our ground troops. I flew three missions on 26 July, one of which was directed against a group of Soviet tanks that was blocking the path of our motorized infantry. The enemy armour was speedily dealt with, leaving the way clear for our spearheads to resume their drive southwards.

Another of this day's three missions was something of a novelty for us: a maritime reconnaissance sweep along the coast of the Sea of Azov. And it was in this unlikely setting that I claimed my second aerial victory when our *Schwarm* was attacked by a gaggle of I-153s over open water some 35km to the south-west of Taganrog. This time success didn't come quite as easily as it had done over Lissichansk back on 9 July. The pilots of this group of Polikarpovs were far more belligerent than their earlier counterparts. They clearly weren't going to be content with making just a few token passes and then shearing off. In fact, they carried out attack after attack on us. Fortunately, their marksmanship did not match their aggression. We suffered no losses but did inevitably collect a number of bullet holes.

Although the Bf 110 was not designed to dogfight with agile little biplanes, we not only managed to hold the enemy machines off, but even succeeded in bringing a couple down during the course of the running fight. If I'm honest, my second victory did also involve a certain amount of luck. I saw one of the Soviet fighters sitting on the tail of another Bf 110. The enemy pilot was concentrating so hard on his intended victim that he didn't spot me curving in towards him until it was far too late. The I-153 stood no chance of survival after taking a full burst from my nose armament and went down into the sea.

On 28 July we were back over *terra firma* and I flew two missions against Soviet artillery emplacements that were bombarding the Don crossings upriver from Rostov. The gun positions had been well camouflaged and we came under heavy ground fire as we searched for them. Luckily there was no sign of the Red Air Force, and so we were able to concentrate fully on the task in hand: finding and silencing the enemy guns. We decided that the best way to go about it was to split the *Schwarm* up and carry out individual searches and attacks. This proved to be the right thing to do. All four of us were familiar with the area from earlier operations and used our knowledge of the terrain to good effect; locating and knocking out the enemy gun positions one by one.

As expected, we weren't allowed to enjoy the delights of Lakademenovka for long, and on 29 July we were ordered to transfer the 100km or so eastwards to Rostov. The city had been secured just four days earlier, together with the large bridge at nearby Bataisk. At Rostov we were far better placed to cover the major crossing points further upstream where the armoured divisions of 1. and 4. *Panzerarmeen* – the original *Panzergruppen* 1–4 of '*Barbarossa*' days having been redesignated 1.–4. *Panzerarmeen* during the winter of 1941/42 – were beginning their thrust down into the Caucasus.

Being that much closer to the scene of the fighting meant that we could spend at least a good hour over the battlefield. It really made a difference. With some half-dozen or more of our aircraft constantly roaring back and forth low above their heads, our troops were afforded some much-needed respite. The enemy's attention was diverted away from them as he concentrated instead on keeping out of the way of our cannon and machine-gun fire.

But the length of time thus spent meant that we had to be very careful with our ammunition in case we exhausted it too quickly. We would therefore intersperse our live strafing runs with dummy attacks. We also switched targets at the last moment and came in from different directions, all at high speed, and all in order to confuse and keep up the pressure on the enemy. This was best done with three or four pairs of aircraft working the area over in unison. It proved a very effective method of supporting our forces as they crossed the Don and advanced on the River Manych, the last major water barrier that stood in their way before the open country of the Caucasus. These missions usually lasted on average about two hours. I flew one such on 30 July and another two the following day.

Our operations may have been arduous, but they represented only a fraction of our day's duties. And they wouldn't have been possible at all were it not for the tireless labours of our dedicated ground crews who toiled unceasingly from dawn till dusk, sweltering through the heat of the midday sun, as they refuelled and re-armed the machines of each returning *Schwarm* or pair, checking and servicing, repairing battle damage where necessary, all the while under time pressure to get the aircraft back into the air again as quickly as possible.

On 1 August 1942 – the eighth anniversary, incidentally, of my joining what was then still known as the *Reichsheer*, the 100,000-man strong army which Germany had been allowed to keep by the victorious Allies of the First World War – I set out with a *Schwarm* on a reconnaissance flight that, for all the wrong reasons, is still vivid in my memory.

The weather when we took off from Rostov at 06.25 hours was far from good. Visibility was poor and the sky partially cloudy. There was a high bank of fog building off to the east – so no lack of meteorological information to be included in my post-op report.

I was unfamiliar with the country to the north-east of Rostov and the absence of any distinctive features in the flat landscape soon saw me getting into difficulties with my navigational map-reading. Our mission was to locate and report on the enemy forces retreating eastwards across the Great Don Bend. Our four aircraft headed north-east flying in loose formation. Due to the combination of low-lying mist and a continuing build-up of high-level fog we kept losing sight of the ground. Apart from the occasional glimpse of one or two vehicles on the roads below, I could detect no signs of any major troop movements. I altered course a number of times in my search for the elusive enemy, but without result; whatever Red Army units were still in the area remained hidden from view.

From time to time I asked my wireless-operator/gunner to mark our current position on his flight map. But this he was apparently unable to do as he was becoming increasingly uncertain as to our exact whereabouts. After a fruitless hour spent searching, I set course back to Rostov – or, at least, I thought I did.

Every now and then I caught sight of a solitary vehicle ploughing along one of the roads or dirt tracks – there wasn't much difference between the two, to be honest – that meandered across the bare expanse of the open steppe. The visibility continued to deteriorate and before long I had lost sight of the ground altogether. Time was passing and my initial feelings of unease were rapidly turning into anxiety. I had absolutely no idea where we were, and the last thing I wanted to do was run out of fuel and end the mission with our four machines sitting on the ground in the middle of nowhere.

Then, quite by chance, there was a break in the cloud and I spotted what appeared to be an airfield below us. I signalled to the other pilots and banked into a wide curve preparatory to touching down. The place appeared so quiet and deserted that I began to worry it might still be in Russian hands. As a precaution, we taxied in single file one close behind the other across to a small cluster of buildings where we made a 180° turn, facing back out towards the take-off line in case we had to make a quick getaway.

We kept our engines running as we had no intention of staying on the ground any longer than was absolutely necessary. We simply wanted directions and then to be on our way again as quickly as possible. I climbed cautiously out of my machine and took in the scene around me. After a few minutes a small group of our own soldiers came strolling out towards us. They were clearly surprised by our unexpected arrival, but were in no kind of hurry.

I beckoned them across to us, while indicating to the other pilots to switch off their engines. Then we all got together to try to sort out the situation. We spread one of our maps out on the ground and attempted, with the help of the soldiers, to pinpoint our location. It wasn't easy. The ground troops were as much in the dark as we were. We had only a very rough idea of where we might be, and they were extremely vague as to their unit's precise position. Finally, and only after a lot of discussion, we decided that we had landed at Morosovskaya – we had unwittingly flown almost halfway to Stalingrad!

We had already spent 115 minutes in the air and so it was high time to start thinking about refuelling. We therefore opted to make the short, twelve-minute hop to Tatsinskaya, which the map told us was only about 45km away to the south-west. After topping up our tanks there, we set off back to Rostov where we finally touched down without further incident at 12.05 hours.

The results of our 'reconnaissance' were meagre, to say the least. The enemy forces had either retired from the area completely or had camouflaged themselves so cleverly that we had failed to spot them, although the latter seemed somewhat unlikely given the flat, featureless nature of the terrain. The weather had not been at all favourable for such a mission, and with no ground navigation aids to guide us our lack of success was not altogether surprising. But there was no hint of censure at debriefing. We were all four back safely. That was the main thing, we were told.

At 14.55 hours we took off again. This time we were heading south-south-east to Belaya-Glina down in the Caucasus where an armoured train was reported to be holding up the leading elements of 1. *Panzerarmee* as they advanced on the important town of Armavir. We had little difficulty in locating and attacking the target, despite its attempt to hide behind a thin line of trees. We returned to Rostov after a two-hour flight and later received a message from the troops on the ground thanking us for our assistance and complimenting us on the accuracy of our bombing.

But there was little time to bask in the glow of 'mission accomplished' and a job well done. After just sixty minutes we were off again on our third and final operation of that eventful day. Our destination was Belaya-Glina once more, but our brief now was to attack the large groups of enemy forces that were withdrawing south-eastwards towards the foothills of the Caucasus Mountains. And twenty-four hours later, on 2 August, I returned to the Belaya-Glina region for a third time, again with orders to attack the retreating enemy.

In some places, however, our forces were again meeting more determined resistance. On 3 and 4 August we flew ground-support missions to Ssalsk and Armavir respectively, both areas where our Panzers were heavily engaged against Soviet armoured units.

And yet, despite the enormous territorial gains our ground forces were making, the overall situation was not developing to our advantage. Hitler had interpreted – or rather, misinterpreted – Marshal Timoshenko's strategic withdrawals across the Don, eastwards towards Stalingrad and south-eastwards down into the Caucasus, as signs of the weakening, if not the imminent collapse, of the entire Soviet Southern Front.

As a consequence, the *Führer* decided that he could well afford to redeploy some of his own forces currently engaged in southern Russia. He transferred the whole of 11. *Armee* up to the northern sector where it was to help in the taking of Leningrad. And with the spectre of an Allied 'Second Front' somewhere along the Channel coast already beginning to exercise his mind, Hitler also ordered a number of élite formations to be withdrawn from the Don area and sent to north-west Europe.

With Army Group South's having been split into two only weeks before – *Heeresgruppe* A for the advance down into the Caucasus, *Heeresgruppe* B for the march on Stalingrad – this further depletion of our forces boded ill for the future. Neither force was strong enough to carry out the tasks demanded of it. The units of *Heeresgruppe* A for example, which we were supporting, were required not only to advance across some 500km of open country in temperatures of up to 50° and then scale the heights of the Caucasus, a mountain range which included Mount Elbrus – at 5,642m the highest peak in Europe – but also to occupy the entire eastern coastline of the Black Sea, thereby 'eliminating the enemy's Black Sea fleet', and capture the oilfields along the Caspian coast.

We did the best we could, flying shuttle missions each and every day, and assisting our army units as effectively as we were able to with the means at our disposal. Our ground crews came under even greater pressure during this period. In addition to keeping our aircraft serviceable, they were also responsible for ensuring that our many moves went smoothly. For such were the distances that we were now having to fly in order to reach some of our more distant targets that we were finding it necessary to make use of additional advanced landing grounds where we could put down to refuel.

As a case in point, after the morning mission of 4 August down to Armavir we had to land at Yegorlik to top up our tanks before making it back to Rostov. And it was the same in the afternoon when we took off at 16.10 hours and headed south, flying some 250km down to the River Kuban, where our troops were encountering fierce resistance as they tried to secure a crossing. Again we had to stop on the way back to refuel at Yegorlik before reaching Rostov.

We flew a similar mission the next day, but on 6 August we made use of Belaya-Glina as an advanced landing ground, putting down to refuel there on both the outward and return flights during yet another operation in support of our Panzers, which were still heavily engaged in the fight for the Kuban crossings.

We took off from Rostov at 04.09 hours the following morning to fly the 100km back down to Yegorlik in readiness for our next round of missions. With the spearheads of 1. *Panzerarmee* having by this time established a toehold on the south bank of the Kuban, they were now facing another water barrier, and this was our target for the day. The River Laba was a fast-flowing tributary of the Kuban, but it was nowhere near as strongly defended as the main stream.

From Yegorlik we were able to maintain a near-unbroken succession of *Schwarm*-strength shuttle missions to the target areas along the Laba. Our constant presence and frequent low-level strafing runs along the line of the river forced the enemy to keep his head down and, as we learned later, were a great help to our troops as they 'bounced' this latest obstacle in their path southwards. We collected quite a number of bullet holes in our aircraft, but fortunately suffered no casualties.

I note from my logbook that I had flown thirty-eight missions from five different airfields and two advanced landing grounds in the month leading up to this 7 August, which illustrates just how mobile and adaptable we had become. But we couldn't have done it without the untiring support of our ground crews. We were totally dependent upon their sterling work and greatly appreciated their efforts. But they received little or no recognition from higher quarters. We could only assume that their labours were not looked upon as deserving of special mention, but were simply regarded as part of their normal duties. The term 'unsung heroes' might have been coined for them.

On 9 August we moved down to Kerch on the eastern tip of the Crimean Peninsula. As most of the 300km from Rostov to Kerch would take us across the Sea of Azov, we were ordered to undertake the transfer flight as a maritime-reconnaissance mission. Although we enjoyed the still relative novelty of another long overwater flight – the late morning sunlight glinting off the waves far below us was a glorious sight – we saw no sign of the enemy. There was no gaggle of unfriendly Polikarpovs this time, and so we had little to report upon our arrival at Kerch at 12.35 hours after nearly two hours in the air.

The next nine days were fairly uneventful. Our aircraft were showing clear signs of wear and tear from their recent heavy use. Nearly all of them required a major service and many were in need of an urgent repair of some sort or another. The short break did us all a world of good. Apart from a few check flights, we spent most of our time relaxing and exploring the surrounding countryside. There was even time to put pen to paper again and write one or two letters home.

On 19 August we were ordered to fly an armed reconnaissance mission of the area around the Black Sea port of Novorosissk. I didn't find it a pleasurable experience. As soon as we crossed over into enemy-held territory we were met by a veritable inferno of Flak. A number of machines, including my own, took hits. An enemy shell blew a sizeable hole in my left wing. The aircraft became difficult to control and my port engine soon gave up the ghost altogether. I was still in the thick of the barrage and it took me quite some time to work my way out of it, being thrown about all the while by near misses from medium and heavy Flak. When I finally emerged we were completely on our own. There was no sign of the other three aircraft of our *Schwarm*. I limped back to Kerch on the one engine. It was a nerve-wracking flight and I breathed a heartfelt sigh of relief upon our safe arrival.

This was to be my one and only operation from the Crimea, for later that same day we were given orders to return to the mainland. Our destination was Frolov, a landing ground located almost in the centre of the Great Don Bend and just 150km away from our new area of operations ... Stalingrad.

It was a good 800km from Kerch to Frolov and so we staged via Armavir. There were no permanent buildings at Frolov. All the Gruppe's activities were conducted in the open air or under canvas. The heat was stultifying, but we had been issued with some rather smart and luxurious tropical tents and quickly made ourselves at home. As well as being almost unbearably hot, the atmosphere at Frolov also proved to be very tense at times, particularly during the hours of darkness when the Red Air Force sent over light aircraft to carry out night harassment raids. But a hastily-dug slit trench soon appeared outside each of our camouflaged tents, offering its occupants at least some degree of protection against these nocturnal visitors.

The ops tent was situated at the edge of the runway, although the word 'runway' is perhaps a little misleading. In reality, Frolov consisted of nothing more than a large flat expanse of very hard, sun-baked steppe. The dispersal points and our field workshop were well separated as a precaution against enemy bombing raids, but all were within a reasonable distance of each other. This was important as the only means we had of getting about was our own two feet. The field kitchen was also nearby, but drinking water had to be brought in by a horse-drawn tanker wagon. In the prevailing heat it was always lukewarm by the time it arrived. Only the first early-morning delivery of the day was still refreshingly cold.

The field telephone was always located close to hand, so that we could be contacted at a moment's notice. Nobody left the base. There was no reason to. One patch of open steppe looked very much like the next patch of open steppe. Nor did we see any signs of the local inhabitants, if indeed there were any.

At 05.25 hours on 23 August 1942 we lifted off from Frolov for our first mission against Stalingrad. We had been briefed to attack any rail traffic we found in the area around the city. We were as yet unfamiliar with the region, of course, and so we first had to get to know our way around this new area of operations. Despite the barren nature of the terrain there were some excellent visual aids to navigation. The sweep of the River Don as it flowed around the Great Don Bend was unmissable, as was the town of Kalach on its banks, over which we would fly on the direct route to Stalingrad.

The landscape was alien, almost sinister. From above, the ground in front of Stalingrad resembled the wrinkled hide of an elephant. We were advised to familiarize ourselves with its contours as quickly as possible – and with good reason. Every fold and dip seemed to be hiding a battery of Flak guns, which threw up a wall of fire every time we passed overhead.

We soon came to recognize the major landmarks between the Great Don Bend and the River Volga – the settlements, the roads and the railway lines – which were essential points of reference for rapid orientation and for reconnaissance purposes. We almost always crossed the Don at Kalach. From here it was just 60km due east to Stalingrad. The city itself stretched for some 40km along the near bank of the Volga. It was divided into roughly two halves. To the north was the factory district, while in the southern, more residential area were the main railway station, the city's Red Square, and the huge grain silo; the latter trio all excellent landmarks for our forthcoming operations.

During the first three weeks of August, while we had been engaged in supporting the units of *Heeresgruppe* A in their drive down into the Caucasus, *Heeresgruppe* B had been carrying out a large-scale pincer movement aimed at eliminating all enemy forces in the Great Don Bend. On 21 August elements of General der Infanterie Walter Seydlitz's LI. *Armeekorps* had fought their way across the 100m-wide River Don to the north of Kalach and had established bridgeheads at Luchinsky and Vertyachy.

And just forty-eight hours later, on 23 August – the day we flew our first mission against Stalingrad – armoured spearheads of 16. *Panzerdivision* were standing on the steep banks of the mighty, two-kilometre wide River Volga at Rynok, the northernmost suburb of Stalin's namesake city.

At Frolov we now came under the command of the famous VIII. *Fliegerkorps*, whose Ju 87 Stukas had formed the Luftwaffe's main close-support force since the very start of the war. We may have been placed under a new command, we may have been operating in a new area, but our missions remained the same as ever: engage the enemy at close quarters, first by dive-bombing and then by ground-strafing.

In the nine days from 23 to 31 August, I flew no fewer than twenty-three such missions. Our targets were predominantly enemy tanks. And for the first time we were carrying 1,000kg bombs. Weighed down with these monsters, we approached our first take-offs very cautiously indeed. Nobody knew for sure how the Bf 110's under-carriage would fare under such a load. Would it be able to stand up to the extra weight? The surface of the steppe may have been rock hard, but it was far from even. Every small bump, every slight hollow could spell disaster.

As a consequence we were all very careful to make our take-offs as smooth and as gentle as possible. Under no circumstances did we want to lift off too early, or with insufficient speed, and risk hitting the ground again with such a dangerous load slung beneath the aircraft's belly. Up until now we had always carried a single 500kg bomb or two 250kg bombs on the fuselage rack, plus an additional 50kg bomb under each wing if required.

It was never easy to manoeuvre into exactly the right position to launch a dive-bombing attack. And the heavier the load you were carrying, the more difficult – and the more crucial – it became. You needed to get it right first time if you had 1,000kg of bomb strapped under your machine. If you tried to pull out at the bottom of a misjudged dive and climb back up for a second attempt, there was a very good chance of the aircraft's wings buckling under the strain, or even parting company with the fuselage altogether. We therefore amended our usual routine slightly, first flying past the target for that little bit longer in order to give us enough time properly to judge the situation before committing ourselves to the 70° dive. We also needed a bit more height to begin with, something in excess of 2,000m at least.

On 31 August 1942 I completed my one-hundredth operational mission of the war. It lasted just over two hours, from 08.18 hours to 10.25 hours. The target area lay to the south of Stalingrad and after carrying out a successful attack I had just set course back to base when I happened to spot a low-flying Ilyushin Il-2 crossing my path far below me. Almost without thinking I instantly put the Me's nose down in a wide diving curve to get on the enemy's tail. I knew that the Il-2 *Sturmovik* was a heavily armoured machine and so wanted to get in as close as possible before opening fire.

The thick armour plating around the Il-2's cockpit may even have worked to my advantage as it severely restricted the pilot's rearward view. He clearly hadn't seen me diving down on him for he was making no attempt to take any evasive action. I was now right behind the ground-hugging *Sturmovik* and a long burst from my 20mm nose cannon immediately sent him smashing into the baked earth. He couldn't have known what hit him. It was my third victory and, once again, luck had played a large part in it – nothing more than a chance encounter, totally unexpected by either participant.

There was little time to celebrate my hundredth mission, for just over an hour after returning to Frolov I was back in the air again. By now I was becoming quite familiar with the situation in the Stalingrad area and so, not expecting to encounter much opposition on this particular sortie, I had agreed to take a war correspondent along with us. Wrong move!

We reached the target area without incident, but as I was lining up for a strafing run the port engine was hit by a stray burst of machine-gun fire. The upper cowling panel came loose and was now standing upright in the airstream, causing the whole machine to shake violently. After a few moments the panel broke off altogether. Fortunately it didn't hit the tailplane, which could have had very nasty consequences. The engine itself was still running and so, all things considered, I decided that the situation was not that serious.

But the reaction of our panic-stricken passenger was something else again. 'Helmut', he screamed at the top of his voice to my wireless-operator/gunner, 'they're shooting at us!' Helmut rose splendidly to the occasion, yelling back equally loudly that they frequently did!

This exchange caused quite a bit of amusement among the other crews when we got back to base. And the damage to the machine meant that I was able to enjoy a day's break while it was being repaired. All in all, 31 August 1942 had been rather an eventful day for me. My tally of one hundred operational flights earned me the Operational Flight Clasp in Gold, of which I was naturally very proud. Little did I realize at the time that this was not even half the total number of operational flights that I would rack up by the end of the war.

September saw the ground fighting grow ever more vicious and intense as our troops closed in on Stalingrad. Many of our operations were flown in support of 4. *Panzerarmee's* advance on the city from the south-west and we witnessed some incredible scenes as savage tank battles were fought at point blank range, almost gun muzzle to gun muzzle.

We were, however, still experiencing a lot of problems in communicating with our forces on the ground. We now had tank-borne *Fliegerverbindungsoffiziere* (air liaison officers) accompanying the armoured units, whose job it was to direct our operations from the ground. But we had great difficulty in understanding each other. From the turrets of their armoured vehicles the *Flivos*, as they were commonly known, had only a worm's-eye view of the events unfolding on the battlefield, whereas we got an entirely different overall picture from the air. It was simply impossible to respond promptly and effectively to the situation reports and target information that we were being fed from the ground.

With the best will in the world, this system was not the answer to our problems. Other factors – the strength of the enemy's defences, both in the air and on the ground, the rapid and often erratic manoeuvring of the opposing sides on the field of battle, and the need to keep our own small formations intact in the air – were all factors in reducing the effectiveness of this method of ground-to-air control.

It seemed that we would have to continue to rely upon our own reconnaissance abilities and powers of observation for some little while longer yet. In this respect, the first reconnaissance sweeps of the day, flown at dawn just as the sun was rising over the eastern steppe, were particularly rewarding. The early-morning light cast long shadows, delineating every wrinkle and fold in the landscape, and throwing into sharp relief targets that would no longer be visible once the sun had climbed higher into the sky. Masters of camouflage the Soviets may have been, but not even they could make solid objects simply disappear.

To the experienced observer these missions made it far easier to detect any changes that may have taken place on the battlefield during the hours of darkness; changes such as freshly-dug trenches, newly-established artillery positions, the massing of armour, or simply the general redeployment of forces. In fact, the first early morning reconnaissance sortie provided a good working basis for the whole of the coming day.

But it wasn't long before we came to realize that our reports of enemy movements frequently went unheeded. They certainly weren't always acted upon. This was discouraging to say the least and on occasion could lead to ill-feeling. Our reconnaissance flights often took us along the line of the Don upriver from Vertyachy. The signs of a steady build-up of Soviet forces along this sector were unmistakeable and we regularly reported the fact.

It seemed clear to us that the Russians were planning to take a leaf out of our book by launching a giant pincer movement to the west of Stalingrad that would isolate the city and trap General Paulus' 6. *Armee* within it. But we were given no orders to concentrate on this obvious point of danger and were invariably instructed to attack other targets altogether. This was presumably due to our superiors' having a completely different grasp of the situation. But we knew our reports to be correct. The tremendous amount of fire we attracted whenever we ventured too close to this sensitive sector was ample testimony to that fact.

Unfortunately, our aircraft were not fitted with cameras and so we had to rely entirely on visual observation and report only on what we had actually seen. Our opinion was rarely sought at debriefings. It was the job of the intelligence staff to evaluate the overall situation from the many such reconnaissance reports that they received from the returning crews.

On 23 September I flew two missions, which took my total to 125. By now we were all beginning to feel the strain and our machines were also showing signs of hard use. Our casualties were mounting – we had lost another Staffelkapitän only five days earlier when Oberleutnant Robert Gebhardt and his wireless-operator/gunner fell victim to enemy ground fire – and our ground crews were having to struggle hard to make good all the battle damage suffered by our aircraft in order to keep the unit's serviceability figures above the minimum acceptable level.

After completing my 125th operational mission I was granted a long spell of home leave. First I had to carry out several check flights and make a few ferry flights, but then my wireless-operator/gunner and I flew down to Krasnodar in the Caucasus where we were to pick up a Bf 110 for ferrying back to Fürth in Germany for a major overhaul. Our joy at the prospect of seeing the homeland again can be imagined. We rushed through the pre-flight formalities as we were eager to be on our way as quickly as possible. It wasn't unheard of for movement orders to be countermanded and leaves to be cancelled at the very last moment. But at 13.05 hours on 29 September we finally lifted off from Krasnodar in a decidedly sickly old crate. Luckily both engines were running smoothly, although almost everything else on board the machine was borderline unserviceable.

The long flight home could only be made in stages, of course. On the first afternoon, after an intermediate stop at Zaparozhye in the Ukraine, we made it as far as Uman. With 952km behind us, that left only another 2,432km to go to Fürth. We covered them all the next day, putting down to refuel at Cracow and Breslau before reaching Fürth at 18.30 hours. There were more formalities to be gone through as we handed our machine over to the Bachmann und Ladewig aircraft repair works but then, at long last, our month's leave could finally begin.

It didn't take me long to get back into the swing of civilian life. I felt my spirits rising with every kilometre closer to Munich the train took me. I had already made plans to fill every moment of my leave and the next four weeks simply flew by. All too soon it was time to bid farewell to my nearest and dearest – who knew how long it would be before I saw them again?

On the afternoon of 27 October 1942 we took off from Fürth refreshed and reinvigorated – our Bf 110 'as good as new' – and set course for Grossenhain, north-west of Dresden, where we landed at 17.23 hours. The next day's leg got us as far as Uman, with intermediate stops at Cracow and Lemberg (Lvov).

We spent the evening at the transit centre in Uman and chatted about our recent experiences while at home on leave and the impressions we had been left with after the last four weeks. During the course of the conversation my wireless-operator/gunner let slip several remarks that made me feel slightly uneasy. He was very circumspect about it, but there was no mistaking his meaning. I gathered that he had no intention of dying a 'hero's death' at any price. Among other things, he described his irritation at seeing so many people at home, people of his own age, who were in so-called 'reserved occupations' and who were blatantly revelling in their safe, secure and comfortable lives.

He confided in me that, in any case, he was planning to marry his fiancée at the earliest possible opportunity, and that they would then spend the rest of their lives together. I doubt that'll be happening any time soon, I thought to myself. The oft-quoted 'early end to the war' didn't appear all that imminent to me. On the Eastern Front, in fact, the prospects of hostilities' ending any time in the foreseeable future were receding rapidly – as we ourselves were about to discover.

On 30 October we departed Uman for Krasnodar, where we landed at 16.18 hours after just one stop for refuelling at Zaparozhye.

We found the entire Gruppe now gathered at Krasnodar. It had been transferred down from the Stalingrad front due to the worsening situation in the Caucasus. *Heeresgruppe* A's southwards advance had lost its initial impetus in the face of stubborn Soviet resistance and our ground troops were struggling hard to attain their objectives. Although they had captured the Soviet naval base of Novorossisk back on 10 September, their repeated attempts to break through to Tuapse – some 130km further to the south and the real key to the Black Sea coastline all the way down to the Turkish border – had failed completely. As too would their advance on the Grozny oilfields 150km from the Caspian Sea.

In addition to their unsuccessful attempts to take Tuapse in the west and Grozny in the east, *Heeresgruppe* A's thinly stretched forces had also been given the near impossible task of crossing the Caucasus Mountains to the south. A small detachment of élite mountain troops *did* manage to scale Mount Elbrus, but this exploit was little more than a propaganda exercise. The photograph of them planting the *Reichskriegsflagge* atop Europe's highest peak was featured on the front pages of countless newspapers and magazines back home. But the main forces' attempts to fight their way over the three major passes across the Caucasus range were all blocked by a combination of fanatical Russian resistance and the raging blizzards that had begun to sweep the higher slopes early in October.

We flew our first two missions out of Krasnodar on 31 October, the day after we got back from leave. Both were directed against enemy positions near Tuapse and both consisted of the usual dive-bombing followed by ground strafing. The one thing I immediately noticed was how much more the Soviets' ground fire had again increased while I had been away. I thought it had been bad before, but it was nothing compared to what we faced over Tuapse. No sooner had we crossed into enemy territory than we found ourselves coming under heavy and sustained fire from all directions.

On the second of the day's two sorties our aircraft took a nasty hit from a medium Flak shell. We had already released our bombs, but had to abandon all ideas of ground-strafing. Despite a badly damaged wing we managed to limp safely back to Krasnodar.

I took part in a further seventeen missions over the course of the next nineteen days. Mostly we flew in *Schwärmen*, delivering the usual mix of dive-bombing followed up by ground-strafing. But two of the operations during this period, which targeted the enemy airfields at Tuapse and Lazarovskaye, were conducted in Gruppe strength involving some thirty aircraft on each occasion.

By mid-November ground operations in the Caucasus had come to a virtual standstill. But on the Stalingrad front all hell had broken loose. The dangerous build-up of enemy units along the line of the Don to the north-west of the city that we had earlier reported on was now complete. And on 19 November strong Soviet forces stormed across the river and smashed a gap in the sector held by the Romanians. Twenty-four hours later the Russians launched a similar assault to the south of Stalingrad, and on 22 November the two arms of the Soviet pincer met at Kalach, cutting off the city and trapping Paulus' entire 6. *Armee* together with a substantial part of 4. *Panzerarmee*.

Our second spell in the Caucasus was thus short-lived, for within days we found ourselves being transferred post-haste back up to the Stalingrad area. Our new base was Tatsinskaya, approximately 402km to the west of the beleaguered city. Despite the hurried nature of our move we were at full operational readiness within hours of our arrival; yet further proof of the invaluable technical and logistical work performed by our ground staff who coped magnificently with our numerous moves during this critical period.

It had suddenly turned very cold and wintry. On 16 November the first snows had fallen in the area between the Don and the Volga and the temperatures had dropped below zero. The sweltering heat of the recent summer was but a distant memory. We no longer slept in our 'tropical' tents but in snug underground bunkers. Surprisingly, the harsh conditions didn't dampen our spirits in the slightest. We continued to eat well and there were few, if any cases of serious illness.

Our operations targeted enemy forces all along the Don front, both to the north and south of Stalingrad. Our tried and tested methods of attack were still as successful as ever, but their effects were purely local. They brought much-needed relief to the troops we were directly supporting, but did nothing to halt the overwhelming mass of enemy forces – reportedly some ten armies in all – that were gradually tightening a steel noose around Stalingrad.

Due to the worsening weather conditions, I flew just ten missions in the eighteen days from 23 November to 10 December 1942. We suffered a number of casualties during this period, not only from the usual enemy ground fire – something we had almost come to regard as an occupational hazard by now – but also from the Red Air Force's bombing raids on Tatsinskaya. It was these latter which presumably prompted our being transferred some 80km *eastwards* to the advanced landing ground at Verbovka – a classic case of out of the frying pan into the fire.

Our operations were now being severely hampered by a dramatic deterioration in the weather. The thermometer had plummeted to minus 38° centigrade, which wasn't doing either us or our machines any good at all. To make matters worse, the situation on the ground was becoming increasingly confused and it was very difficult to differentiate between friend and foe in the frozen landscape. Nor was our new base as safe as it might be. We were already coming under long-range artillery fire from the north. We clearly couldn't remain here at Verbovka for long; another move had to be in the offing.

On 18 December I was scheduled for the early morning mission and so went to wake my wireless-operator/gunner. But Helmut told me that he wasn't feeling at all well and intended to see the medical officer with a request to be admitted into hospital. I had to find a replacement in a hurry and young Gefreiter Schmidt jumped at the chance to fly the mission with me. After saying goodbye to Helmut I dashed across to the ops room to be briefed.

I didn't burden my new wireless-operator/gunner with too many instructions as I didn't want to make him feel nervous. We duly took off at 06.58 hours. The target was almost on our doorstep and we landed back at Verbovka just thirty-one minutes later – that's how close to the fighting front we were.

As we were making our way across to debriefing the enemy artillery opened up again and we ended up crawling on all fours. After submitting my report I was informed that we had received orders to transfer at once to Millerovo, which lay about 140km to the north-west of us. There was no time to lose. I hastily packed my kit and hurried back out to my aircraft.

As we were taxiing out to the take-off line I spotted Helmut standing with a small group of other personnel beside some parked aircraft. They all had their kitbags on the ground next to them. As I waved goodbye a second time from the cockpit I recalled our chat in the Uman transit centre on our way back from our last leave. Helmut had seemingly got his wish – he was returning early to Germany after all.

At 08.53 hours, less than ninety minutes after landing from our morning mission, we lifted off from Verbovka again and set course for Millerovo. There was a blanket of fog some 300m high off to the west, but otherwise the weather was fine at first. It grew steadily worse during the flight, but we encountered no major problems and touched down safely at a snow-covered Millerovo some forty minutes later.

Just two hours after landing at Millerovo I was ordered up on my next mission. It promised to be a tricky one. The Gruppen-kommandeur informed me that Higher Command weren't entirely sure where the Soviets had broken through along the Don front due north of Millerovo, nor how wide were the gaps that had been torn in our lines. This was the sector held by another of our allies, the Italians. My brief was first and foremost to carry out a thorough reconnaissance of the area, and secondly to engage any enemy formations that we found this side of the river. With poor visibility and heavy snow showers, conditions were not exactly ideal for this kind of mission.

Immediately after taking off I ordered the four machines of the *Schwarm* to keep in tight formation as I could foresee the weather only getting worse which, in fact, it very quickly did. I therefore decided that we should split up and continue the flight in two separate pairs. The other pair eased away and was soon lost to sight. I wasn't too concerned as they knew what the primary purpose of our mission was. Every now and then I contacted them to find out their position, only to be told: 'Above the clouds, heading west, will put down at the first airfield we find.' Well, I thought to myself, I suppose that's one way of dealing with an awkward situation.

Meanwhile, my wingman and I were nearing the Don, which we crossed at Boguchar. The landscape lay under a thick carpet of snow and I couldn't make out very much at all. No troops, no signs of movement; just terrible visibility. But then, quite suddenly, a whole mass of armoured vehicles appeared out of the gloom below us and we immediately came under heavy fire. They were heading south-west, and so clearly weren't ours.

Once we were safely past them, we quickly reversed course and, as the low clouds prevented us from gaining enough height for a dive-bombing attack, released our bombs in a long, shallow dive over the rearmost vehicles of the enemy force before strafing the leading columns as we skimmed low over their heads.

Once clear of their fire we resumed our search in a northerly direction and soon came across small groups of what had to be Italian troops struggling south through the deep snowdrifts. We could only imagine what they were suffering, but all we could do was to get back to base as quickly as possible and report what we had seen. That, however, was easier said than done. In fact, it was all but impossible. The snow was coming down even harder and visibility was almost nil. Nor could we resort to blind-flying, as there were no ground navigational aids in this part of the world.

We battled on southwards, my wingman sticking close to me. Fortunately, I had taken the precaution of memorizing what few railway lines there were in the region and it wasn't too long before I caught a glimpse of a tell-tale row of telegraph poles sticking out of the snow. Telegraph poles tended to run alongside railway tracks and so I decided to follow them.

I partially lowered the aircraft's flaps and set the propellers to fine pitch. Instructing my wingman to do the same, I carefully reduced height until we were flying almost level with the tops of the poles. The countryside hereabouts was slightly hilly and in these atrocious conditions there was always the risk that we might inadvertently make contact with the ground. Should this happen, our present configuration – flaps partly extended, props in fine pitch – would improve our chances of pulling off a successful belly landing.

After some little while I recognized a distinctive bend in the line of the railway. I knew from my study of the maps that if we made a sharp turn to port here we would have Millerovo in front of us. And so it proved. Filled with relief, I prepared for landing and was soon safely down. My wingman was not so lucky. He belly-landed just short of the field.

Nobody at Millerovo had been expecting us in such atrocious conditions. Not knowing what was happening to the north of them, the ops room staff were understandably getting a little bit jittery. My report was therefore received with more than the usual interest and passed on to higher quarters without a moment's delay. I was informed in return that our second pair was also safe and sound. They had landed at a field some way off to the west and were waiting for an improvement in the weather before returning to Millerovo.

In the middle of the debriefing the ops room clerk interrupted us with some urgent news that had just come in. The aircraft carrying my old wireless-operator/gunner had crashed in bad weather near Rostov. All the occupants had been killed. So Helmut never did make it home. The news affected me deeply. I had lost a good comrade and a true friend. I would not find his like again.

The next day I flew another armed-reconnaissance sortie over the same northern sector, this time in slightly better conditions. The enemy was pouring across the Don in huge numbers. Of the Italians there was no sign. A few hours later I was sent off a second time with specific orders to attack a Soviet armoured force advancing south of Boguchar.

On 22 December I carried out another two missions. They were again armed-reconnaissance sweeps whose purpose was to try to obtain a clearer picture of the confused fighting that was now raging along the Don front. As it turned out, they would also prove to be the last two missions I was to fly in Russia.

We celebrated Christmas Eve in a somewhat unlikely fashion. The nearby small township of Millerovo was ablaze. We were surrounded by the enemy and there wasn't a soul about. During the afternoon, in a token display of military preparedness, we were ordered to occupy the slit trenches that had been dug along the eastern edge of the field. But in the evening the order was rescinded. We couldn't clamber out of the freezing cold trenches fast enough, and made ourselves comfortable in a well-heated barracks hut instead.

Luckily, the unit that had been based here before us had left large stocks of food and alcohol behind when they left, so we weren't short of provisions and could really indulge ourselves. Once the festivities got under way the temperature in the hut – and our spirits – both rose several degrees higher. And so passed Christmas Eve 1942: far from home in a wooden hut in the icy wastes of Russia with the enemy all around us.

On Christmas Day morning I took off for Krasnodar in the Caucasus, where I had been ordered to report to Geschwader HQ. Upon arrival in Krasnodar I was informed that I was being posted to Kampfgeschwader 40, a bomber group based in France. HQ was not able to give me any details as to when I was to report to my new unit, nor what my duties were to be. I was simply told that I would have to break my journey in Berlin and go along to the *Reichsluft-fahrtministerium* (RLM – the Air Ministry) where I would be able to obtain all the necessary information and documentation for myself.

On 26 December I flew back up to Millerovo. I landed there at 14.10 hours and had just enough time to pick up my chief mechanic who was ready and waiting for me. After a hectic ten minutes I was back in the air again. Millerovo was under heavy bombardment and could no longer be held. The Gruppe had almost completed its transfer the 95km south-west to Voroshilovgrad and only a small rearguard party still remained at Millerovo.

I didn't fly any operational missions during the two days I spent at Voroshilovgrad, but I was required to carry out several short ferry flights gathering up Bf 110s from nearby fields and depots to bolster our depleted complement of serviceable aircraft.

December 28th was occupied in saying my farewells to all my friends and comrades at Voroshilovgrad and Krasnodar. In total, I had made no fewer than 158 operational flights during my two spells of duty on the Eastern Front with the famous 'Wasps': the first 39 as a member of the original Schnellkampfgeschwader 210 in 1941, and the remainder with the redesignated Zerstörergeschwader 1 in 1942. All had been flown as part of the Luftwaffe's tactical air command in support – either direct or otherwise – of our troops in the field as they fought some of the fiercest battles, both offensive and defensive, of the campaign to date.

But now my time in Russia was at an end. On 29 December 1942, with a new wireless-operator/gunner, the Berliner Karl Schröder, in the seat behind me, I took off from Voroshilovgrad and flew down to Taganrog on the Sea of Azov ready to begin my transfer flight to the west, to pastures not just new, but totally unknown.

Chapter 11

Kampfgeschwader 40

We had a stroke of luck in Taganrog. They had a machine there that had a number of major defects and urgently needed ferrying to Cracow for a complete overhaul. I was warned that it would probably be very tricky to fly, but I jumped at the opportunity. At least we would be spared the long, tedious journey by rail through the endless wintry landscape of Russia. Once we reached Cracow it wasn't all that much further by train to Berlin – and hopefully that part of the journey wouldn't involve any nasty surprises.

So, at 11.27 hours on 29 December 1942, we – my new wireless-operator/gunner and myself, that is – lifted off from Taganrog for the first stage of our flight home, which would take us as far as Uman. The engineering officer at Taganrog hadn't been exaggerating. The Bf 110's many faults made it an absolute beast to handle. And this, together with the less-than-ideal weather conditions, demanded the utmost concentration on my part.

As we crabbed steadily west-north-west from Taganrog I kept a constant and watchful eye on the instruments. The first opportunity I had of checking whether we were still on the correct course came as we flew over the large hydro-electric dam across the Dnieper at Zaparozhye. Not only were we on course, we were also making surprisingly good time. At 13.17 hours, less than two hours after leaving Taganrog, we put down at Uman.

With the first 670km safely behind us, I was anxious to get on and complete the second 760km leg to Cracow while it was still light. So just thirty-three minutes later we were back in the air again, fully tanked-up and on our way to Cracow, where we landed after an uneventful flight that had taken us exactly two hours. With the Bf 110 duly delivered, it was next stop Berlin.

Once in Berlin I reported forthwith to the RLM as ordered. I was received most cordially and an Oberst explained the reason for my transfer and what my new duties were to be. When I heard what it was all about, I couldn't help wondering whether the powers-that-be hadn't perhaps overestimated my abilities more than a little.

Based on the French Biscay coast, Kampfgeschwader 40 was the Luftwaffe's only long-range maritime bomber unit. Equipped with four-engined Focke-Wulf Fw 200 *'Condors'*, it flew missions far out over the Atlantic hunting and attacking Allied merchant shipping. The unit operated in close collaboration with the Kriegsmarine, supporting the latter's U-boat packs by shadowing Allied convoys and relaying details of the vessels' position, course and speed.

Many of the U-boats were also based at ports along the French Biscay coast and of late they had been coming under ever more frequent attack from Allied anti-submarine aircraft as they crossed the Biscay at the start of, or returning from their Atlantic patrols. KG 40 had therefore now been given the additional task of providing more direct support for the U-boats by flying air cover as they ran the 'Biscay gauntlet' on their way to and from the open ocean.

The Geschwader's *'Condor'* bombers were the wrong aircraft for this extra commitment. What was needed was a long-range heavy fighter with the endurance to fly lengthy overwater patrols out over the Biscay – in short, a *Zerstörer*.

And just such a machine was available. The C-6 was the very latest *Zerstörer* variant of the multi-role Junkers Ju 88. Several early examples had already undergone trials on the Biscay front during the previous summer, and now a whole new Gruppe had just been formed to operate as part of KG 40. The young crews selected to fly the heavily-armed Ju 88C-6s would need to be skilled not only in air combat, but also in blind-flying and navigation if they were to undertake long overwater missions in all weathers. Specialized training would be required to prepare them for this dual role, which is why a couple of experienced pilots, myself and one other, had been drafted in from established *Zerstörer* units to act as instructors.

On 6 January 1943 I reported to IV./KG 40 based at Châteaudun, just over 100km to the south-west of Paris. The IV. Gruppe of a Kampfgeschwader generally served as a kind of 'in-house' operational training unit and was usually stationed somewhere quiet in a rear area where it could give a final polish to crews fresh out of training school and prepare them for the realities of operational service with one of the Geschwader's three front-line Gruppen.

It felt a little strange at first to be at Châteaudun among all those 'bomber boys' but, apart from certain reservations, everybody was very helpful, for which I was most grateful. The other *Zerstörer* pilot posted to Châteaudun with me was wearing the Knight's Cross around his neck; a sure sign that he had a lot of combat experience under his belt.

We were both resolved to make a success of our new and somewhat challenging assignment and so we put our heads together to work out a suitable training programme that would encompass both long-range navigation *and* air combat. Our proposals were accepted without question and we started working with our first group of trainees on 13 January 1943.

But before that I had to undergo conversion on to the Ju 88C-6 myself. This proved to be a fairly simple process, initially involving just five take-offs adding up to a grand total of thirty-five minutes' flying time. Then, a few days later, I went up on a 26-minute familiarization flight in the company of a Junkers' works pilot, which gave me all the confidence I needed to be able to handle this superlative machine. By sheer coincidence, the Junkers' pilot had been one of the instructors at the *Fliegerschule* Magdeburg who had taught me blind-flying back in 1935. We got to chatting about old times and both had a good laugh now about one particularly terrifying training flight we had made through a ferocious thunderstorm.

Herr Seibert really put the Ju 88 through its paces, performing some very impressive aerobatics. I was amazed by the machine's excellent manoeuvrability; so essential for our future operations – and so different from our rather sluggish old Bf 110s. Even more impressive, perhaps, was the Ju 88's single-engined performance and its ability to roll while in a fast shallow dive with *both* engines switched off! I couldn't wait to try out the machine's exceptional qualities for myself.

For the initial part of our training programme we were also given some elderly Bücker Bü 131 '*Jungmann*' biplanes. It was a new lease of life for these venerable primary trainers, but they were to prove remarkably useful. We could teach – at least in principle – all the individual basic manoeuvres that needed to be mastered if one was to survive, let alone be successful, in air combat. We could also put into practice all the tactical theories taught in the classroom in a much more economical and far less risky fashion than if we had let our partially trained pupils loose on the thirsty, high-powered Ju 88s. The sight of our tiny two-seat biplanes bumbling about the field may have raised more than a few smiles on the faces of the resident four-engined bomber crews, but the results we achieved very soon proved the effectiveness of our methods.

The flying training programme that we had come up with was based to a great extent on that taught at the *Zerstörerschule* Schleissheim, but with one or two additions of our own relating specifically to our trainees' future operational role. All our first batch of pilots already held the C-2, or 'Advanced Military Pilot's Licence', and all were qualified in blind-flying. Our programme therefore focussed largely on air combat exercises and the various disciplines these entailed. The theoretical side of the course dealt primarily with the special requirements needed for operations over the Biscay.

Training activities took up practically all of my time, but I enjoyed every minute of it. An extra bonus was the fact that we were based in central France where the climate, despite its being midwinter, seemed positively balmy after what I had just been through in Russia.

But as the months passed and the spring of 1943 slowly gave way to summer our training schedules began to suffer increasing disruption from ever more frequent air-raid warnings as Allied bombers – RAF mediums and USAAF heavies – stepped up their daylight attacks on French targets. Enemy fighters were also becoming noticeably more active, not only escorting the bomber raids in large numbers, but also flying intruder sweeps of their own deep into France, both by day and by night.

It was proving more and more difficult to keep to our regular training exercises in the face of these constant interruptions. Things would be much easier if we were transferred to a less hostile environment. In fact, there was no reason for us to remain at

Châteaudun as we were no longer an integral part of Kampf-geschwader 40. In August our Staffel, 10./KG 40, had been redesignated to become 3./*Erg.Z.Gr* – in other words, the third Staffel of the *Ergänzungs-Zerstörergruppe*, or Heavy-fighter Advanced Training and Replacement Wing.

Our redesignation had been just one part of a general restructuring of *Zerstörer* training, all of which now came under the control of the one *Ergänzungs-Zerstörergruppe*, whose four component Staffeln were each equipped with a different type of aircraft – the Bf 110, Me 210 (and Me 410), Ju 88C-6 and Me 410 respectively – which were used for training crews for specific front-line *Zerstörer* units. The Gruppe was based in the Brunswick area of northern central Germany. The Gruppenstab, 1. and 4. Staffeln all operated out of Braunschweig-Broitzem, while our 3./Erg.Z.Gr was to join 2. Staffel at Braunschweig-Waggum.

I flew my last training sortie out of Chateaudun on 23 October 1943 and nine days later, on 1 November, departed France with my wireless-operator Karl Schröder and our new gunner Alfred Müller – the Ju 88C-6 carried a crew of three – for Braunschweig-Waggum, where we landed at 14.05 hours.

It took a day or two to get used to operating under 'Homeland conditions' with all the rules and restrictions that that involved. But we soon found our feet again and, after a short orientation flight to familiarize ourselves with the field and its immediate surroundings, training was resumed on 4 November.

The programme itself, both the theoretical and the practical, remained little changed. But our job was now becoming immeasurably more difficult as the young crews being turned out by the flying training schools were no longer being given the thorough grounding of earlier trainees. They lacked many of the basic skills, let alone any advanced qualifications, and fell far below the standards of the more experienced crews we had been training at Châteaudun.

To add further to our problems, it was not long before the increasing tempo of Allied air attacks began to disrupt our activities in the Brunswick area too. It was very difficult to make up for all the hours of training lost whenever enemy aircraft were reported to be in the vicinity. The number of serious accidents involving our young crews increased at an alarming rate, creating painful gaps in the Staffel's ranks.

Shortly after our transfer to Braunschweig-Waggum, Hauptmann Günther Moltrecht, who had commanded the Staffel since its inception as 10./KG 40, was posted away. I was appointed Kapitän in his stead and duly promoted to the rank of Hauptmann on 1 January 1944.

It so happened that one of the Gruppen of my old Geschwader, ZG 1 – the 'Wasps' – was also based at Braunschweig-Broitzem for a short while during this period. II./ZG 1 had been pulled out of Russia soon after the fall of Stalingrad, serving next in the Mediterranean theatre and then on the French Atlantic coast. Of late, the Gruppe had been part of the Defence of the Reich organization, stationed in Austria to combat the US heavy bombers flying up from Italy to attack targets in the south-easternmost areas of the Reich.

I was invited over to Broitzem to have dinner with them one evening and jumped at the opportunity to see some of my old comrades again. Sadly, I discovered that many of them had been killed since our days together on the Eastern Front. We spent half the night discussing the situation facing our Luftwaffe as Allied air power went from strength to strength. My comrades' main concern was the enemy's overwhelming technical superiority, against which they had no effective answer. After a brief flirtation with the disastrous Me 210, they were back flying the Bf 110. And while they were now equipped with the latest 'G' variant, the design itself was a good ten years old. The flaws in its initial concept as a long-range, twin-engined strategic day fighter were still very much in evidence.

Its failings in the offensive role had been laid bare in the Battle of Britain when it had been able to escort bombers to distant objectives, but had then proven almost totally incapable of protecting those same bombers from the RAF's single-engined fighters once over the target area.

In the daylight defensive role the Bf 110's shortcomings were equally apparent. It could fly long distances to intercept approaching US heavy bombers. It was sturdy enough to carry extra-large calibre cannons and rocket launchers. But these heavy anti-bomber weapons impaired its already marginal manoeuvrability even further, which made it easy prey for Allied escorting fighters and meant it was rarely able to penetrate the fighter screen to get at the bombers it was intended to destroy.

Not surprisingly, the Gruppe had suffered some grievous losses and, to compound its difficulties, here too the new crews being drafted in to replace its casualties were becoming ever younger, less experienced and less adequately trained to survive the murderous aerial battles being fought in defence of the homeland.

On 4 March 1944 the *Erg.Z.Gr.* was transferred *en bloc* from the Brunswick area down to Illesheim, an airfield some 50km to the west of Nuremberg where, it was hoped, our training schedules would not be subject to quite as much disruption from enemy air activity. The station personnel at Illesheim gave us every help and support. We settled in very quickly and resumed training with the minimum of delay.

Unfortunately, although the skies around Illesheim remained reasonably free from enemy incursions, the number of accidents we were suffering continued to rise. As a result we were soon forced to adjust the tempo of the training programme to make allowances for the relative inexperience of the crews being sent to us.

As can be imagined, this was not always easy, as the previous service history of each new arrival was different. We no longer received complete intakes of trainees straight from flying school – all with the same amount and level of training behind them – but rather a collection of individuals from various sources: youngsters fresh from training school, long-serving flying instructors, pilots and crews from second-line units, and veteran flyers from disbanded operational Staffeln and Gruppen. This inevitably made the training process more difficult, more complicated and more protracted.

By now the tide of war was changing dramatically, and not in Germany's favour. On the Eastern Front our armies were giving ground on all three main sectors. To the south, Anglo-American forces were firmly established in Italy. And in the West it could only be a matter of time before the enemy launched a cross-Channel invasion.

Nearer to home, the Luftwaffe's training arm seemed to be undergoing constant reorganization. At the end of March 1944 the Stab of the *Ergänzungs-Zerstörergruppe*, already in its third incarnation, was disbanded yet again. Of its four component Staffeln, 1./*Erg.Z.Gr.* was also disbanded. The other three, 2., 3. and 4./*Erg.Z.Gr*, while remaining together at Illesheim, were each placed under the command of one of the three front-line Zerstörer-geschwader still in existence (ZGs 26, 1 and 76 respectively) albeit on a semi-autonomous basis. I thus found myself back in the ZG 1 fold, now as the Staffelkapitän of the Geschwader's own training and replacement unit, which was given the designation *Ergänzungs-staffel/ZG* 1.

None of this administrative shuffling affected our training regime at Illesheim in the slightest, however. In fact, we received additional personnel and aircraft, which allowed us to turn out even more new Ju 88 crews ready for operational service. Our flying training programme was extended to include more navigational exercises to prepare the trainees for the long overwater flights that awaited them after their transfer to one of the Geschwader's front-line Staffeln.

The theoretical side of the programme was also expanded in an effort to close the gaps left by the trainees' rather perfunctory schooling to date, particularly in the fields of navigation and communications. The Staffel was kept extremely busy and the results we were achieving were acknowledged on more than one occasion by messages of appreciation from our superiors.

As a Hauptmann in command of a semi-autonomous Staffel subordinated directly to the Geschwaderstab, I was acting more in the role of a Gruppenkommandeur with all the authority and rights – but also all the responsibilities – that that office carried with it. And these responsibilities were not made any easier by the distance that separated us from Geschwaderstab HQ, which was currently located at Lorient on the French Biscay coast.

The war was entering a critical phase and most of us were convinced that things could only get worse in the weeks ahead. We had to make strenuous efforts to overcome the mounting difficulties that we were beginning to encounter, but every single member of the Staffel turned to with a will. Supply shortages were made good by some very inventive improvisation, and training flights were sometimes carried out in ways and under conditions that could only be described as 'unorthodox'. But despite all the problems, we managed to keep to our schedules and continued to produce Ju 88 crews trained to the best of our ability.

There were, however, two things that were both painful and hard to bear, and over which we had no control whatsoever. The first resulted from the inevitable tragedies of the times we were living through – tragedies that hit some of us very hard indeed. One of our number might perhaps receive official notification that his entire family had been killed in an air raid, another that his brother or some other close relative had fallen in battle, and a third that his house and all his worldly goods had been destroyed by enemy action.

The rest of us did everything we could to help alleviate our comrades' suffering, often bending the rules almost to the point of breaking when it came to issuing leave passes and the organizing of emergency transport. Although each such case was of course a deeply personal matter, the common burden of grief brought us all closer together as a unit and hopefully helped in some small way to ease the victim's pain.

The second thing was our total inability to counter the growing number of enemy air raids now occurring in the Nuremberg area and the sense of helplessness that this engendered. The terrible feeling of being under constant threat and not being able to do anything about it made the veterans among us long to get back into action. We couldn't help thinking of all the hours previously spent on operations. They may have been arduous, very often highly dangerous, but at least we were hitting back. Our evening get-togethers in the officers' mess nearly always revolved around this very issue, and the discussions were invariably tinged with not a little pessimism about the future.

On 5 June 1944 I received orders to fly to Lorient to attend a meeting with the Geschwaderkommodore of ZG 1, Oberstleutnant Erich von Selle. I took off late that same afternoon and set course westwards. Burdened by anxieties about our current situation, I began turning over in my mind a list of the items and equipment that could make our job a little easier, thinking that I might perhaps get the opportunity to put in a request for them while at Geschwader HQ. But after just thirty minutes in the air my thoughts were rudely interrupted when one of the engines started playing up. I had no option but to turn round and limp back to Illesheim, where I landed at 18.40 hours.

Early next morning I tried again. When I lifted off at 04.50 hours the weather was far from good. The field was covered in low cloud and it was raining heavily. I wasn't too unhappy about the miserable conditions, however. Flying through thick cloud meant that there was less likelihood of our bumping into roving enemy fighters, a danger always to be reckoned with along the route to the French Atlantic coast.

For routine flights such as this there were certain regulations laid down by the authorities regarding course, height and communications procedures that had to be obeyed. Failure to do so increased the risk of being fired upon by our own side, so one always took great care to comply.

The excellent flying characteristics of the Ju 88 were proving their worth yet again. The machine responded immediately to the slightest touch on the controls. Ignoring the weather outside, it wasn't hard to keep the aircraft on track by use of the instruments alone. Both engines were purring away quite happily. If things continued like this we could settle down to enjoy a quiet and comfortable flight.

I held course for the so-called *Zaberner Senke*, a low-lying area of land in the otherwise mountainous Vosges region of Lower Alsace to the north-west of Strasbourg. If the weather conditions when we got to the *Senke*, or depression, were still as bad as they had been ever since leaving Illesheim, I planned to cross it at low level, as we were strictly prohibited from flying over this area either in or above solid cloud.

I couldn't help noticing that our wireless-operator, an old sweat who rarely got into a flap about anything, was becoming increasingly uneasy as we neared the Rhine. I glanced back at him from time to time, but he was hunched over his sets, earphones clamped to his head, concentrating intently on the dials and switches in front of him like I had never seen him concentrate before.

In the meantime the clouds below us were beginning to break up and we caught our first sight of the ground. Our thorough pre-flight planning had paid off. We were exactly where our calculations said we should be.

But then our wireless-operator suddenly started yelling 'MYO, MYO' over and over again at the top of his voice. There was no mistaking his meaning; 'MYO' was the three-letter code group indicating the presence of hostile aircraft in the area. But I was sceptical. What would enemy aircraft be doing over here this early in the day, and in such miserable conditions?

The wireless-operator's repeated warnings couldn't simply be ignored, however. A decision had to be made about what course of action we should take – we were, after all, a three-man crew. To my mind, an intermediate landing didn't seem to be warranted. For one thing, there were still enough clouds around for us to hide in if need be. And there was always the alternative option of diving down to treetop height to escape detection, a ploy that had proved effective often enough in such situations in the past.

But the clouds continued to thin and had soon vanished almost entirely. By this time the Rhine was far behind us and the French countryside beneath our wings was basking in a golden morning glow. It presented a scene of such utter peace and tranquillity that it was hard to imagine the presence of enemy aircraft, let alone the possibility of sudden life-or-death air combat.

But the wireless-operator was becoming ever more insistent. I was none too pleased about his loud hollering, as I had always preferred to have calm and quiet in the cockpit. But his obvious anxiety finally prompted me to decide that now was the moment to get the Ju 88 down on the deck and start some serious low-level flying. The large numbers of hostile aircraft being reported in neighbouring areas was more than a little worrying. We needed to be vigilant and not take unnecessary chances.

Once safely down at ground level I had to concentrate hard in order to avoid hitting any high-tension cables, tall buildings, trees or other such obstacles. Fortunately, I knew this area well and decided that my best bet would be to make for the airfield at Tours. But where exactly were all these reported enemy aircraft? Were they, in fact, about to attack Tours? Was a carpet of bombs perhaps raining down on the field at this very moment? These were eventualities that I had to consider, of course. But they didn't change my mind about trying to land at Tours. There weren't any other suitable airfields in the immediate vicinity and now that I had made my decision I didn't want to run any further risks by staying in the air longer than I had to.

By now we were rapidly approaching Tours and it was time to gain a little height and prepare for landing. The airfield was situated on the higher northern bank of the River Loire overlooking the town. I could see nothing suspicious as I circled to land and a few minutes later we touched down. All seemed quiet – almost too quiet – and so I lost no time in getting off the runway and taxiing over towards the edge of the field.

Before we reached it I suddenly spotted a lone motorcycle combination heading in our direction. The steel-helmeted rider astride the bike signalled to us to follow him. While we were doing so he continued to gesticulate vigorously, which struck me as rather odd.

We rolled to a stop and had hardly got the ventral hatch open before the clearly nervous airman was standing there shouting up at us in a loud voice that could we please hurry and get under cover as they were expecting an air raid at any moment. We needed no second bidding, although we still weren't quite sure what all the fuss was about. Then the airman dropped his bombshell, asking in some agitation whether we were aware that the invasion had begun shortly after midnight, that all flying had been suspended and that aircraft were only being allowed to take off with special permission. The answer to that was simple: no, we hadn't been aware.

It was the morning of 6 June 1944. The Allies had launched their invasion and we were sitting on Tours airfield. Those were the facts. What was to be done about it; that was the question. The invasion beaches were some 250km away to the north of us and so, as far as I could see, there was no reason to get too excited just yet.

Without our really having noticed it, it was turning into a very warm day. The wind had dropped and the air was almost unnaturally still. Once the aircraft had been secured we drove down into Tours to see the town commandant. He greeted us in a friendly enough fashion and proceeded to explain the situation, or as much of it as he knew, in a few brief sentences. He then went on to outline certain new rules and regulations that had automatically come into force now that the invasion had started.

This wasn't an awful lot to go on, and so I tried to get in touch with the Geschwaderstab in Lorient by phone. Under the present circumstances, I realized this might take quite some while and, in fact, it wasn't until the following day that I was able to get through. I was told that we weren't allowed to take off for the time being. So this meant we couldn't continue our flight to Lorient, nor could we return to Illesheim. No amount of reasoned argument could sway the officer on the other end of the line. We were staying put.

Fortunately, the hotel we were billeted in was not far from the commandant's office, which meant that I could at least keep in close touch. After several more attempts I finally managed to contact Lorient again, and this time speak to the Geschwaderkommodore in person. His orders were straight to the point: I was to return to Illesheim at once and carry on with my training duties as before while awaiting developments on the invasion front. So it was back to business as usual, at least for the time being.

At 04.50 hours on the morning of 8 June we took off from Tours for the two-hour return flight to Illesheim. We encountered no problems on the way, although we did notice that the reports of enemy air activity were now far more numerous than those being broadcast forty-eight hours earlier.

At Illesheim we immediately got back down to training and continued to achieve some good results. The growing number of air raid warnings caused frequent disruptions and made our task that much harder, but they didn't impact upon the training programme to any significant extent. We simply improvised and adapted, juggling the times, locations, duration and content of our training exercises to compensate for the inevitable delays we were suffering.

The Staffel had been slowly but steadily increasing in size over the past months and by this stage had more than fifty aircraft on strength. They operated both by day and by night. The majority of them were Ju 88C-6s, of course, but we had also been given a number of Siebel Si 204s. The Siebel was originally a twin-engined, eight-passenger light transport machine, which subsequently saw extensive service as a flying classroom for wireless and navigation training. We still retained several of our old Bücker Bü 131s as well. These continued to do valuable duty in the preliminary training role.

In addition to growing in strength and size, the Staffel had also expanded geographically. Back in April we had established a small training detachment at Mont-de-Marsan in south-west France, from where we could give our fully-trained crews a first taste of operational flying over the Bay of Biscay.

At Illesheim meanwhile we were concentrating primarily on navigation and air-to-ground communications training. We regularly sent crews on lengthy exercises up to Rahmel in East Prussia where they could practise their overwater navigation skills in the less unfriendly skies above the Baltic Sea. We had set up our own ground radio station in a barn not far from the airfield at Illesheim. From here we could monitor each crew's progress as they flew up to Rahmel. We would receive a constant flow of signals from the aircraft reporting its position, which we could then track and check for accuracy against our own maps.

We found too that the Siebel Si 204 made an excellent advanced blind-flying trainer. It was fully instrumented for self-bearing navigational exercises and equipped for radio-beam approaches, the forerunners of today's ILS, or Instrument Landing System. As an added bonus, its Argus engines used far less fuel than our notoriously thirsty Ju 88s, which was an important factor in these increasingly straitened times.

But no amount of improvisation on our part could now counter the increasingly critical war situation and the effects it was having on our activities. The news from the Normandy front was not good and this, combined with a build-up of enemy air activity over the southern Biscay area, meant that we had to pull our detachment out of Mont-de-Marsan. The field had already been subject to several small-scale attacks from the air. And while these had not seriously disrupted training, the writing was clearly on the wall.

I flew to Mont-de-Marsan for the last time on 1 July 1944 to tidy up the final few details of our three months' occupancy of the base, and returned to Illesheim the following day. Another valuable plank in our carefully-constructed training edifice had been removed.

Within the Staffel there were growing doubts about the prospects for the future. More and more questions were being asked – guardedly, of course – as to what chances, if any, we still had of bringing about a change for the better in the overall war situation. Unfortunately, I had no answer to that. All I could do was to try to ensure that the Staffel's morale stayed high. And luckily I had firm foundations to build on. My instructing staff were a very close-knit bunch. They all got on remarkably well together, both on-duty and off. Our comradeship and mutual trust had seen us through many a sticky patch in the past and would no doubt continue to do so in the future.

I had a surprise visit from the top brass during the second week of July. The General der Jagdflieger arrived unannounced at Illesheim and I was ordered to report to him immediately. Generalleutnant Adolf Galland wasted few words. But before disclosing the reason for his unexpected visit, he ordered me to cease all flying and recall those machines currently engaged in exercises. Although totally mystified, I complied at once.

The General then quite bluntly informed me that our Ju 88 Staffel was to be disbanded forthwith and the pilots retrained on single-seaters for daylight fighter operations! This decision came as a direct result of the deteriorating war situation, I was told. It had been taken at the very highest level and brooked no argument. All available remaining resources now had to be channelled into the defence of the homeland and that included, first and foremost, those twin-engined heavy fighter, or *Zerstörer*, units that were still in existence in one form or another.

Truth be told, I was not at all unhappy about the General der Jagdflieger's news. At least something was happening. A new task awaited us and I couldn't wait to get started. For some reason I can no longer recall, the General's departure was then delayed and I had the rare opportunity to talk to him on his own for the best part of two hours. He opened up a little during the course of the conversation and gave me a fascinating glimpse of the present situation as he saw it.

The Allied invasion of Normandy could no longer be contained, let alone be driven back into the sea. We had to accept the fact that large areas in the West were going to be lost to the advancing enemy armies. In the air the Luftwaffe faced a mammoth struggle, and our only hope of turning the tide was first to strengthen our defences in order to buy time. This had to done by every means available if the Reich's towns and cities weren't to be reduced to rubble and ashes before the onset of the coming winter.

The General was therefore planning to create many more new fighter units for the daylight defence of the homeland – a total of 2,000 operational aircraft in all. The American bomber streams that were now parading almost with impunity into the furthermost corners of the Reich had to be stopped in order to give our forces and our industries the necessary breathing space to prepare for the next round of the battle. The possibilities for setting up such a fighter force were there, although – as he himself freely admitted – his plan hadn't found universal approval among the topmost echelons of the Luftwaffe.

Heartened by the General's words, I set about the task of disbanding the Staffel. The pilots would have to attend a conversion course in preparation for single-engined fighter operations. The wireless-operators and gunners were to be posted elsewhere, many to ground duties. All our stores and technical equipment had to be handed in, and our Ju 88C-6s ferried up to a holding unit at Salzwedel.

Within a matter of days everything had been done. On 14 July 1944 I led the aircraft of the *Ergänzungsstaffel/Zerstörergeschwader* 1 for one last time on the nearly 400km flight north from Illesheim to Salzwedel. The field that I remembered so well from my days as a flying instructor had been changed almost beyond recognition by the war. There was a grey, sombre air about the place. Not a trace of the carefree pre-war atmosphere remained. It took me quite some time to get used to the once familiar surroundings again and I found it an altogether depressing experience.

The formalities involved in handing over our Ju 88C-6s were fairly straightforward and quickly dispensed with. And as we had been given very little information as to what we were to do next regarding the activation of our new Geschwader, the first few days at Salzwedel were not exactly bustling with activity.

But then, quite unexpectedly, I found myself caught up in a most unusual situation. During the night of 20/21 July I was woken by a loud hammering on the door of my quarters. I mumbled enter, whereupon one of the signals clerks burst in and thrust a red teleprinter message into my hand, saying that it was most important and required immediate attention. I glanced at the contents – which seemed to consist mainly of a long list of names – without really taking them in, then turned over and promptly went back to sleep.

A little while later the field telephone on my bedside locker rang. The station commander was on the other end of the line. He asked me to come and see him, adding that, given the seriousness of the situation, I should do so immediately and without delay. Before ringing off he said in a friendly, almost conspiratorial tone of voice: 'I think we understand each other, don't we?' I could only assume that he was speaking in a political sense which, in fact, I didn't understand at all.

I quickly got into my uniform and hurried across to the station HQ building to find out what was going on. There I found myself face to face with an extremely affable, grey-haired Major who must have been about the same age as my father. He put me in the picture at once. Apparently there was a power struggle going on between the leading political and military figures in Berlin following a bungled attempt to assassinate the Führer. He then read me a list of names of those high-ranking officers whose orders were *not* to be obeyed.

I could not conceal my utter astonishment. I found it difficult to accept the fact that such a coup could have taken place without any sort of prior warning. It was simply impossible. I had a thousand questions to ask, but the Major brushed them aside, adding that it was very likely that the situation would develop into an armed confrontation between the opposing factions within the armed services. Had it really come to this – brother taking up arms against brother? After all these years of fighting shoulder to shoulder for a common cause? For me the whole idea was unthinkable.

I did not raise the alarm among my own unit immediately. I needed first to make some sort of sense in my own mind of what was obviously still a very confused and volatile situation. I therefore returned to my quarters, where I found two further teleprinter messages awaiting me. Both were brief and to the point; one repeating the list the Major had read out to me naming those individuals whose orders were to be ignored, and the other confirming that, as the assassination attempt had failed, there was no change in the leadership of the Reich.

As far as I was concerned, that meant that everything remained more or less the same as before. I decided to turn in again for a few more hours, leaving instructions to be woken at 5.00 hours. Early the next morning I ordered the men to fall in and explained the bare essentials of the situation to them – not that I knew much more than that myself. I did, however, warn them to be extra vigilant and I also had the ground staff prepare our aircraft for immediate take-off, just in case. As we were still in the middle of reorganizing the unit and I did not yet have any direct means of communication with our new Geschwaderstab, I was left very much to my own devices. I had to act independently, but that didn't worry me unduly – it was something I had had to do often enough in the past.

A few days after the abortive coup, the transitional phase between disbanding our old Staffel and activating the new was complete. It marked the end of another chapter in my Luftwaffe flying career. That chapter had begun in December 1942 as the Battle of Stalingrad was approaching its climax, and had ended with the events of the now historic 20 July 1944 plot. In between, the world had witnessed the titanic Panzer battle at Kursk in July 1943 – which many now regard as the true turning point of the war on the Eastern Front – and had seen the western Allies storm ashore on the beaches of Normandy on D-Day, 6 June 1944.

Although I did not fly any operations during those tumultuous times, I had been kept fully occupied training countless new crews for front-line service. It had been an exacting but rewarding task. Now I was looking forward with fresh hope and renewed confidence to my next role: back on operations flying single-seat Bf 109 fighters as a Staffelkapitän with the newly-activated Jagdgeschwader 4.

Chapter 12
Jagdgeschwader 4

Although officially first established in the summer of 1944, Jagd-geschwader 4 could in fact trace its roots back more than two years to the end of April 1942 when some half-dozen Bf 109s of 1./JG 77 were withdrawn from the Crimean front and transferred back to Romania for rest and re-equipment prior to being sent to North Africa.

The Messerschmitts were still in Romania early in June when a detachment of American B-24 Liberator bombers *en route* to China via the Middle East landed in Egypt. Here they were detained and, on 12 June 1942, used to carry out a low-level dawn bombing raid on the Romanian oilfields at Ploesti.

Although the results achieved by the thirteen Liberators were described as 'negligible', the attack rang warning bells in the corridors of power in Berlin. The oil from the Ploesti fields was vital to the Wehrmacht. And while little damage had been done, the 12 June raid was a worrying sign that the Romanian oilfields were no longer immune from Allied long-range bombers flying up from the Mediterranean.

Immediate steps were taken to strengthen the area's defences. One of the first measures was to cancel the onward transfer of 1./JG 77's Bf 109s to North Africa. Instead, they were retained in Romania where they formed the nucleus of the so-called '*Ölschutzstaffel Ploesti*', or 'Ploesti Oil Protection Squadron'. But a single understrength Staffel was obviously not sufficient for the task in hand and so, over the course of the next few weeks, many more pilots were transferred in, from JG 77 and elsewhere, to join the original six. These newcomers were used not only to reinforce the '*Ölschutzstaffel*', but also to form a second, entirely new Staffel.

In August 1942 this latter was designated as 1./JG 4. At the same time the now greatly expanded '*Ölschutzstaffel*' was divided into two halves to become 2. and 3./JG 4. A little later a fourth Staffel, manned entirely by Romanian Air Force personnel, was added to the unit. And at the beginning of January 1943 a Gruppenstab was activated.

Alongside their Romanian allies, I./JG 4 formed the Luftwaffe's major contribution to the aerial defence of the Ploesti oilfields. And when the enemy did finally return in strength – some 175 Libyan-based Liberators attacked Ploesti on 1 August 1943 – the Gruppe gave a good account of itself, claiming ten of the forty-one American bombers downed in combat.

At the end of 1943 I./JG 4 was transferred to Italy. Here it would remain until August 1944, when it was recalled to Kassel-Rothwesten in Germany where, in the aftermath of the Normandy landings and the escalation of the daylight bombing offensive against the Reich, a completely new Jagdgeschwader was in the process of formation.

Jagdgeschwader 4 was to be composed of three (later four) Gruppen, each of four Staffeln. Its second Gruppe had almost as convoluted an early history as I./JG 4. It had originated out of a proposal by one Major Hans-Günter von Kornatzki for what he termed a *Sturmstaffel* – literally a 'Storm squadron' – equipped with heavily-armed and armoured Focke-Wulf Fw 190s, which would be strong enough to punch their way through to the American four-engined bombers and shoot them down with their heavy-calibre 30mm cannon. Should they fail to do so, the *Sturm* pilot was expected to ram the enemy machine and bring it down by severing part of a wing or the tail unit.

Calls for volunteers had gone out in the autumn of 1943 and *Sturmstaffel* 1 saw its first action on 11 January 1944. Early results were so encouraging that it was not long before it was decided to create two wholly new *Sturmgruppen*. The original *Sturmstaffel* 1 provided the nucleus for one of these: II.(*Sturm*)/JG 4, which was to be commanded by the recently promoted Oberstleutnant von Kornatzki. After a lengthy period spent working up and awaiting delivery of their specially modified Fw 190s, II.(*Sturm*)/JG 4 was finally declared operational at Welzow in the late summer of 1944.

In contrast to the first two Gruppen, III./JG 4's origins were simple in the extreme. It was created from scratch using personnel drawn mainly from the now disbanded III./ZG 1. In line with the post-Normandy restructuring of the Luftwaffe's fighter arm, the new Gruppe was to be made up of four Staffeln – 9., 10., 11. and 12. – and I was appointed Kapitän of the senior Staffel: 9./JG 4.

On the morning of Sunday 23 July 1944 I took off from Salzwedel in one of the last remaining Siebel Si 204s left to us after the disbandment of the *Ergänzungsstaffel* and flew up to Rotenburg an der Wümme, an airfield some 35km to the east of Bremen, to take up my duties. On arrival I was pleased to see a lot of old faces whom I had known during my days with Zerstörergeschwader 1 on the Eastern Front, and who had likewise been ordered to report to the new unit being formed at Rotenburg. That afternoon the first thing we did was to all get together in the mess for a long chat about the current situation in general and the part we would be playing in it.

From some of the remarks made it was clear that many of those present felt an underlying sense of apprehension about our common future. Among the things we discussed were the developments of the past twelve months. And while these had hardly been favourable to us, we decided that the build-up of Luftwaffe strength – every Jagdgeschwader being increased from nine component Staffeln to sixteen, for example – justified fresh hope and a certain cautious optimism on our part. The Luftwaffe High Command had given this expansion programme the code-name '*Phönix*', which was more than a little apt, for we really *were* going to have to rise out of the ashes of what had gone before.

Another subject that came under discussion on that first afternoon in the mess was the differences between fighter and bomber pilots. As quite a sizeable proportion of the pilots seconded to the Gruppe had also come from now-defunct bomber units, we were naturally curious as to their suitability for their new role. The characteristics of a bomber and a fighter pilot were fundamentally opposed. Put in the simplest of terms, one was the hunted and the other the hunter. Both faced their own particular kinds of danger on an almost daily basis. And the longer they survived on ops, the more deeply ingrained their manner of flying became.

But this was not an insuperable problem. It all depended on the individual involved. If a pilot had been properly taught and had mastered the art of flying, he could be retrained to develop new skills and techniques. And that was our first priority: to train our motley intake of *Zerstörer* and bomber pilots and turn them into proficient single-engined fighter pilots.

To do so we transferred the 40km or so from Rotenburg down to Hoya, south of Bremen, on 11 August for three weeks of intensive training. It was during this period, on 23 August, that we received a visit from the General der Jagdflieger, who was making a tour of all the units currently working up prior to taking their place as part of his new and expanded fighter arm. Generalleutnant Galland explained in some detail what our future tasks were to be and expressed his firm conviction that the combined strength of the force he was assembling would be able to stop the streams of US heavy bombers from parading at will across Germany once and for all.

On 31 August the Gruppe moved to its first operational base, the satellite field at Alteno about 90km to the south-east of Berlin. Although now officially on a war footing, we continued with our training, rounding off an intensive programme with a series of formation exercises flown in both Staffel and Gruppe strength. By its close each pilot had clocked up an average of close on twenty-five flying hours familiarizing himself on the Bf 109G. I myself had flown thirty-three training exercises totalling exactly 22 hours and 46 minutes.

Unfortunately, circumstances – by which I mean the increasingly parlous war situation – did not allow us any more time. And the quality of our training also suffered somewhat from the fact that, apart from our Gruppenkommandeur, Hauptmann Friedrich Eberle – who had served throughout the war to date in a succession of operational and training roles – there were hardly any experienced single-engine fighter pilots among our number to show us the ropes. Our combat readiness was inevitably limited by these two factors. But a sense of determination and a resolution to do well could be felt throughout the Gruppe and we all looked forward to our first operation with quiet confidence.

Getting to grips with the enemy, however, was to prove harder than we had imagined. On the morning of 8 September reports began coming in of a large force of '*Viermots*' – American four-engined heavy bombers – nearing the Reich's borders. It was not yet clear exactly where they were heading for. By this stage of the war the Americans were regularly sending more than a thousand bombers on raids over Germany. But they were rarely all aiming for the same target. The bomber streams would more often than not separate into smaller formations of several hundred bombers apiece – each with its own screen of escorting fighters – which, during the latter stages of their approach, would alter course and dogleg to different targets many kilometres apart.

This was done not only to cause the most widespread damage possible, but also to confuse and split our defences. Such tactics certainly made our ground-controllers' job that much harder. On occasion they could not be sure of the intended target until the first bombs were actually falling.

Such was the case on 8 September 1944, when two of the enemy's primary targets were almost 300km apart. At Alteno we weren't scrambled until shortly after midday. But ground control must have quickly realized that there was no chance of our catching any of the American formations for we were recalled to base after just twenty minutes in the air. Exactly the same thing happened the following day when the bombers struck at a number of targets along the Rhine. This time we were scrambled at 10.20 hours, but then ordered back to Alteno after a fruitless chase that had lasted little more than thirty minutes.

Then came Monday, 11 September 1944.

At around 09.00 hours we received the first reports of large numbers of enemy bombers assembling over England. This indicated that yet another heavy raid was in the offing. We were summoned to a quick briefing and by 09.30 hours had been called to cockpit readiness to await developments. But a good hour was to pass, an hour of increasing tension, before a green flare arced into the sky to signal take-off.

The machines of Hauptmann Eberle's Gruppenstab were the first into the air. I watched the cloud of dust they kicked up on the far side of the field as they started to roll. Then it was the turn of my

9. Staffel. Release brakes, push the throttle forward, and rapidly gather speed as we raced across the grass. All sixteen of us got away cleanly and without mishap; the other three Staffeln following close on our heels.

In order not to waste precious seconds when given the order to scramble, the Staffeln did not taxi out to the start line in orderly fashion one after the other. Instead, we each took off in quick succession straight from our dispersal areas and headed out directly across the field. As the four Staffelns' dispersals were spaced at intervals around the perimeter of the field this meant, of course, that their take-off runs were made from all four points of the compass. This was not without a certain amount of risk. It required the utmost concentration from the pilots, and timing was all-important. The practice we had put in paid off, however. Fortunately, there was only a slight wind and the weather was good. Everything went like clockwork. What looked like being our first combat mission had got off to a promising start.

Being among the first to take off, I had been able to watch the whole procedure. It made an impressive sight as the entire Gruppe, some seventy fighters in all, rapidly rose into the air. Now began the process of getting into formation as we climbed away from Alteno and set course for Finsterwalde, the rendezvous point for the mixed battle group of which we were to be part. The climb to our operating altitude of 8,000m was of necessity slow and steady in order to allow the machines flying on the outer flanks of the formation to get into position.

This too went off without incident. We were in good formation, heading for Finsterwalde and gradually gaining altitude all the while. Everything was going according to plan. There had been no recall. Surely nothing could go wrong now. I began to relax. But then the voice of the Gruppenkommandeur, Hauptmann Eberle, suddenly sounded in my earphones: "'Lupine Eins' from "Lupine Anton", take over command, fuel transfer pump malfunctioning, am returning to base.'

I hadn't been expecting this. As senior Staffelkapitän I now found myself leading the entire Gruppe. Although not very comfortable about it, I would simply have to do the best I could. I acknowledged the Kommandeur's transmission with the single word '*Viktor*' – the radio code for 'message received and understood' – and then immediately contacted ground control for instructions. Armed with the necessary information regarding course and altitude, I led the Gruppe the remaining few kilometres south towards the rendezvous point at Finsterwalde.

Here we met up with the other units of the battle group, among them the Fw 190s of Oberstleutnant von Kornatzki's II.(*Sturm*)/JG 4 up from Welzow who, like us, were flying their first combat mission on this day. Overall leadership of the battle group, which I estimated to be about 250 aircraft strong, had been entrusted to the Geschwaderstab of JG 11, a veteran Defence of the Reich fighter unit commanded by Major Günther Specht. The 27-victory Specht had been shot down and wounded in action against RAF bombers over the North Sea in the opening months of the war. Despite the loss of an eye, he returned to ops during the Battle of France and since that time had led an active and varied career. Awarded the Knight's Cross in April 1944, he had been appointed Geschwaderkommodore of JG 11 a month later.

After a successful rendezvous over Finsterwalde, the airfield currently occupied by Stab JG 11, we continued to fly southwards, still steadily climbing the whole time. Everybody was feeling the tension, but there was as yet no sign of the American formation. By now an almost unbroken blanket of cloud had closed in beneath us and I had only a rough idea of our position. There was little chatter over the R/T. We didn't want to alert the enemy to our presence any more than was absolutely necessary.

The sun was almost full in our faces. Despite our excellent goggles, its glare was proving extremely troublesome. It was very hard to stare for any length of time into the achingly blue bowl of the sky searching for the first signs of the enemy. Not only that, we also had to check our instruments at regular intervals – particularly the oxygen supply gauge, which was vital at the height we were now flying. And, unavoidably, it always took a few moments for our eyes to adjust from the outside glare before we could properly make out the instrument panel; moments when we were, quite literally, flying blind.

By now well over an hour had passed since we had rendezvoused over Finsterwalde – but still no sign of the enemy. The tension was becoming almost unbearable. We were all very conscious of the fact that today was the first time for more than four months that our Reich's Defence fighters had risen in any great strength to challenge the American *'Viermots'*. It was the culmination of the General der Jagdflieger's efforts to rebuild his shattered forces after the mauling they had received in the post-invasion fighting over Normandy.

We were also fully aware that the High Command was pinning high hopes on the outcome of today's mission. We were determined to make it a resounding success. But the minutes were ticking by. We had already been in the air for the best part of two hours now, trying to find the elusive enemy bomber formations. Time – and our fuel – were both getting dangerously short.

At long last, however, the ground controller's voice sounded over the radio with the message we had all been desperately waiting to hear: "*Dicke Autos*" ['large cars', the code for heavy bombers] in front of you heading east ...' I acknowledged, but still couldn't see anything. The sky ahead of us remained obstinately empty. I was getting more and more worried. The one thing I feared above all else at this moment would be to fail to find the enemy. The next few minutes were an eternity. But, try as I might, I couldn't see a sign of them.

Then I gradually became aware of a myriad little pinpoints of light twinkling in the far distance – bright sunlight glinting off glass and metal surfaces!

Keeping my eyes firmly fixed on this glittering patch of sky, I reported the sighting to ground control and followed this up with a loud '*Pauke, Pauke!*' over the R/T, warning the Gruppe's pilots to prepare for imminent action. Making doubly sure that my own guns were charged, I led all four Staffeln in a wide sweeping curve that would get us into position behind and slightly above the American bombers just as we had been taught during our recent training.

Now that the enemy had at last been found and the attack was about to begin, all the tension that I had been feeling disappeared in an instant. I was concentrating totally on the job in hand. As my 9. Staffel was leading the Gruppe, I had my choice of targets from among the gently undulating mass of bombers now growing rapidly larger in our sights.

I selected a formation of bombers that was flying a little lower than the main body of enemy machines and which seemed, at the moment, to be devoid of any fighter cover. This, I reckoned, would give us the best chance of delivering one concentrated attack and inflicting the most damage before diving away without interference from either the higher bomber formations or from any enemy fighters that might be lurking around.

Approaching in a shallow dive, we were by now fast closing in on the enemy. Muzzle flashes from the tail guns and upper turrets of the B-17s showed that they were already blazing away at us, but I waited until the range was down to about 200m before opening fire.

The next few seconds are impossible to describe in any coherent manner. I remember giving a few brief bursts of cannon fire and seeing my chosen victim gently slide away from its fellows trailing a thin banner of smoke. But then everything became a kaleidoscopic blur of fragmentary images: bombers exploding in mid-air, others rearing up almost vertically before tumbling helplessly earthwards, torn-off wings spinning through the air, thick clouds of black smoke, stabbing jets of flame, a crazy patchwork of tracer fire, blossoming parachutes – an absolute inferno!

Our large battle group had no hope of re-forming after this one initial scything pass. At our present altitude of very nearly 8,000m our machines simply didn't have the reserves of power needed to get back into any kind of coherent formation in time to carry out a second concerted attack on the bombers and, to make matters worse, we were now under attack ourselves from a horde of American Mustang fighters that had suddenly appeared as if out of nowhere.

Although we had first made contact with the bombers somewhere to the south-west of Chemnitz, the Gruppe was now scattered all over the sky and I was still not sure of our exact position. Wherever I looked there seemed to be dozens of tiny black dots twisting and turning as small groups of fighters clashed in individual dogfights. I was not challenged, however, and so was able to find my way safely back to Alteno where I touched down after a mission that had lasted exactly 150 minutes.

As other pilots returned and were debriefed it soon became apparent that we had succeeded in delivering the devastating blow to the enemy that we had hoped for. The Gruppe's initial claims amounted to nearly twenty B-17s, plus a handful of fighters, well over half of which were subsequently confirmed.

Not surprisingly, 9. Staffel had reaped the lion's share, being credited with eight of the bombers during our opening pass, while 10. Staffel following close behind us had got five. Although I had not been aware of it at the time, both 11. and 12. Staffeln had been bounced by Mustangs before they reached the bombers and had failed to gain any victories.

And while today's mission had also been the first for the Fw 190s operating under their new designation as II.(*Sturm*)/JG 4, many of the pilots of our sister Gruppe had already seen action as members of the specialist anti-bomber *Sturmstaffel* 1. It was therefore hardly surprising that they had achieved even greater success, with a confirmed total of twenty-three B-17s!

I should perhaps point out, however, that a third of the thirty-six bombers claimed by our two Gruppen – including my own – were so-called '*Herausschüsse*'. An '*Herausschuss*', literally a 'shooting-out', was the term used to describe a bomber so severely damaged that it was unable to remain in formation but was forced to drop away from the protection of its box and struggle on alone as best it could.

'*Herausschüsse*' were therefore not classed as kills *per se*, but they did contribute to the points system which the Luftwaffe employed to determine the award of decorations. Thus the confirmed destruction of a heavy bomber earned the victorious fighter pilot four points, whereas an '*Herausschuss*' was rewarded with two. And any pilot who subsequently chanced upon the victim of an earlier '*Herausschuss*' and gave the lone straggler the final *coup de grâce* was awarded just one point.

But we had paid a high price for our success. Our III. Gruppe alone had suffered nine pilots killed and five wounded. And with many others having to bail out or crash-land, our losses in aircraft were even higher: twenty-seven Bf 109s lost or written-off and a further four damaged. The figures for II.(*Sturm*)/JG 4 were comparable. Our baptism of fire had cost us very nearly half our strength!

Despite these catastrophic losses in men and machines, we were sent up again less than twenty-four hours later when another large formation of enemy bombers was reported to be approaching the Reich's borders. Taking off from Alteno shortly before 10.00 hours, we were this time ordered to fly not south-eastwards, but to the north-west in the direction of Magdeburg.

After nearly an hour's steady climbing we were passing to the north of Magdeburg – where, incidentally, I had first taken to the air more than nine years earlier – when we spotted contrails in the distance off to the south-west near Halberstadt. Despite our depleted numbers – we were again being accompanied by the Fw 190s of II.(*Sturm*)/JG 4, but today we could barely muster forty machines between us – we manoeuvred into an attacking position behind one of the bomber boxes. But this time the escorting Mustangs were ready and waiting for us.

Fortunately my 9. Staffel escaped the worst of their onslaught as we were flying a little lower than the rest of the Gruppe. This gave us just enough time for two quick passes at the B-17s, which netted us three '*Herausschüsse*'. I was credited with one of them, while a young Unteroffizier claimed the other two. Although there was no opportunity for another concerted attack, we continued to harry the bombers for the next ten minutes as they ploughed their way towards Magdeburg. During this time the Staffel managed to bring down three B-17s, plus another '*Herausschuss*'.

These were the only bombers claimed by the Gruppe during this mission. And again they had cost us dear: eight pilots killed, two wounded and ten aircraft lost. For the second day in a row we had suffered 50 per cent casualties. How long could we go on like this?

The Fw 190s of II.(*Sturm*)/JG 4 had again performed better than us. They had been credited with thirteen bombers against just four of their own killed and one wounded. But one of the four fatalities was their Gruppenkommandeur, Oberstleutnant Hans-Günter von Kornatzki, the officer widely acknowledged as the 'Father of the *Sturm* idea'. After his aircraft had been damaged by return fire from the group of B-17s that he was attacking, von Kornatzki had attempted an emergency landing in open country to the north-west of Halberstadt, only to hit some power lines and lose his life in the resultant crash.

On the morning of 13 September, for the third time in as many days, we again began to get reports of yet another large formation of American bombers coming in across the North Sea. Any hopes of a respite were soon dashed when we received orders to take off and intercept the enemy. It was a stark reflection of our grievous losses of the last two days that the Gruppe was only able to put seven aircraft into the air – a tenth of the number that had scrambled just forty-eight hours earlier.

Under the circumstances, it was perhaps just as well that our small force failed to make contact with the enemy armada. The American bombers were heading down into the southern part of the Reich and were thus at the very limit of our range. Despite constant guidance from ground control, nearly three hours of assiduous searching in bad weather conditions brought no results and we were ordered to land at Erfurt to refuel before flying back to Alteno.

This day marked the end of Generalleutnant Galland's ambitious scheme to bring a halt to the American daylight bomber offensive by delivering a series of knockout blows from his massed fighter forces. Admittedly, not every one of his painstakingly rebuilt Defence of the Reich Jagdgruppen had suffered to the extent that we had, but the Luftwaffe's overall rate of loss was unsustainable. The task was beyond us. The dream was over.

The next three days remained quiet. There were no enemy incursions and we made good use of the pause to start rebuilding our strength. But we weren't left alone for long. On 17 September we unexpectedly received orders to transfer the nearly 400km due west from Alteno to Bad Lippspringe. The Allies had apparently launched a large-scale airborne assault between Eindhoven and Arnhem in eastern Holland very near to the German border.

As part of the response to this new threat, the Luftwaffe immediately despatched five Defence of the Reich Jagdgruppen, including our own, closer to the area of the landings. We had two tasks to perform. One was to prevent any airborne reinforcements or supplies from reaching the troops on the ground by intercepting and destroying the Allies' transport aircraft, and the other was to strafe those troops already down and fighting to break out of the landing and drop zones.

This had all the makings of another very difficult and costly assignment. Our recent brief period of retraining on single-seaters had concentrated almost exclusively on preparing us for high-altitude anti-bomber missions. Now we were expected to operate at medium to ground level against what would undoubtedly be strong opposition from enemy fighters and Flak. I had at least some knowledge of ground-support operations from my time as a Bf 110 pilot on the Eastern Front. But for the majority of the Gruppe's younger pilots this would be a totally new and unfamiliar experience.

Over the last seventy-two hours we had more than tripled the number of serviceable fighters that we had been able to send up on 13 September's fruitless search for the American bombers. Thus at 17.20 hours on 17 September – the opening day of the Allied airborne operation – twenty-four of our Bf 109s lifted off from Alteno for the 110-minute flight to Bad Lippspringe.

At 10.43 hours the following morning we took off for our first patrol of the Eindhoven-Arnhem corridor. Our brief was to search for any enemy transport aircraft attempting to drop supplies to the airborne troops fighting on the ground, but the blue skies remained empty. We had to content ourselves with ground strafing the landing zones – destroying a number of abandoned gliders in the process – and targeting those neighbouring areas of woodland where enemy activity had been reported. We returned to Bad Lippspringe with neither kills nor losses to report. But the mission had at least served to give our youngsters a first taste of low-level operations.

The next afternoon, 19 September, it was the same story. We spent some ninety minutes vainly searching the skies for the enemy, but again they were nowhere to be found. Somewhat mystified by the apparent lack of air support the Allied troops on the ground were getting, we landed back at Bad Lippspringe empty-handed.

On 20 September we put up just sixteen fighters; four *Schwärme* taking off at 08.45 hours, but with equally disappointing results. They too returned after a ninety-minute patrol without having made contact with the still elusive enemy. Although, in mitigation, the bright blue skies of the past couple of days had by this time given way to cloud and poor visibility, which admittedly made the hunt that much more difficult.

The weather continued to worsen and we were not called upon to fly our next mission until 24 September, when we formed part of a force of more than sixty fighters tasked with escorting a formation of bomb-carrying Fw 190s in an attack on the pontoon bridge over the River Waal at Nijmegen.

We duly took off from Bad Lippspringe shortly after 08.00 hours as ordered, but the Focke-Wulfs failed to show up at the rendezvous point. After circling the area for some little while we were instructed to head north and strafe the Oosterbeek perimeter just outside Arnhem where the last of the enemy airborne troops were still holding out.

Although the Allied airborne threat to the Arnhem bridge had been successfully contained by our ground forces, the main body of the enemy advancing up from the south was plentifully equipped with Flak weapons and this mission cost the Gruppe its first two Arnhem casualties: one pilot being reported missing, believed killed, and another being wounded, both from 11. Staffel.

It wasn't until the afternoon of 25 September that we finally encountered the enemy in the air. It was our second operation of the day and once again we were part of a larger mixed force, some sixty-five fighters in all, whose mission was to provide support for our troops fighting on the ground to the west of Arnhem. Our Gruppe's particular brief was again to provide close escort for the Fw 190 fighter-bombers that made up part of the formation.

The weather had deteriorated even further. When we took off from Bad Lippspringe at 17.00 hours it was into low-lying cloud and frequent heavy showers of rain. By the time we were approaching the target area the cloud base had lifted slightly but visibility was still very poor.

We were north-east of Nijmegen and had just flown over the unmistakable fork in the Rhine where it split into two as it entered Holland to become the Neder-Rijn and the River Waal, when we bumped into a large number of American medium bombers and their even larger screen of escorting fighters. As soon as they spotted us most of the enemy fighters peeled away from their charges and dived down to attack our formation. All thoughts of our own mission had to be abandoned as we turned to meet the threat and within seconds the cloudy sky was a whirling mass of separate, vicious little dogfights.

The two *Schwärme* that I was leading were flying at an altitude of only some 600m. This was quite a lot lower than the others and before the American fighters reached us I suddenly saw a small group of RAF Spitfires passing just beneath us on an opposite heading. I shouted a warning. But it was too late. The Spitfires had made a fast climbing turn and were already sitting on our tails. Our rearmost man immediately went down in flames as we broke sharply to port and tried to turn the tables by getting behind our opponents. But the British pilots were clearly an experienced bunch and had anticipated our move. Now it was every man for himself.

I had latched onto one of the Spitfires but couldn't keep him in my sights long enough to get in an effective burst. For the best part of ten minutes we twisted and turned in ever more violent manoeuvres, each trying to gain the upper hand until, finally, we lost sight of each other in the squally rain and scudding cloud. My first brush with the RAF after five years of war had been a disappointing and un-satisfactory affair.

My two *Schwärme* had become completely scattered during the fight with the Spitfires and we made our way back to Bad Lippspringe singly or in pairs. At debriefing I subsequently learned that the Gruppe had just one victory to show for the day's mission: an American Mustang fighter shot down by a pilot of 10. Staffel. We had more success twenty-four hours later, however, claiming three RAF Typhoon fighter-bombers in the Arnhem area for the loss of one of our own.

It was not until 27 September, when the Battle of Arnhem was to all intents and purposes over, that RAF Spitfires began to appear in any significant numbers – as we quickly found out to our cost. That afternoon we had been ordered to carry out a ground-strafing mission against concentrations of enemy troops south of the Neder-Rijn, but were bounced by Spitfires as we crossed the German-Dutch border. We managed to down two of the RAF fighters, but lost two of our own pilots killed – both from my 9. Staffel – plus three others wounded.

It was a similar situation two days later when we were sent to attack enemy fighter-bombers reported to be active in the Arnhem area. We were again met by large numbers of English and American fighters and although we claimed three Spitfires and a P-47 Thunderbolt, we lost four more of our own comrades; two killed and two reported missing.

In the short time that we had been in action against the RAF's Spitfires I must admit that I had developed a very healthy respect for them. In my opinion the RAF had the best pilots in the world. The courage, aggression and skill they showed in combat was beyond compare. By this late stage of the war the average RAF pilot was unquestionably better than our own. Our Jagdgruppen contained far too many inadequately-trained youngsters who were ill-prepared for front-line service. Nor must one forget the aircraft we were flying. There is no doubt in my mind that the later marks of Spitfire were far superior to our by now rather tired Bf 109s, certainly as far as engine performance was concerned.

On the morning of 2 October we flew our last operation over the Arnhem bridgehead area. It was another ground-support mission and after finding and shooting up some enemy armoured vehicles we all returned safely to Bad Lippspringe at 11.20 hours.

The next two days were taken up by a protracted and piecemeal return to Alteno. But by the early afternoon of 4 October we were all back at our old base and soon found ourselves in the thick of Defence of the Reich operations once again.

On the morning of 6 October came the by now all-too-familiar reports of enemy bomber activity. We were first brought to cockpit readiness and then scrambled shortly after 10.30 hours. Our orders were to head for Finsterwalde, where we were to rendezvous with the Fw 190s of II.(*Sturm*)/JG 4. Having met up, our two Gruppen set course north-westwards to intercept the incoming bombers. After little more than an hour we had our first sighting of the American '*Viermots*' to the west of Berlin.

During the pre-op briefing back at Alteno it had been stressed that our primary task was to provide top cover for the Focke-Wulfs of II. Gruppe. But the enemy's escorting fighters were a little slow off the mark on this occasion, which allowed us simply to follow the Fw 190s down in the usual wide sweeping curve that put us into the ideal position for a stern attack.

The results were devastating. In the space of just five minutes the pilots of II.(*Sturm*)/JG 4 claimed no fewer than twenty-two B-17s! Close on their heels, our Gruppe added a further five bombers – including two '*Herausschüsse*' – and two P-51 fighters at the cost of two of our own number killed. It was one of the last major successes we would score in Defence of the Reich operations.

Twenty-four hours later our two Gruppen were again in action, but – although part of a much larger force – with far less impressive results. The Fw 190s were able to claim seven bombers in the engagement to the north of Weimar, whereas we were credited with a single P-51 Mustang, again for the loss of two of our own.

The rest of October remained surprisingly free of incident as far as we were concerned. The Gruppe failed to achieve any victories and suffered just one casualty. The latter was a pilot of my 9. Staffel who was posted missing, believed shot down and killed, on 16 October.

Our mission on that date had been noteworthy in two respects. Firstly, we were accompanied by the Bf 109s of I./JG 4 which had, until now, been serving under *Luftwaffenkommando West* and had played no part in the Defence of the Reich campaign and, secondly, our opponents were not the heavy bombers of the US 8th Air Force based in England, but their counterparts of the 15th Air Force flying up from Italy to attack targets in the one-time Czech territories.

The relative dearth of action during the latter half of October had enabled the Gruppe to rebuild its strength. By the end of the month we again had an establishment of over fifty fighters; a mixture of the latest Bf 109G variants plus a handful of the new Bf 109Ks. But this was on paper. The reality in terms of our serviceability returns was somewhat different.

On 2 November, for example, when Jagdgeschwader 4 flew its first operation with a full complement of four Gruppen – a new IV./JG 4 had been added to our ranks on 20 October simply by redesignating the existing II./JG 5 – we were hard pressed to put more than half of those fifty fighters into the air. But, given the enemy's overwhelming numerical superiority, it was almost immaterial whether we sent up twenty-five or fifty of our own fighters in opposition. As it was, we suffered five casualties, three killed and two wounded, without achieving a single victory on this date.

I had been granted a short spell of home leave at the end of October – my last home leave of the war – and so missed the 2 November mission. But I returned to Alteno a week or so later to find that changes were afoot. It was not only in the air that the Allies enjoyed the advantage. Five months had passed since the Normandy landings and the enemy's ground forces were now getting dangerously close to the Reich's western borders in many places. The first Germany city, Aachen, had in fact already been occupied by the Americans.

On 19 November we therefore received orders to leave Alteno and transfer west to an airfield nearer the Rhine. Here our task would be to help relieve some of the pressure on our hard-pressed ground forces by engaging the fighter-bombers that were supporting the enemy's advance through eastern France. But preparations for the move were almost immediately interrupted by an emergency scramble and instructions to head down towards Prague to intercept a formation of heavy bombers reported to be flying up from Italy. Having failed to locate the enemy force, we returned to Alteno some two hours later only to find that the weather had closed in, making the planned transfer impossible.

It was perhaps indicative of the confusion and uncertainty beginning to surround our future deployment that when we did finally make the move the following day we were sent not westwards, but down to Erfurt, near Weimar, where we were given brief instruction in the use of the new and improved 'Y-System' of ground control.

Twenty-four hours later our new-found knowledge was put to the test. The weather had worsened considerably during the night and the Erfurt runway was being lashed by heavy rain when our twenty-plus Bf 109s began taking off at around 11.00 hours to intercept an incoming force of heavy bombers.

The 'Y-System' came into operation the moment we were off the ground, with the controller ordering us to climb on a north-easterly bearing through the thick rain clouds. Although we were of course unaware of it at the time, one of the bomber formations was heading for the oil refineries at Merseburg, which was only about 80km to the north-east of Erfurt, and we were being directed straight towards it.

Little more than fifteen minutes later, while still climbing, we emerged from the clouds only to be set upon by a swarm of P-51 Mustangs. We lost eight fighters – over a third of our strength – in the ensuing action, with one pilot killed and four wounded. In return, our Gruppe submitted claims for four B-17s and one Mustang destroyed. Exactly how many bombers were actually shot down is no longer certain. But whatever the number, they were the last to be credited to Jagdgeschwader 4 during the unit's involvement in Defence of the Reich operations.

After our mauling at the hands of the Mustangs we were ordered to land first at Esperstedt before returning to Erfurt later that same afternoon. Another five days were to pass before, on 26 November, we were finally transferred to the Western Front. Our destination was Biblis, an airfield close to the Rhine south of Darmstadt.

At Biblis we were no longer part of the Defence of the Reich command. We now found ourselves subordinated to the *Jagdflieger- führer Mittelrhein* (Fighter Commander Middle Rhine), the tactical fighter air command responsible for supporting ground operations on the central sector of the Western Front. But although now officially employed in a tactical role – our primary tasks being to combat the enemy's fighter-bombers, as well as to fly ground-attack missions of our own – we were also expected to take part in Defence of the Reich operations as and when the situation demanded.

In order to do this our Bf 109s needed to be able to fly and fight in two different configurations. But our ever-resourceful ground crews quickly mastered the art of converting our machines from one role to the other in a matter of minutes.

In the event, they weren't called upon to demonstrate their skills as we didn't participate in any further Defence of the Reich missions and our role remained purely one of ground-support. Most of our new young pilots were totally unsuited for such operations, however. They hadn't been given the necessary prior training. But there was an easy solution to this problem. We simply kept them on the ground and didn't schedule them to fly operations. We had far more pilots than serviceable aircraft in any case. But this didn't go down at all well with many of the youngsters. Despite their inexperience, they were full of fighting spirit and felt that they were being unfairly held back.

I still remember one particular case very well. One young pilot, barely nineteen years of age and newly posted to my Staffel, kept asking me why I wasn't allowing him to take part in our operations. 'Too few aircraft and tough missions that require a lot of experience', was my stock reply. And this was putting it mildly. Our missions weren't just tough, they were murderous.

I was therefore always very careful about which of my pilots I selected to fly. But one day this young Unteroffizier's father came to visit him at Biblis. He chatted to his son and his comrades and, quite naturally, I was introduced to him too. He took the opportunity to enquire about his son's not yet having flown any combat missions. I offered him the same explanation that I had given his son – the current situation was so dangerous that only the most experienced pilots stood any chance of survival against the overwhelming might of the enemy. But he wouldn't let the matter drop, and so I told him that on the next operation which, in my opinion, promised even the slightest reduction of possible risk, I would let his son accompany us. The opportunity arose far sooner than I could have imagined.

During the first half of December 1944 our entire Gruppe had been credited with just one solitary victory: a P-47 Thunderbolt downed during a sweep west of Cologne on 12 December. But all that was about to change when, four days later, Hitler launched his last great gamble in the west – a massive counter-offensive through the Ardennes.

In the early hours of 16 December our armoured spearheads smashed through the thinly-held American lines in a number of places. The enemy troops were confused and disorganized. Many were in full retreat. The fluidity of the situation on the ground meant that the American fighter-bombers would have great difficulty in distinguishing friend from foe amongst the densely wooded hills and valleys of the Ardennes region. And this, together with the poor weather conditions would, I hoped, help to reduce both their numbers and their effectiveness.

A mission on the first day of the ground offensive had achieved little, with neither victories nor losses to record. But if I expected the same on 17 December I was to be sadly disappointed. The Gruppe took off from Biblis at 09.25 hours and set course north-westwards for the battle area. After half-an-hour in the air we had just flown over Malmédy in Belgium on the northern shoulder of the breakthrough when our small formation of about twenty Bf 109s was met by a much larger force of P-47 Thunderbolts.

The encounter immediately erupted into a series of fierce individual dogfights. The action over the high ground to the east of Malmédy must have lasted the best part of thirty minutes in all, but in the poor visibility and low-hanging cloud it was difficult to know exactly what was going on. It was only at debriefing back at Biblis that a balance could be drawn. Once again the Gruppe had lost a third of its aircraft: six Bf 109s shot down, plus a seventh badly damaged and forced to make a belly-landing. Three of our pilots had been killed. Only one of them was a member of my 9. Staffel – the youngster who had so desperately wanted to fly a mission with us.

In return we had brought down three of the enemy, one of which I had accounted for with a quick burst of cannon and machine-gun fire as he appeared out of the gloom and sailed unsuspectingly straight through my line of sight. Perhaps he too had been a beginner, eager to join the fight but lacking the experience to survive the lethal reality of air combat.

But experience alone was no guarantee of safety, as I was to find out myself just forty-eight hours later. After being debriefed at Biblis, we were ordered to stand by for another transfer. That same afternoon we then made the short 20km hop northwards to Darmstadt-Griesheim, a field we would henceforth share with the Bf 109s of I. Gruppe. And it was from Griesheim that we took off shortly after mid-day on 19 December for a so-called *'freie Jagd'* sweep – a roving patrol – of the Ardennes area with orders to seek out and attack targets of opportunity.

After rendezvousing with other units over Frankfurt, our four *Schwärme* crossed the Rhine south of Koblenz and headed for the scene of the fighting in the wooded hills beyond the German-Belgian border. The persistently poor weather conditions again forced us to keep to a fairly low altitude, which made a mission of this kind all the more difficult. Despite flying a zigzag course beneath the lowering cloud base we were unable spot any targets. But then, on the plus side, neither did we meet any opposition in the air – or, at least, not at first.

We could tell from the hubbub in our headphones that there were hostile aircraft somewhere in the vicinity, but down as close to the trees as we were we couldn't see any sign of them. Then control called us directly to inform us that twenty-plus enemy fighters had been reported in the Koblenz region flying in a westerly direction. This meant they were heading straight for us. Our formation leader immediately gave the order to climb up through the cloud to intercept the approaching enemy.

As I broke through the cloud layer I saw a host of black dots rapidly bearing down on me and a split-second later I was bang in the middle of a mass of American Thunderbolts that were obviously heading for home. I was totally alone – the others hadn't yet emerged from the clouds – surrounded by at least a squadron of enemy fighters!

The Thunderbolts were no doubt as equally surprised by my sudden appearance in their midst. They quickly encircled me and, without any conscious action on my part, I almost at once found myself sitting on the tail of one of them. I wasn't more than 30m away from the enemy machine at most. And at that range I couldn't miss. My opening salvo of cannon fire tore large pieces off the P-47 and it immediately burst into flames.

To avoid colliding with the blazing Thunderbolt I climbed away above him in a sharp right-hand curve, then straightened out for an instant to orientate myself. But that was an instant too long. Ahead of me I caught a momentary glimpse of another Thunderbolt climbing steeply directly towards me, its wings two bright lines of flickering fire as the enemy pilot let fly at me with all eight of his heavy machine-guns. There was an almighty bang. My windscreen was covered in oil, and for a second or two I was totally blind.

I instinctively flipped the Me onto its back and went down almost vertically – back into the safety of the clouds – in an effort to make good my escape. I pulled the small yellow lever beneath the windscreen. A jet of aviation fuel sprayed the windscreen, clearing the armoured glass of its thick film of oil and enabling me to see again. By now I was getting dangerously close to the ground but fortunately I had already begun to pull out of the dive while still in the shelter of the cloud, otherwise I might have come to a sticky end there and then.

As it was, I levelled out into a narrow valley just below the crest of a wooded ridge. None of the enemy had attempted to follow me down; at least, I couldn't see anybody. But the constant stream of reports in my headphones told me that there were still a lot of enemy fighters about. So, keep a sharp eye out!

The next thing on the agenda was to check how the machine handled. The Me seemed to be flying smoothly enough, but the engine had obviously suffered some damage. The oil and coolant temperature gauges were rising at a disturbing rate. I would have to be prepared for an emergency landing at any time. The minutes dragged by. But once safely back across the Rhine I was more than relieved to see the Frankfurt Autobahn. Not only would this make an ideal emergency landing strip if the need arose, it also helped me establish my bearings.

The machine was still flying well. I had eased back on the throttle in order to be able get as far south as possible in the direction of Griesheim. Ground-control was still issuing reports of enemy air activity in the region, but my luck held and I wasn't spotted.

A small town appeared below me. There wasn't a roof left intact. I could look down into the interiors of the destroyed buildings – into people's homes – even right down into the cellars of some of them. It was a sobering and deeply perturbing experience to see destruction on such a scale.

I had been searching for Frankfurt-Rebstock airfield, thinking I could perhaps put down there. But it wasn't proving easy to find, and the old crate was still flying. So why give up just yet? With Frankfurt behind me, it wasn't long before I saw Darmstadt on the horizon, and then Griesheim just a few kilometres beyond off to the south-west. I radioed ahead to flying control to inform them of my condition and to let them know that I had now also discovered that I couldn't lower my undercarriage. The hydraulic system must have been damaged and the emergency manual handwheel wasn't working either. I was told that fire tenders and an ambulance would be standing by in case I needed help after belly-landing.

The field was covered in a light haze. Approaching from a height of about 500m, I reduced speed as much as I dared and entered a gentle curve, hoping to float in for a precision landing close to where the emergency services were waiting. Luckily, as I slowed down, first one and then the other undercarriage leg dropped and locked into position – two green lights! – and I was able to make a near perfect three-pointer. The brakes had had it, of course, and I didn't finally roll to a stop until the far end of the field. The ground crew were quickly on the scene. The looks on their faces as they surveyed the damage to my trusty old bird was a sight to behold. They later counted eighty-two bullet holes in her. I hadn't suffered so much as a scratch.

I then had another close shave on one of our very next missions. We had taken off in separate *Schwärmen* as usual and again had orders to rendezvous with machines of other Gruppen over Frankfurt before heading for the Ardennes. I was leading the rearmost *Schwarm* and had my job cut out to remain in visual contact with those ahead of us. I couldn't afford to close up on them too tightly, as I also had to maintain a constant watch for any signs of enemy aircraft in the surrounding airspace, as well as keep a check on our own course and position. Due to the poor visibility and the low altitude at which we were flying, this latter wasn't at all easy and I only had a rough idea of where we actually were.

There was still a lot of movement on the ground and consequently we hadn't been given a precise briefing. Our orders were simply: patrol the area to the south of Düren and engage enemy troops by carrying out low-level attacks on targets of opportunity. In other words, find your own targets – shades of the Eastern Front all over again!

And then suddenly, and without any warning, the aircraft at the head of the leading *Schwarm* burst into flames. A moment later a second machine went plummeting down like a blazing torch. We had unwittingly flown straight over a heavily defended enemy position hidden in a steep-sided valley. From our height of only 200m we had not spotted it until we were almost on top of it, by which time it was far too late to take avoiding action.

We were enveloped in a dense web of tracer and hemmed in on all sides by the bursts of exploding Flak shells. I felt my Bf 109 take several hits. It no longer responded fully to the controls. The entire machine was rattling and shaking. Our formation quickly fell apart as we all tried to reverse course and head back eastwards to friendly territory. In a situation like this it was every man for himself. Any damaged machine was on its own. The others were in no position to offer any defensive fire to cover its withdrawal.

I was attempting to keep my wounded bird on an easterly heading. I had only a very vague idea of where I was. I was pinning all my hopes on 'Old Father Rhine', which I would have to cross at some point. And, sure enough, it wasn't long before I spotted the broad ribbon of the Rhine ahead of me, looking grey and leaden beneath the overcast sky. The tops of many of the hills lining its banks were hidden in cloud.

The aircraft was now shaking violently the whole time and I prepared myself for the worst. But the Me was still flying, even though it was taking every bit of muscle power in my right leg to hold it roughly on course. The tail surfaces had been so badly damaged that it required all my strength to counteract its force by keeping the machine in a constant bank. Thankfully, the engine hadn't been hit – it was still running normally – but the fuselage, tail and wings had all taken a real beating.

I continued to crab south for what seemed like hours before finally landing at Darmstadt with the last of my strength. Another difficult and costly mission was over. I was unwounded, but the Me was a write-off. By this stage the Gruppe desperately needed to make good its recent heavy losses in men and machines. As a result we were stood down for a week; a very welcome and necessary break after the attrition of the last few days.

Towards the end of December, while the Gruppe was still off ops, I received orders to attend a formation leaders' course at the *Verbandsführerschule G.d.J.* (General of Fighters' School for Formation Leaders) at Königsberg/Neumark, an airfield some 80km to the north-east of Berlin. I thus missed the now notorious Operation '*Bodenplatte*' ('Baseplate'), the Luftwaffe's ill-fated attempt to regain air superiority over the Western Front by attacking the Allies' tactical air bases in the Low Countries and eastern France.

Flown on the early morning of New Year's Day, 1 January 1945, by fighters from no fewer than eleven Jagdgeschwader, plus elements from a number of other units, the aim of '*Bodenplatte*' was to break the back of Allied tactical air power on the mainland of Europe. And while more than 300 Allied aircraft were reportedly destroyed, and almost another 200 damaged, it proved to be a Pyrrhic victory for the Luftwaffe. We ourselves lost 217 fighters, plus many more damaged, with 213 of our pilots killed, missing or captured.

Such a war of attrition was one that we could not hope to win. While the Allies were quickly able to replace their losses from their vast pool of resources, '*Bodenplatte*' sounded the death-knell for our fighter arm. If Generalleutnant Galland still harboured any lingering hopes of a knockout blow against the Americans' high-flying heavy bombers, they had been dashed once and for all. His force had been squandered on a series of costly low-level attacks for no lasting gain and would never again pose any serious threat to the enemy.

Each of the eleven Jagdgeschwader involved in '*Bodenplatte*' had been assigned its own specific target airfield or airfields and these had been attacked with varying degrees of success. Unfortunately, our Geschwader's performance had been the poorest of all. Although all four Gruppen – nearly seventy machines in total – took part in the operation, they completely failed to find their assigned target, the airfield at Le Culot to the south-east of Brussels. It is not known how many Allied aircraft JG 4's pilots destroyed or damaged on the ground in their attacks on other airfields in and around the Belgian capital, but their aerial claims amounted to just one: an Auster light spotter aircraft of the RAF. Against this they suffered twenty pilots killed, missing or captured, plus five wounded – once again the Geschwader had lost over a third of its number.

I. and III./JG 4 had put up a combined force of thirty-five Bf 109s from the base we shared at Darmstadt-Griesheim. I. Gruppe provided the bulk of these fighters, twenty-six against our Gruppe's nine, but as their Kommandeur was currently grounded, it was our Gruppenkommandeur, Hauptmann Friedrich Eberle, who had been selected to lead the formation. All went well until shortly after crossing the front lines near Malmédy. Here the Bf 109s suddenly came under concentrated Flak fire. And it was at this point that Hauptmann Eberle's nine machines abruptly altered course and, for some inexplicable reason, retired eastwards. This action was to have some very unpleasant consequences, with Hauptmann Eberle subsequently standing trial charged with cowardice in the face of the enemy.

Attending the formation leaders' school at Königsberg/Neumark, I was far removed from these events on the Western Front. The first *Verbandsführerlehrgang* (Formation Leaders' Training Course) had been organized back in November 1943 as a precaution against the increasing number of fighter unit leaders being lost in the early months of the American daylight bombing offensive. Since that time the situation that had at first been simply a matter of concern had grown into crisis proportions. The recent '*Bodenplatte*' operation alone had cost the Luftwaffe three Geschwaderkommodore, five Gruppenkommandeure and no fewer than fourteen Staffelkapitäne.

In the last twelve months the original Formation Leaders' Training Course had undergone a number of changes in designation, location and commanding officers. The current commander was Major Günther Rall, one of the Luftwaffe's most renowned, experienced and – with a phenomenal 274 victories to his credit – successful fighter pilots. He was ably assisted by a staff of equally capable and knowledgeable instructors on both the theoretical and the practical sides of the course. They were all very proficient and we gained many a fresh insight into the demands and responsibilities of leadership in the air.

The 'pupils' all had a lot of combat experience under their belts and many sported the highest awards for bravery. For a brief while we even had among our number the highest scoring fighter pilot of all – one Hauptmann Erich '*Bubi*' Hartmann – before he was urgently recalled to his unit on the Eastern Front.

The flying programme was kept short and was used mainly to demonstrate the latest tactical developments. This was particularly useful for the trainees on the element leaders' course, which was being run in parallel to our own.

The theoretical side of the curriculum was excellent. Based on experience gained from all the fighting fronts, it offered a comprehensive and fascinating overview of the direction the air war had taken to date. Given the current situation, however, there was unfortunately very little practical use to which this newly acquired fund of knowledge could be put.

Of particular interest was a talk given by a guest speaker on the preparations for, and conduct of the Ardennes counter-offensive, which had been launched in a completely new way. Unlike the Wehrmacht's earlier campaigns, the Battle of the Ardennes did not kick off with a massed set-piece advance by large bodies of troops and armour, which stood absolutely no chance of remaining undiscovered by enemy reconnaissance, but rather with carefully separated combat groups and small formations that were able to make full use of the local terrain to remain undetected.

Those of us who had been flying over the Ardennes area on an almost daily basis had certainly spotted no signs of the massive build-up of forces taking place below us. Nor, obviously, had the enemy – otherwise our initial successes would not have been so spectacular. As later became apparent, total surprise had been achieved and the confusion sown behind the American lines was widespread.

It was not until the weather improved at the start of the second week of the offensive, allowing the enemy to deploy his over-whelming air power, that the situation began to change. Square metre after square metre of the battlefield was ploughed up by bombs until there was nothing left moving, and only then did the Americans begin to launch their own devastating counter-attacks. Nothing short of a strong and effective aerial umbrella could have enabled our ground troops to continue their advance westwards, and this we were no longer able to provide. The offensive faltered and withered, and with it our hopes of turning the tide of the war on the Western Front.

Alongside the many discussions we had on the Luftwaffe's purely aerial commitments, there was also an exchange of experiences and opinions on ground-support operations. And here our views were very much at odds. I won't go into details here – this is a subject that would fill an entire book on its own – suffice it to say that, at that time, the majority agreed with the then General der Jagdflieger, who declared that the skies had first to be swept clean of all opposition before any thought could be given to other forms of operational requirements.

We were also especially interested in hearing all about the latest technical developments in ground-control procedures, although here too we were unable to derive any real benefits from the knowledge gained. It was again far too late to put in place the necessary measures.

It must also be said the subject of ground-to-air cooperation was not covered in any great depth. The reason for this was no doubt partly due to the very strict secrecy which prevented any meaningful discussions on the subject. But I also got the impression that there was very little inclination to embrace these latest technical innovations. The fighter fraternity placed much more value on freedom of movement, hunting the enemy and engaging him in one-to-one combat, rather than being held on an invisible electronic leash under the guidance of some faceless ground-controller.

Another subject touched upon was the economics of warfare and the Reich's external foreign trade relationships with other nations. This helped us understand a little better the economical involvement between the warring and neutral states and the consequent supply bottlenecks this imposed upon our enemies. Interesting and informative as this subject was, its relevance in our present dire situation was again questionable, to say the very least. And it wasn't long before harsh reality intervened.

On 12 January 1945 the Red Army launched a major offensive on the Eastern Front. Our course was terminated a few days early and we were ordered to return to our units forthwith. For me this meant travelling by rail, via Berlin and Frankfurt am Main, to Altenstadt, the airfield some 30km to the north-east of Frankfurt where my 9. Staffel was based – or, rather, had been based. For when I finally arrived there on the night of 29 January the nest was empty apart from a small rear party and a few unserviceable Bf 109s. The Staffel had decamped six days earlier for the Eastern Front; more specifically for Drewitz, a field just over 100km to the south-east of Berlin.

On the morning of 2 February I took off from Altenstadt in one of the Bf 109s that the mechanics had managed to get airworthy again and set off for Drewitz to rejoin 9. Staffel and the rest of III. Gruppe. I landed there at 10.25 hours to discover that quite a number of changes had taken place during my five weeks' absence.

The most obvious of these was the change in command. Although he had been acquitted of the charge of cowardice during *'Bodenplatte'*, Hauptmann Eberle had been relieved of command of III./JG 4 on 8 January and moved to a staff position. His place at the head of the Gruppe was taken by Hauptmann Gerhard Strasen, whose operational career had begun with JG 26 on the Channel front in 1942. The following year he had been transferred to JG 77 in the Mediterranean theatre. After recovering from wounds received in action against B-17s over Italy, he was then appointed Geschwader-Adjutant of JG 77 in December 1943, the office he held until becoming the new Gruppenkommandeur of III./JG 4.

One thing that hadn't changed, however, was the continuing disparity in numbers between the pilots on strength and the aircraft available for them to fly. At Drewitz by the start of February the Gruppe had no more than a dozen serviceable Bf 109s, but nearly twice that number of pilots. Despite this, I was able to undertake my first sortie in this new area of operations on the afternoon of my arrival.

My target was a large body of Red Army troops near Züllichau. They were reported to be advancing on the River Oder, which lay only some 20km in front of them. Two winters ago I was supporting our ground forces as they fought their way towards the River Volga and Stalingrad. Now I was trying to prevent the Russians from reaching the River Oder, the last major water barrier before Berlin. It was a chilling reminder, if any were needed, of just how dramatically the tide of war had changed, and a clear indication that the final phase of the conflict was about to begin.

In all, I flew a total of eighteen missions during the thirteen days I spent at Drewitz. By 5 February the Red Army had reached the banks of the Oder less than 50km from Berlin and had thrown bridgeheads across the river to the north and south of the fortified cities of Küstrin and Frankfurt-an-der-Oder. Our efforts were directed against these bridgeheads and the troops moving up to consolidate them. The missions we flew were hard and costly. During these two weeks the Gruppe suffered four pilots killed and double that number of aircraft destroyed or damaged; casualties that we could ill afford, given our already weakened and depleted state.

Having gained their footholds on the western bank of the Oder, the Russians were determined to defend them at all costs. Our attempts to contain them were hampered by the extremely poor flying conditions. We often had great difficulty in establishing our own positions from those of the enemy. We nearly always flew in *Schwarm* strength, and even then it was hard to keep in contact with each other. Nor had the Red Army lost any of its ability to make use of camouflage, and a lot of our time had to be spent searching for prospective targets.

To complicate matters yet further, we were never entirely sure how many of our own people – military or civilian – were still holed up in the numerous villages and farmsteads that dotted the countryside on either side of the Oder. This was also a problem when we detected movements on the roads – were they convoys of horse-drawn enemy troops, or columns of refugees fleeing westwards?

Russian fighters were increasingly in evidence, but they caused us little trouble. They still showed few signs of aggression. Why this was so, we couldn't understand. Perhaps they wanted to keep their strength in reserve for the last great battle to come.

By 13 February it was clearly time for us to start looking for another base. With the Oder now behind them, Red Army forces were rapidly pushing westwards and getting dangerously close to Drewitz. I was ordered to take the Gruppe's Bf 108 courier machine and reconnoitre a clutch of airfields and landing grounds some kilometres to the west of us to find a suitable new location from which we could operate without fear of being overrun. The following morning I duly set off to try my luck at Gahro, Alteno and Jüterbog-Damm. The results were not all that encouraging, but the landing strip outside Jüterbog, some 60km to the south of Berlin, seemed to offer the best prospects.

At 08.10 hours on the morning of 15 February I therefore took off from Drewitz to make the transfer to Jüterbog; or, at least, that was my intention. But I had hardly got off the ground before my engine started coughing and spluttering. Moments later it gave up altogether. There wasn't time for lengthy deliberation; something had to be done, and done quickly. So, as practised and preached so often in the past, it was a case of keeping my eyes peeled for a suitable spot for an emergency landing while, at the same time, going through all the usual cockpit drills required in just such an emergency.

Luckily, all went reasonably well. After one or two bumps and bounces, which didn't do a lot for my backbone, the Bf 109 finally slid to a stop on its belly. Now all I had to do was find someone who could give me a lift back to Drewitz. It shouldn't take long. The whole flight from take-off to touch down had lasted barely ten minutes.

Once back at Drewiz I had another go at getting to Jüterbog. This time I was more successful, hitching a lift with the rear party in one of the last cars just about to set off on the 100km journey. On the way we passed streams of refugees all heading west to escape the advancing Red Army. The sight of this tide of human misery – women, children and the elderly – affected me deeply. Powerless to help, unable to do anything to relieve their obvious suffering, it was a truly horrifying experience to have to drive past them for kilometre after endless kilometre. It was from this moment on that I began to experience real apprehension. How was it all going to end?

In Jüterbog there was yet more confusion as to our future employment. It took quite a while before we were declared operational again. The whole situation was full of doubt and uncertainty. I flew only one combat mission while at Jüterbog. This was on 8 March when Geschwaderkommodore Oberstleutnant Michalski and his wingman, both flying Fw 190D-9 *'Langnasen'* – 'Long noses'; so called because the D-9, the latest version of the Focke-Wulf fighter, was the first variant to be powered by a Junkers Jumo liquid-cooled engine in a lengthened nacelle – led sixteen of our Gruppe's Bf 109s up on a bomber-escort mission.

Our charges were about a dozen Junkers Ju 88s and Ju 188s of Kampfgeschwader 200, a specialist bomber unit equipped with a variety of aircraft and advanced weaponry. Among today's group were four of the so-called *'Mistel'* ('Mistletoe') composites. These consisted of a single-engined fighter sitting on struts atop an unmanned Ju 88 bomber packed with high explosives. When nearing the objective, the pilot of the fighter would release the bomber component and use radio-guidance to steer it onto its target. The *'Mistel'* was a cumbersome contraption, but it packed a lethal punch, causing extensive damage and leaving a huge crater wherever it hit.

On this particular mission the bombers' targets were the two pontoon bridges the Red Army had thrown across the River Oder at Göritz, about 10km upstream from Küstrin. On the approach flight our force encountered a number of Soviet Yak-9 fighters but, again, these showed little inclination to engage us in combat. I do not know the results of the bombing – the '*Mistel*' was a notoriously difficult weapon to deliver accurately on target – but all four *Schwärme* of our Gruppe returned safely to Jüterbog. The day's only aerial success had been a Yak-9 claimed by the Geschwaderkommodore.

To keep ourselves busy and prevent demoralization from setting in, we whiled away the long days at Jüterbog by organizing what can only be described as a sort of self-help welfare programme. After all, none of us knew what the immediate future held. We each had our own private thoughts on the subject, no doubt, and had a picture in our own minds of what the coming weeks and months would bring. But discussing such matters openly kept the bonds of comradeship strong.

The dearth of operational activity at Jüterbog meant that, by the close of March, the Gruppe was still at full strength with a complement of more than sixty pilots. Aircraft numbers still lagged behind, however, with just over forty machines serviceable. But these deceptively healthy totals were more than offset by the crippling lack of fuel, which was now keeping many units anchored to the ground.

The fuel situation was, in fact, so critical that rumours had been floating around for some time that our Geschwader was to be deactivated. They appeared to be confirmed when first I. Gruppe, and then IV. Gruppe, were disbanded within four days of each other at the end of March/beginning of April. A few of the more experienced of their pilots were selected for conversion training and future service on the revolutionary Me 262 twin-jet fighter. Some were posted across to us. But the majority of their personnel were remustered as ground troops.

Many of the two units' Bf 109s were also handed over to us, which seemed to suggest that we had been granted a stay of execution. And, indeed, just forty-eight hours later we received orders to transfer down to Löbnitz, a field about 40km to the north of Leipzig. Here – together with the Fw 190s of II. Gruppe, which had likewise been transferred down from the Berlin area to nearby Mörtitz – we would be facing not eastwards, but westwards. Our new task: to support the army units in the Mühlhausen region that were desperately trying to halt the Americans' advance across Thuringia towards the River Elbe and a link-up with the Russians.

I made the 80-kilometre flight from Jüterbog to Löbnitz on 7 April. It was a shock to realize just how much progress the Americans had made since crossing the Rhine. If they continued to advance at this rate it could only be a matter of weeks, if not days, before they made contact with the Red Army and the Reich was split in two.

But such was the chaos and confusion of these closing stages of the war that on 12 April, after just five days at Löbnitz, we were summoned back north to Mark Zwuschen, an airfield little more than 15km away from Jüterbog, the base we had vacated less than a week earlier.

Although we continued to carry out the occasional low-level attack on American troops and transport – on 14 April, for example, the Gruppe despatched more than fifty of its Bf 109s to strafe American convoys in the Magdeburg area – at Mark Zwuschen we were once again facing the Russians. With the Red Army preparing for its final onslaught on Berlin, the war in the air had suddenly become more bitter and ferocious. The scarlet-nosed Yaks of 'Stalin's Eagles', the Red Air Force's élite Guards fighter units, were very much in evidence and clearly spoiling for a fight. They displayed none of the reluctance that we had noticed in our earlier brushes with their less colourful comrades.

Despite being faced with this much stiffer opposition, I nonetheless managed to claim three victories in the space of just seventy-two hours while at Mark Zwuschen. The first of these occurred late on the morning of 16 April – the day the Soviets launched their all-out attack on Berlin – during a lengthy *freie Jagd* sweep to the south and east of the capital. We had taken off at 10.30 hours and it was some forty-five minutes later, when we were approaching Küstrin towards the end of the mission, that I happened to spot a low-flying Airacobra. The Russian pilot was presumably busy scanning the ground for a suitable target, for he failed to see me until it was too late and I was able to send him down without undue difficulty.

The following day I managed to claim a second victory, albeit during a mission of a very different kind altogether. During the course of March senior Luftwaffe officers had toured airfields asking for volunteers to fly suicide missions. Unlike the earlier *Sturm* pilots who, in their heavily-armoured Fw 190s, had stood every chance of surviving a mid-air collision, what was being sought now were pilots who were prepared to forfeit their lives by deliberately crashing their machines into specific targets of strategic importance.

This proposal, which was a direct equivalent of Japan's infamous '*Kamikaze*' missions, had emanated from Göring himself and a surprising number of pilots – estimates put the figure at around 100 in all – answered their Commander-in-Chief's call. They ran the gamut from experienced veterans with many years of front-line service behind them, to newly trained youngsters fresh out of flying school. Their reasons for volunteering were equally diverse. For some, committed National Socialists who had grown up under the Third Reich and knew no other regime, it was purely ideological; a way of inflicting certain damage on the enemy. For others it was a personal matter – a loved one, perhaps, or even an entire family, wiped out in an Allied bombing raid or by the advance of the Red Army.

And the unit given the task of providing the fighter escort for many of these hapless souls on their final flight was Jagdgeschwader 4.

I was involved in two such missions, protecting these '*Kamikaze*' pilots in their bomb-laden machines. It is hard to describe how I felt, knowing that I was escorting them to their deaths. They had no hope of returning and were as good as lost the moment they pushed the throttle forward to start their take-off runs.

It was at 18.35 hours on 17 April that a small group of us lifted off from Mark Zwuschen for the 15-kilometre hop to nearby Jüterbog Altes Lager where the 'SO' pilots – 'SO' for '*Selbstopfer*', or 'self-sacrifice' – were based. On arrival we circled above Jüterbog a few times, waiting and watching as our charges took off and slowly climbed up towards us in their overloaded fighters. We had been told that, in order to be able to carry more explosives, they had been given only enough fuel to reach their target and that none of them was wearing a parachute – this really was the end for them.

What was going through their minds as we set course north-eastwards for their final 120km flight to the Oder crossings near Frankfurt can only be imagined. I remember one of them in particular. He seemed to be having trouble screwing up his courage to go through with the mission. He edged up close alongside me several times during the approach flight. But once over the target he too flipped over onto one wing and followed his comrades down, slamming into the ground close to the banks of the River Oder in a terrible fireball.

As we escorts turned for home, a gaggle of inquisitive Russian fighters came nosing up to us, probably attracted by the columns of thick black smoke rising from the explosions below, and it was one of these, a Yak-3, that gave me my second victory.

On 18 April I then made it three in three days. At 12.30 hours, despite reports of marauding American P-47s in the vicinity of the field, I took off at the head of a small group of our Bf 109s for a ground-attack mission against Russian troops closing in on Berlin. Once we had dropped our bombs, we were to carry out a *freie Jagd* sweep of the Fürstenwalde area between the capital and the Oder. And it was here that we bumped into an untidy formation of Soviet Il-2 '*Sturmovik*' ground-assault aircraft clearly engaged in a similar mission to our own. The '*Sturmoviki*' were being escorted by a large number of fighters. A fierce battle developed, which quickly broke up into the usual series of individual dogfights, during the course of which I was able to get in several bursts of cannon fire at one of the ground-hugging Il-2s and bring it down.

There was a story behind my short string of successes. Not all aerial encounters with the enemy ended in the victory expected. A pilot could twist and turn according to all the rules in the book, open fire on his opponent at point-blank range, and still fail to bring him down. What was the reason for this? We racked our brains, discussed it at great length between ourselves, but never did come up with a satisfactory answer.

I couldn't help but notice that one of the most successful Feldwebeln of my 9. Staffel would sit quietly listening to us with a slight smile on his face as we bandied ideas and theories back and forth. In the end I had to ask him what he found so amusing. In his usual relaxed manner he proceeded to explain in simple terms that although all the standard gunnery manuals and lessons in deflection shooting were no doubt excellent in purely theoretical terms, they weren't much use in practice.

He then described his own method of achieving success in aerial combat. What you had to do in a dogfight, he said, was to let the enemy aircraft disappear for an instant beneath the nose of your own machine before opening fire, otherwise all your shots would be wasted on thin air behind your opponent's tail. I could see the sense in that. It sounded both plausible and very straightforward. So I tried it for myself and it worked – Braun had been right!

By this time Mark Zwuschen was coming under increasing threat; not just from aerial attacks by both American and Russian fighter-bombers, but also from the Soviet ground forces spearheading the southern arm of the Red Army's giant pincer movement that was about to snap shut on Berlin.

On 19 April we therefore transferred some 150km to the north-west of the capital, well outside the ring of encirclement, to Redlin, a satellite field of the Rechlin experimental station. From here we flew a number of missions over the Greater Berlin area. The fighting for the capital was fast approaching its climax and many of our attacks were directed against enemy troops and armour in the Oranienburg sector to the north of Berlin. We also carried out armed reconnaissance and *freie Jagd* sweeps of the same area, during the course of which I managed to claim three more enemy aircraft, all Soviet Yak-3 fighters.

The first went down during a free-for-all over Oranienburg on 23 April. Four days later, while escorting Fw 190 '*Jabos*' of a ground-attack unit to targets in Berlin, we again tangled with Yak-3s, which provided me with my twelfth and penultimate victory of the war. The last was scored during another escort mission to Berlin late on the morning of 29 April. Feldwebel Hans Braun's dogfight rule of thumb – let your enemy disappear beneath your nose – had served me well yet again.

With the war all too clearly in its death throes, a growing sense of real trepidation began to descend on the Gruppe. Nobody voiced their concerns in so many words, but anxiety about the future was written on everyone's face.

General der Flieger Martin Fiebig, the AOC of *Luftwaffen-kommando Nordost* (Air Force Command North-east), arrived unexpectedly at the field towards the end of April. We all gathered round him in a semi-circle. He addressed us in an avuncular manner, conceding that the war was lost and that it was only a matter of days, possibly of hours, before the Red Army overran our area. He went on to thank us for our loyalty, our devotion to duty and for the comradeship that had seen us through good times and bad. He then ordered us to get all the unit's female personnel away to the safety of the Western Allies without delay in order to save them from falling into the hands of Soviet troops and all the unspeakable horrors that would mean. We complied immediately and succeeded in saving them all.

On 30 April we transferred the 35km south-east from Redlin to Wittstock, but remained here for only a few hours – just long enough for us to undertake a brief sweep of the Neustrelitz area – before retiring back past Redlin all the way to Parchim, little more than 80km south-east of the Baltic port of Lübeck.

At 05.35 hours the following morning, 1 May 1945, I took off with my wingman for a weather-reconnaissance flight over Berlin. The weather conditions above the smoking ruins of the capital were in fact good, but below us there was nothing but a vast expanse of rubble – a scene of utter destruction with few recognizable landmarks. On the way back to Parchim we had one last inconclusive encounter with Soviet fighters.

And thus ended my 212th and final operational mission of the war – entry number 5,918 in my flying logbook ... a logbook that had begun with a little Focke-Wulf trainer bouncing over the grass at Magdeburg exactly ten years and four days earlier.